C-1476   CAREER EXAMINATION SERIES

This is your
PASSBOOK for...

Senior Engineer

Test Preparation Study Guide
Questions & Answers

COPYRIGHT NOTICE

This book is SOLELY intended for, is sold ONLY to, and its use is RESTRICTED to individual, bona fide applicants or candidates who qualify by virtue of having seriously filed applications for appropriate license, certificate, professional and/or promotional advancement, higher school matriculation, scholarship, or other legitimate requirements of education and/or governmental authorities.

This book is NOT intended for use, class instruction, tutoring, training, duplication, copying, reprinting, excerption, or adaptation, etc., by:

1) Other publishers
2) Proprietors and/or Instructors of "Coaching" and/or Preparatory Courses
3) Personnel and/or Training Divisions of commercial, industrial, and governmental organizations
4) Schools, colleges, or universities and/or their departments and staffs, including teachers and other personnel
5) Testing Agencies or Bureaus
6) Study groups which seek by the purchase of a single volume to copy and/or duplicate and/or adapt this material for use by the group as a whole without having purchased individual volumes for each of the members of the group
7) Et al.

Such persons would be in violation of appropriate Federal and State statutes.

PROVISION OF LICENSING AGREEMENTS – Recognized educational, commercial, industrial, and governmental institutions and organizations, and others legitimately engaged in educational pursuits, including training, testing, and measurement activities, may address request for a licensing agreement to the copyright owners, who will determine whether, and under what conditions, including fees and charges, the materials in this book may be used them. In other words, a licensing facility exists for the legitimate use of the material in this book on other than an individual basis. However, it is asseverated and affirmed here that the material in this book CANNOT be used without the receipt of the express permission of such a licensing agreement from the Publishers. Inquiries re licensing should be addressed to the company, attention rights and permissions department.

All rights reserved, including the right of reproduction in whole or in part, in any form or by any means, electronic or mechanical, including photocopying, recording, or by any information storage and retrieval system, without permission in writing from the Publisher.

Copyright © 2025 by
National Learning Corporation

212 Michael Drive, Syosset, NY 11791
(516) 921-8888 • www.passbooks.com
E-mail: info@passbooks.com

PASSBOOK® SERIES

THE *PASSBOOK® SERIES* has been created to prepare applicants and candidates for the ultimate academic battlefield – the examination room.

At some time in our lives, each and every one of us may be required to take an examination – for validation, matriculation, admission, qualification, registration, certification, or licensure.

Based on the assumption that every applicant or candidate has met the basic formal educational standards, has taken the required number of courses, and read the necessary texts, the *PASSBOOK® SERIES* furnishes the one special preparation which may assure passing with confidence, instead of failing with insecurity. Examination questions – together with answers – are furnished as the basic vehicle for study so that the mysteries of the examination and its compounding difficulties may be eliminated or diminished by a sure method.

This book is meant to help you pass your examination provided that you qualify and are serious in your objective.

The entire field is reviewed through the huge store of content information which is succinctly presented through a provocative and challenging approach – the question-and-answer method.

A climate of success is established by furnishing the correct answers at the end of each test.

You soon learn to recognize types of questions, forms of questions, and patterns of questioning. You may even begin to anticipate expected outcomes.

You perceive that many questions are repeated or adapted so that you can gain acute insights, which may enable you to score many sure points.

You learn how to confront new questions, or types of questions, and to attack them confidently and work out the correct answers.

You note objectives and emphases, and recognize pitfalls and dangers, so that you may make positive educational adjustments.

Moreover, you are kept fully informed in relation to new concepts, methods, practices, and directions in the field.

You discover that you are actually taking the examination all the time: you are preparing for the examination by "taking" an examination, not by reading extraneous and/or supererogatory textbooks.

In short, this PASSBOOK®, used directedly, should be an important factor in helping you to pass your test.

SENIOR ENGINEER

DUTIES

This position involves professional level work in connection with the preparation, design, development, construction or inspection of engineering projects, plans and specifications in the engineering department. The work is performed under the general direction of a higher level engineering or administrative employee. Depending upon the job assignment, the incumbent may supervise the work of subordinate professional, sub-professional or technical employees or else work independently in developing and/or reviewing plans and specifications to community development projects. Does related work as required.

SCOPE OF THE EXAMINATION

The written test designed to evaluate knowledge, skills and /or abilities in the following areas:
1. Principles and practices of civil engineering;
2. Engineering plans; specifications and estimates;
3. Methods and materials of construction;
4. Surveying principles and practices, including map interpretation;
5. Building construction principles, practices and materials;
6. Preparing written material; and
7. Supervision.

HOW TO TAKE A TEST

I. YOU MUST PASS AN EXAMINATION

A. WHAT EVERY CANDIDATE SHOULD KNOW

Examination applicants often ask us for help in preparing for the written test. What can I study in advance? What kinds of questions will be asked? How will the test be given? How will the papers be graded?

As an applicant for a civil service examination, you may be wondering about some of these things. Our purpose here is to suggest effective methods of advance study and to describe civil service examinations.

Your chances for success on this examination can be increased if you know how to prepare. Those "pre-examination jitters" can be reduced if you know what to expect. You can even experience an adventure in good citizenship if you know why civil service exams are given.

B. WHY ARE CIVIL SERVICE EXAMINATIONS GIVEN?

Civil service examinations are important to you in two ways. As a citizen, you want public jobs filled by employees who know how to do their work. As a job seeker, you want a fair chance to compete for that job on an equal footing with other candidates. The best-known means of accomplishing this two-fold goal is the competitive examination.

Exams are widely publicized throughout the nation. They may be administered for jobs in federal, state, city, municipal, town or village governments or agencies.

Any citizen may apply, with some limitations, such as the age or residence of applicants. Your experience and education may be reviewed to see whether you meet the requirements for the particular examination. When these requirements exist, they are reasonable and applied consistently to all applicants. Thus, a competitive examination may cause you some uneasiness now, but it is your privilege and safeguard.

C. HOW ARE CIVIL SERVICE EXAMS DEVELOPED?

Examinations are carefully written by trained technicians who are specialists in the field known as "psychological measurement," in consultation with recognized authorities in the field of work that the test will cover. These experts recommend the subject matter areas or skills to be tested; only those knowledges or skills important to your success on the job are included. The most reliable books and source materials available are used as references. Together, the experts and technicians judge the difficulty level of the questions.

Test technicians know how to phrase questions so that the problem is clearly stated. Their ethics do not permit "trick" or "catch" questions. Questions may have been tried out on sample groups, or subjected to statistical analysis, to determine their usefulness.

Written tests are often used in combination with performance tests, ratings of training and experience, and oral interviews. All of these measures combine to form the best-known means of finding the right person for the right job.

II. HOW TO PASS THE WRITTEN TEST

A. NATURE OF THE EXAMINATION

To prepare intelligently for civil service examinations, you should know how they differ from school examinations you have taken. In school you were assigned certain definite pages to read or subjects to cover. The examination questions were quite detailed and usually emphasized memory. Civil service exams, on the other hand, try to discover your present ability to perform the duties of a position, plus your potentiality to learn these duties. In other words, a civil service exam attempts to predict how successful you will be. Questions cover such a broad area that they cannot be as minute and detailed as school exam questions.

In the public service similar kinds of work, or positions, are grouped together in one "class." This process is known as *position-classification*. All the positions in a class are paid according to the salary range for that class. One class title covers all of these positions, and they are all tested by the same examination.

B. FOUR BASIC STEPS

1) Study the announcement

How, then, can you know what subjects to study? Our best answer is: "Learn as much as possible about the class of positions for which you've applied." The exam will test the knowledge, skills and abilities needed to do the work.

Your most valuable source of information about the position you want is the official exam announcement. This announcement lists the training and experience qualifications. Check these standards and apply only if you come reasonably close to meeting them.

The brief description of the position in the examination announcement offers some clues to the subjects which will be tested. Think about the job itself. Review the duties in your mind. Can you perform them, or are there some in which you are rusty? Fill in the blank spots in your preparation.

Many jurisdictions preview the written test in the exam announcement by including a section called "Knowledge and Abilities Required," "Scope of the Examination," or some similar heading. Here you will find out specifically what fields will be tested.

2) Review your own background

Once you learn in general what the position is all about, and what you need to know to do the work, ask yourself which subjects you already know fairly well and which need improvement. You may wonder whether to concentrate on improving your strong areas or on building some background in your fields of weakness. When the announcement has specified "some knowledge" or "considerable knowledge," or has used adjectives like "beginning principles of…" or "advanced … methods," you can get a clue as to the number and difficulty of questions to be asked in any given field. More questions, and hence broader coverage, would be included for those subjects which are more important in the work. Now weigh your strengths and weaknesses against the job requirements and prepare accordingly.

3) Determine the level of the position

Another way to tell how intensively you should prepare is to understand the level of the job for which you are applying. Is it the entering level? In other words, is this the position in which beginners in a field of work are hired? Or is it an intermediate or advanced level? Sometimes this is indicated by such words as "Junior" or "Senior" in the class title. Other jurisdictions use Roman numerals to designate the level – Clerk I, Clerk II, for example. The word "Supervisor" sometimes appears in the title. If the level is not indicated by the title, check the description of duties. Will you be working under very close supervision, or will you have responsibility for independent decisions in this work?

4) Choose appropriate study materials

Now that you know the subjects to be examined and the relative amount of each subject to be covered, you can choose suitable study materials. For beginning level jobs, or even advanced ones, if you have a pronounced weakness in some aspect of your training, read a modern, standard textbook in that field. Be sure it is up to date and has general coverage. Such books are normally available at your library, and the librarian will be glad to help you locate one. For entry-level positions, questions of appropriate difficulty are chosen – neither highly advanced questions, nor those too simple. Such questions require careful thought but not advanced training.

If the position for which you are applying is technical or advanced, you will read more advanced, specialized material. If you are already familiar with the basic principles of your field, elementary textbooks would waste your time. Concentrate on advanced textbooks and technical periodicals. Think through the concepts and review difficult problems in your field.

These are all general sources. You can get more ideas on your own initiative, following these leads. For example, training manuals and publications of the government agency which employs workers in your field can be useful, particularly for technical and professional positions. A letter or visit to the government department involved may result in more specific study suggestions, and certainly will provide you with a more definite idea of the exact nature of the position you are seeking.

III. KINDS OF TESTS

Tests are used for purposes other than measuring knowledge and ability to perform specified duties. For some positions, it is equally important to test ability to make adjustments to new situations or to profit from training. In others, basic mental abilities not dependent on information are essential. Questions which test these things may not appear as pertinent to the duties of the position as those which test for knowledge and information. Yet they are often highly important parts of a fair examination. For very general questions, it is almost impossible to help you direct your study efforts. What we can do is to point out some of the more common of these general abilities needed in public service positions and describe some typical questions.

1) General information

Broad, general information has been found useful for predicting job success in some kinds of work. This is tested in a variety of ways, from vocabulary lists to questions about current events. Basic background in some field of work, such as sociology or economics, may be sampled in a group of questions. Often these are principles which have become familiar to most persons through exposure rather than through formal training. It is difficult to advise you how to study for these questions; being alert to the world around you is our best suggestion.

2) Verbal ability

An example of an ability needed in many positions is verbal or language ability. Verbal ability is, in brief, the ability to use and understand words. Vocabulary and grammar tests are typical measures of this ability. Reading comprehension or paragraph interpretation questions are common in many kinds of civil service tests. You are given a paragraph of written material and asked to find its central meaning.

3) Numerical ability

Number skills can be tested by the familiar arithmetic problem, by checking paired lists of numbers to see which are alike and which are different, or by interpreting charts and graphs. In the latter test, a graph may be printed in the test booklet which you are asked to use as the basis for answering questions.

4) Observation

A popular test for law-enforcement positions is the observation test. A picture is shown to you for several minutes, then taken away. Questions about the picture test your ability to observe both details and larger elements.

5) Following directions

In many positions in the public service, the employee must be able to carry out written instructions dependably and accurately. You may be given a chart with several columns, each column listing a variety of information. The questions require you to carry out directions involving the information given in the chart.

6) Skills and aptitudes

Performance tests effectively measure some manual skills and aptitudes. When the skill is one in which you are trained, such as typing or shorthand, you can practice. These tests are often very much like those given in business school or high school courses. For many of the other skills and aptitudes, however, no short-time preparation can be made. Skills and abilities natural to you or that you have developed throughout your lifetime are being tested.

Many of the general questions just described provide all the data needed to answer the questions and ask you to use your reasoning ability to find the answers. Your best preparation for these tests, as well as for tests of facts and ideas, is to be at your physical and mental best. You, no doubt, have your own methods of getting into an exam-taking mood and keeping "in shape." The next section lists some ideas on this subject.

IV. KINDS OF QUESTIONS

Only rarely is the "essay" question, which you answer in narrative form, used in civil service tests. Civil service tests are usually of the short-answer type. Full instructions for answering these questions will be given to you at the examination. But in case this is your first experience with short-answer questions and separate answer sheets, here is what you need to know:

1) Multiple-choice Questions

Most popular of the short-answer questions is the "multiple choice" or "best answer" question. It can be used, for example, to test for factual knowledge, ability to solve problems or judgment in meeting situations found at work.

A multiple-choice question is normally one of three types—
- It can begin with an incomplete statement followed by several possible endings. You are to find the one ending which *best* completes the statement, although some of the others may not be entirely wrong.
- It can also be a complete statement in the form of a question which is answered by choosing one of the statements listed.

- It can be in the form of a problem – again you select the best answer.

Here is an example of a multiple-choice question with a discussion which should give you some clues as to the method for choosing the right answer:

When an employee has a complaint about his assignment, the action which will *best* help him overcome his difficulty is to
   A. discuss his difficulty with his coworkers
   B. take the problem to the head of the organization
   C. take the problem to the person who gave him the assignment
   D. say nothing to anyone about his complaint

In answering this question, you should study each of the choices to find which is best. Consider choice "A" – Certainly an employee may discuss his complaint with fellow employees, but no change or improvement can result, and the complaint remains unresolved. Choice "B" is a poor choice since the head of the organization probably does not know what assignment you have been given, and taking your problem to him is known as "going over the head" of the supervisor. The supervisor, or person who made the assignment, is the person who can clarify it or correct any injustice. Choice "C" is, therefore, correct. To say nothing, as in choice "D," is unwise. Supervisors have and interest in knowing the problems employees are facing, and the employee is seeking a solution to his problem.

2) True/False Questions

The "true/false" or "right/wrong" form of question is sometimes used. Here a complete statement is given. Your job is to decide whether the statement is right or wrong.

SAMPLE: A roaming cell-phone call to a nearby city costs less than a non-roaming call to a distant city.

This statement is wrong, or false, since roaming calls are more expensive.
This is not a complete list of all possible question forms, although most of the others are variations of these common types. You will always get complete directions for answering questions. Be sure you understand *how* to mark your answers – ask questions until you do.

V. RECORDING YOUR ANSWERS

Computer terminals are used more and more today for many different kinds of exams.
For an examination with very few applicants, you may be told to record your answers in the test booklet itself. Separate answer sheets are much more common. If this separate answer sheet is to be scored by machine – and this is often the case – it is highly important that you mark your answers correctly in order to get credit.
An electronic scoring machine is often used in civil service offices because of the speed with which papers can be scored. Machine-scored answer sheets must be marked with a pencil, which will be given to you. This pencil has a high graphite content which responds to the electronic scoring machine. As a matter of fact, stray dots may register as answers, so do not let your pencil rest on the answer sheet while you are pondering the correct answer. Also, if your pencil lead breaks or is otherwise defective, ask for another.

Since the answer sheet will be dropped in a slot in the scoring machine, be careful not to bend the corners or get the paper crumpled.

The answer sheet normally has five vertical columns of numbers, with 30 numbers to a column. These numbers correspond to the question numbers in your test booklet. After each number, going across the page are four or five pairs of dotted lines. These short dotted lines have small letters or numbers above them. The first two pairs may also have a "T" or "F" above the letters. This indicates that the first two pairs only are to be used if the questions are of the true-false type. If the questions are multiple choice, disregard the "T" and "F" and pay attention only to the small letters or numbers.

Answer your questions in the manner of the sample that follows:

32. The largest city in the United States is
    A. Washington, D.C.
    B. New York City
    C. Chicago
    D. Detroit
    E. San Francisco

1) Choose the answer you think is best. (New York City is the largest, so "B" is correct.)
2) Find the row of dotted lines numbered the same as the question you are answering. (Find row number 32)
3) Find the pair of dotted lines corresponding to the answer. (Find the pair of lines under the mark "B.")
4) Make a solid black mark between the dotted lines.

VI. BEFORE THE TEST

Common sense will help you find procedures to follow to get ready for an examination. Too many of us, however, overlook these sensible measures. Indeed, nervousness and fatigue have been found to be the most serious reasons why applicants fail to do their best on civil service tests. Here is a list of reminders:

- Begin your preparation early – Don't wait until the last minute to go scurrying around for books and materials or to find out what the position is all about.
- Prepare continuously – An hour a night for a week is better than an all-night cram session. This has been definitely established. What is more, a night a week for a month will return better dividends than crowding your study into a shorter period of time.
- Locate the place of the exam – You have been sent a notice telling you when and where to report for the examination. If the location is in a different town or otherwise unfamiliar to you, it would be well to inquire the best route and learn something about the building.
- Relax the night before the test – Allow your mind to rest. Do not study at all that night. Plan some mild recreation or diversion; then go to bed early and get a good night's sleep.
- Get up early enough to make a leisurely trip to the place for the test – This way unforeseen events, traffic snarls, unfamiliar buildings, etc. will not upset you.
- Dress comfortably – A written test is not a fashion show. You will be known by number and not by name, so wear something comfortable.

- Leave excess paraphernalia at home – Shopping bags and odd bundles will get in your way. You need bring only the items mentioned in the official notice you received; usually everything you need is provided. Do not bring reference books to the exam. They will only confuse those last minutes and be taken away from you when in the test room.
- Arrive somewhat ahead of time – If because of transportation schedules you must get there very early, bring a newspaper or magazine to take your mind off yourself while waiting.
- Locate the examination room – When you have found the proper room, you will be directed to the seat or part of the room where you will sit. Sometimes you are given a sheet of instructions to read while you are waiting. Do not fill out any forms until you are told to do so; just read them and be prepared.
- Relax and prepare to listen to the instructions
- If you have any physical problem that may keep you from doing your best, be sure to tell the test administrator. If you are sick or in poor health, you really cannot do your best on the exam. You can come back and take the test some other time.

VII. AT THE TEST

The day of the test is here and you have the test booklet in your hand. The temptation to get going is very strong. Caution! There is more to success than knowing the right answers. You must know how to identify your papers and understand variations in the type of short-answer question used in this particular examination. Follow these suggestions for maximum results from your efforts:

1) Cooperate with the monitor

The test administrator has a duty to create a situation in which you can be as much at ease as possible. He will give instructions, tell you when to begin, check to see that you are marking your answer sheet correctly, and so on. He is not there to guard you, although he will see that your competitors do not take unfair advantage. He wants to help you do your best.

2) Listen to all instructions

Don't jump the gun! Wait until you understand all directions. In most civil service tests you get more time than you need to answer the questions. So don't be in a hurry. Read each word of instructions until you clearly understand the meaning. Study the examples, listen to all announcements and follow directions. Ask questions if you do not understand what to do.

3) Identify your papers

Civil service exams are usually identified by number only. You will be assigned a number; you must not put your name on your test papers. Be sure to copy your number correctly. Since more than one exam may be given, copy your exact examination title.

4) Plan your time

Unless you are told that a test is a "speed" or "rate of work" test, speed itself is usually not important. Time enough to answer all the questions will be provided, but this does not mean that you have all day. An overall time limit has been set. Divide the total time (in minutes) by the number of questions to determine the approximate time you have for each question.

5) Do not linger over difficult questions

If you come across a difficult question, mark it with a paper clip (useful to have along) and come back to it when you have been through the booklet. One caution if you do this – be sure to skip a number on your answer sheet as well. Check often to be sure that you have not lost your place and that you are marking in the row numbered the same as the question you are answering.

6) Read the questions

Be sure you know what the question asks! Many capable people are unsuccessful because they failed to *read* the questions correctly.

7) Answer all questions

Unless you have been instructed that a penalty will be deducted for incorrect answers, it is better to guess than to omit a question.

8) Speed tests

It is often better NOT to guess on speed tests. It has been found that on timed tests people are tempted to spend the last few seconds before time is called in marking answers at random – without even reading them – in the hope of picking up a few extra points. To discourage this practice, the instructions may warn you that your score will be "corrected" for guessing. That is, a penalty will be applied. The incorrect answers will be deducted from the correct ones, or some other penalty formula will be used.

9) Review your answers

If you finish before time is called, go back to the questions you guessed or omitted to give them further thought. Review other answers if you have time.

10) Return your test materials

If you are ready to leave before others have finished or time is called, take ALL your materials to the monitor and leave quietly. Never take any test material with you. The monitor can discover whose papers are not complete, and taking a test booklet may be grounds for disqualification.

VIII. EXAMINATION TECHNIQUES

1) Read the general instructions carefully. These are usually printed on the first page of the exam booklet. As a rule, these instructions refer to the timing of the examination; the fact that you should not start work until the signal and must stop work at a signal, etc. If there are any *special* instructions, such as a choice of questions to be answered, make sure that you note this instruction carefully.

2) When you are ready to start work on the examination, that is as soon as the signal has been given, read the instructions to each question booklet, underline any key words or phrases, such as *least, best, outline, describe* and the like. In this way you will tend to answer as requested rather than discover on reviewing your paper that you *listed without describing*, that you selected the *worst* choice rather than the *best* choice, etc.

3) If the examination is of the objective or multiple-choice type – that is, each question will also give a series of possible answers: A, B, C or D, and you are called upon to select the best answer and write the letter next to that answer on your answer paper – it is advisable to start answering each question in turn. There may be anywhere from 50 to 100 such questions in the three or four hours allotted and you can see how much time would be taken if you read through all the questions before beginning to answer any. Furthermore, if you come across a question or group of questions which you know would be difficult to answer, it would undoubtedly affect your handling of all the other questions.

4) If the examination is of the essay type and contains but a few questions, it is a moot point as to whether you should read all the questions before starting to answer any one. Of course, if you are given a choice – say five out of seven and the like – then it is essential to read all the questions so you can eliminate the two that are most difficult. If, however, you are asked to answer all the questions, there may be danger in trying to answer the easiest one first because you may find that you will spend too much time on it. The best technique is to answer the first question, then proceed to the second, etc.

5) Time your answers. Before the exam begins, write down the time it started, then add the time allowed for the examination and write down the time it must be completed, then divide the time available somewhat as follows:
    - If 3-1/2 hours are allowed, that would be 210 minutes. If you have 80 objective-type questions, that would be an average of 2-1/2 minutes per question. Allow yourself no more than 2 minutes per question, or a total of 160 minutes, which will permit about 50 minutes to review.
    - If for the time allotment of 210 minutes there are 7 essay questions to answer, that would average about 30 minutes a question. Give yourself only 25 minutes per question so that you have about 35 minutes to review.

6) The most important instruction is to *read each question* and make sure you know what is wanted. The second most important instruction is to *time yourself properly* so that you answer every question. The third most important instruction is to *answer every question*. Guess if you have to but include something for each question. Remember that you will receive no credit for a blank and will probably receive some credit if you write something in answer to an essay question. If you guess a letter – say "B" for a multiple-choice question – you may have guessed right. If you leave a blank as an answer to a multiple-choice question, the examiners may respect your feelings but it will not add a point to your score. Some exams may penalize you for wrong answers, so in such cases *only*, you may not want to guess unless you have some basis for your answer.

7) Suggestions
    a. Objective-type questions
        1. Examine the question booklet for proper sequence of pages and questions
        2. Read all instructions carefully
        3. Skip any question which seems too difficult; return to it after all other questions have been answered
        4. Apportion your time properly; do not spend too much time on any single question or group of questions

5. Note and underline key words – *all, most, fewest, least, best, worst, same, opposite*, etc.
6. Pay particular attention to negatives
7. Note unusual option, e.g., unduly long, short, complex, different or similar in content to the body of the question
8. Observe the use of "hedging" words – *probably, may, most likely*, etc.
9. Make sure that your answer is put next to the same number as the question
10. Do not second-guess unless you have good reason to believe the second answer is definitely more correct
11. Cross out original answer if you decide another answer is more accurate; do not erase until you are ready to hand your paper in
12. Answer all questions; guess unless instructed otherwise
13. Leave time for review

   b. Essay questions
   1. Read each question carefully
   2. Determine exactly what is wanted. Underline key words or phrases.
   3. Decide on outline or paragraph answer
   4. Include many different points and elements unless asked to develop any one or two points or elements
   5. Show impartiality by giving pros and cons unless directed to select one side only
   6. Make and write down any assumptions you find necessary to answer the questions
   7. Watch your English, grammar, punctuation and choice of words
   8. Time your answers; don't crowd material

8) Answering the essay question

Most essay questions can be answered by framing the specific response around several key words or ideas. Here are a few such key words or ideas:

M's: manpower, materials, methods, money, management
P's: purpose, program, policy, plan, procedure, practice, problems, pitfalls, personnel, public relations
   a. Six basic steps in handling problems:
   1. Preliminary plan and background development
   2. Collect information, data and facts
   3. Analyze and interpret information, data and facts
   4. Analyze and develop solutions as well as make recommendations
   5. Prepare report and sell recommendations
   6. Install recommendations and follow up effectiveness

   b. Pitfalls to avoid
   1. *Taking things for granted* – A statement of the situation does not necessarily imply that each of the elements is necessarily true; for example, a complaint may be invalid and biased so that all that can be taken for granted is that a complaint has been registered

2. *Considering only one side of a situation* – Wherever possible, indicate several alternatives and then point out the reasons you selected the best one
3. *Failing to indicate follow up* – Whenever your answer indicates action on your part, make certain that you will take proper follow-up action to see how successful your recommendations, procedures or actions turn out to be
4. *Taking too long in answering any single question* – Remember to time your answers properly

IX. AFTER THE TEST

Scoring procedures differ in detail among civil service jurisdictions although the general principles are the same. Whether the papers are hand-scored or graded by machine we have described, they are nearly always graded by number. That is, the person who marks the paper knows only the number – never the name – of the applicant. Not until all the papers have been graded will they be matched with names. If other tests, such as training and experience or oral interview ratings have been given, scores will be combined. Different parts of the examination usually have different weights. For example, the written test might count 60 percent of the final grade, and a rating of training and experience 40 percent. In many jurisdictions, veterans will have a certain number of points added to their grades.

After the final grade has been determined, the names are placed in grade order and an eligible list is established. There are various methods for resolving ties between those who get the same final grade – probably the most common is to place first the name of the person whose application was received first. Job offers are made from the eligible list in the order the names appear on it. You will be notified of your grade and your rank as soon as all these computations have been made. This will be done as rapidly as possible.

People who are found to meet the requirements in the announcement are called "eligibles." Their names are put on a list of eligible candidates. An eligible's chances of getting a job depend on how high he stands on this list and how fast agencies are filling jobs from the list.

When a job is to be filled from a list of eligibles, the agency asks for the names of people on the list of eligibles for that job. When the civil service commission receives this request, it sends to the agency the names of the three people highest on this list. Or, if the job to be filled has specialized requirements, the office sends the agency the names of the top three persons who meet these requirements from the general list.

The appointing officer makes a choice from among the three people whose names were sent to him. If the selected person accepts the appointment, the names of the others are put back on the list to be considered for future openings.

That is the rule in hiring from all kinds of eligible lists, whether they are for typist, carpenter, chemist, or something else. For every vacancy, the appointing officer has his choice of any one of the top three eligibles on the list. This explains why the person whose name is on top of the list sometimes does not get an appointment when some of the persons lower on the list do. If the appointing officer chooses the second or third eligible, the No. 1 eligible does not get a job at once, but stays on the list until he is appointed or the list is terminated.

X. HOW TO PASS THE INTERVIEW TEST

The examination for which you applied requires an oral interview test. You have already taken the written test and you are now being called for the interview test – the final part of the formal examination.

You may think that it is not possible to prepare for an interview test and that there are no procedures to follow during an interview. Our purpose is to point out some things you can do in advance that will help you and some good rules to follow and pitfalls to avoid while you are being interviewed.

What is an interview supposed to test?

The written examination is designed to test the technical knowledge and competence of the candidate; the oral is designed to evaluate intangible qualities, not readily measured otherwise, and to establish a list showing the relative fitness of each candidate – as measured against his competitors – for the position sought. Scoring is not on the basis of "right" and "wrong," but on a sliding scale of values ranging from "not passable" to "outstanding." As a matter of fact, it is possible to achieve a relatively low score without a single "incorrect" answer because of evident weakness in the qualities being measured.

Occasionally, an examination may consist entirely of an oral test – either an individual or a group oral. In such cases, information is sought concerning the technical knowledges and abilities of the candidate, since there has been no written examination for this purpose. More commonly, however, an oral test is used to supplement a written examination.

Who conducts interviews?

The composition of oral boards varies among different jurisdictions. In nearly all, a representative of the personnel department serves as chairman. One of the members of the board may be a representative of the department in which the candidate would work. In some cases, "outside experts" are used, and, frequently, a businessman or some other representative of the general public is asked to serve. Labor and management or other special groups may be represented. The aim is to secure the services of experts in the appropriate field.

However the board is composed, it is a good idea (and not at all improper or unethical) to ascertain in advance of the interview who the members are and what groups they represent. When you are introduced to them, you will have some idea of their backgrounds and interests, and at least you will not stutter and stammer over their names.

What should be done before the interview?

While knowledge about the board members is useful and takes some of the surprise element out of the interview, there is other preparation which is more substantive. It *is* possible to prepare for an oral interview – in several ways:

1) Keep a copy of your application and review it carefully before the interview

This may be the only document before the oral board, and the starting point of the interview. Know what education and experience you have listed there, and the sequence and dates of all of it. Sometimes the board will ask you to review the highlights of your experience for them; you should not have to hem and haw doing it.

2) Study the class specification and the examination announcement

Usually, the oral board has one or both of these to guide them. The qualities, characteristics or knowledges required by the position sought are stated in these documents. They offer valuable clues as to the nature of the oral interview. For example, if the job involves supervisory responsibilities, the announcement will usually indicate that knowledge of modern supervisory methods and the qualifications of the candidate as a supervisor will be tested. If so, you can expect such questions, frequently in the form of a hypothetical situation which you are expected to solve. NEVER go into an oral without knowledge of the duties and responsibilities of the job you seek.

3) Think through each qualification required

Try to visualize the kind of questions you would ask if you were a board member. How well could you answer them? Try especially to appraise your own knowledge and background in each area, *measured against the job sought*, and identify any areas in which you are weak. Be critical and realistic – do not flatter yourself.

4) Do some general reading in areas in which you feel you may be weak

For example, if the job involves supervision and your past experience has NOT, some general reading in supervisory methods and practices, particularly in the field of human relations, might be useful. Do NOT study agency procedures or detailed manuals. The oral board will be testing your understanding and capacity, not your memory.

5) Get a good night's sleep and watch your general health and mental attitude

You will want a clear head at the interview. Take care of a cold or any other minor ailment, and of course, no hangovers.

What should be done on the day of the interview?

Now comes the day of the interview itself. Give yourself plenty of time to get there. Plan to arrive somewhat ahead of the scheduled time, particularly if your appointment is in the fore part of the day. If a previous candidate fails to appear, the board might be ready for you a bit early. By early afternoon an oral board is almost invariably behind schedule if there are many candidates, and you may have to wait. Take along a book or magazine to read, or your application to review, but leave any extraneous material in the waiting room when you go in for your interview. In any event, relax and compose yourself.

The matter of dress is important. The board is forming impressions about you – from your experience, your manners, your attitude, and your appearance. Give your personal appearance careful attention. Dress your best, but not your flashiest. Choose conservative, appropriate clothing, and be sure it is immaculate. This is a business interview, and your appearance should indicate that you regard it as such. Besides, being well groomed and properly dressed will help boost your confidence.

Sooner or later, someone will call your name and escort you into the interview room. *This is it.* From here on you are on your own. It is too late for any more preparation. But remember, you asked for this opportunity to prove your fitness, and you are here because your request was granted.

What happens when you go in?

The usual sequence of events will be as follows: The clerk (who is often the board stenographer) will introduce you to the chairman of the oral board, who will introduce you to the other members of the board. Acknowledge the introductions before you sit down. Do not be surprised if you find a microphone facing you or a stenotypist sitting by. Oral interviews are usually recorded in the event of an appeal or other review.

Usually the chairman of the board will open the interview by reviewing the highlights of your education and work experience from your application – primarily for the benefit of the other members of the board, as well as to get the material into the record. Do not interrupt or comment unless there is an error or significant misinterpretation; if that is the case, do not hesitate. But do not quibble about insignificant matters. Also, he will usually ask you some question about your education, experience or your present job – partly to get you to start talking and to establish the interviewing "rapport." He may start the actual questioning, or turn it over to one of the other members. Frequently, each member undertakes the questioning on a particular area, one in which he is perhaps most competent, so you can expect each member to participate in the examination. Because time is limited, you may also expect some rather abrupt switches in the direction the questioning takes, so do not be upset by it. Normally, a board member will not pursue a single line of questioning unless he discovers a particular strength or weakness.

After each member has participated, the chairman will usually ask whether any member has any further questions, then will ask you if you have anything you wish to add. Unless you are expecting this question, it may floor you. Worse, it may start you off on an extended, extemporaneous speech. The board is not usually seeking more information. The question is principally to offer you a last opportunity to present further qualifications or to indicate that you have nothing to add. So, if you feel that a significant qualification or characteristic has been overlooked, it is proper to point it out in a sentence or so. Do not compliment the board on the thoroughness of their examination – they have been sketchy, and you know it. If you wish, merely say, "No thank you, I have nothing further to add." This is a point where you can "talk yourself out" of a good impression or fail to present an important bit of information. Remember, *you close the interview yourself*.

The chairman will then say, "That is all, Mr. _____, thank you." Do not be startled; the interview is over, and quicker than you think. Thank him, gather your belongings and take your leave. Save your sigh of relief for the other side of the door.

How to put your best foot forward

Throughout this entire process, you may feel that the board individually and collectively is trying to pierce your defenses, seek out your hidden weaknesses and embarrass and confuse you. Actually, this is not true. They are obliged to make an appraisal of your qualifications for the job you are seeking, and they want to see you in your best light. Remember, they must interview all candidates and a non-cooperative candidate may become a failure in spite of their best efforts to bring out his qualifications. Here are 15 suggestions that will help you:

1) **Be natural – Keep your attitude confident, not cocky**

If you are not confident that you can do the job, do not expect the board to be. Do not apologize for your weaknesses, try to bring out your strong points. The board is interested in a positive, not negative, presentation. Cockiness will antagonize any board member and make him wonder if you are covering up a weakness by a false show of strength.

2) **Get comfortable, but don't lounge or sprawl**

Sit erectly but not stiffly. A careless posture may lead the board to conclude that you are careless in other things, or at least that you are not impressed by the importance of the occasion. Either conclusion is natural, even if incorrect. Do not fuss with your clothing, a pencil or an ashtray. Your hands may occasionally be useful to emphasize a point; do not let them become a point of distraction.

3) **Do not wisecrack or make small talk**

This is a serious situation, and your attitude should show that you consider it as such. Further, the time of the board is limited – they do not want to waste it, and neither should you.

4) Do not exaggerate your experience or abilities
In the first place, from information in the application or other interviews and sources, the board may know more about you than you think. Secondly, you probably will not get away with it. An experienced board is rather adept at spotting such a situation, so do not take the chance.

5) If you know a board member, do not make a point of it, yet do not hide it
Certainly you are not fooling him, and probably not the other members of the board. Do not try to take advantage of your acquaintanceship – it will probably do you little good.

6) Do not dominate the interview
Let the board do that. They will give you the clues – do not assume that you have to do all the talking. Realize that the board has a number of questions to ask you, and do not try to take up all the interview time by showing off your extensive knowledge of the answer to the first one.

7) Be attentive
You only have 20 minutes or so, and you should keep your attention at its sharpest throughout. When a member is addressing a problem or question to you, give him your undivided attention. Address your reply principally to him, but do not exclude the other board members.

8) Do not interrupt
A board member may be stating a problem for you to analyze. He will ask you a question when the time comes. Let him state the problem, and wait for the question.

9) Make sure you understand the question
Do not try to answer until you are sure what the question is. If it is not clear, restate it in your own words or ask the board member to clarify it for you. However, do not haggle about minor elements.

10) Reply promptly but not hastily
A common entry on oral board rating sheets is "candidate responded readily," or "candidate hesitated in replies." Respond as promptly and quickly as you can, but do not jump to a hasty, ill-considered answer.

11) Do not be peremptory in your answers
A brief answer is proper – but do not fire your answer back. That is a losing game from your point of view. The board member can probably ask questions much faster than you can answer them.

12) Do not try to create the answer you think the board member wants
He is interested in what kind of mind you have and how it works – not in playing games. Furthermore, he can usually spot this practice and will actually grade you down on it.

13) Do not switch sides in your reply merely to agree with a board member
Frequently, a member will take a contrary position merely to draw you out and to see if you are willing and able to defend your point of view. Do not start a debate, yet do not surrender a good position. If a position is worth taking, it is worth defending.

14) Do not be afraid to admit an error in judgment if you are shown to be wrong

The board knows that you are forced to reply without any opportunity for careful consideration. Your answer may be demonstrably wrong. If so, admit it and get on with the interview.

15) Do not dwell at length on your present job

The opening question may relate to your present assignment. Answer the question but do not go into an extended discussion. You are being examined for a *new* job, not your present one. As a matter of fact, try to phrase ALL your answers in terms of the job for which you are being examined.

Basis of Rating

Probably you will forget most of these "do's" and "don'ts" when you walk into the oral interview room. Even remembering them all will not ensure you a passing grade. Perhaps you did not have the qualifications in the first place. But remembering them will help you to put your best foot forward, without treading on the toes of the board members.

Rumor and popular opinion to the contrary notwithstanding, an oral board wants you to make the best appearance possible. They know you are under pressure – but they also want to see how you respond to it as a guide to what your reaction would be under the pressures of the job you seek. They will be influenced by the degree of poise you display, the personal traits you show and the manner in which you respond.

ABOUT THIS BOOK

This book contains tests divided into Examination Sections. Go through each test, answering every question in the margin. We have also attached a sample answer sheet at the back of the book that can be removed and used. At the end of each test look at the answer key and check your answers. On the ones you got wrong, look at the right answer choice and learn. Do not fill in the answers first. Do not memorize the questions and answers, but understand the answer and principles involved. On your test, the questions will likely be different from the samples. Questions are changed and new ones added. If you understand these past questions you should have success with any changes that arise. Tests may consist of several types of questions. We have additional books on each subject should more study be advisable or necessary for you. Finally, the more you study, the better prepared you will be. This book is intended to be the last thing you study before you walk into the examination room. Prior study of relevant texts is also recommended. NLC publishes some of these in our Fundamental Series. Knowledge and good sense are important factors in passing your exam. Good luck also helps. So now study this Passbook, absorb the material contained within and take that knowledge into the examination. Then do your best to pass that exam.

EXAMINATION SECTION

EXAMINATION SECTION
TEST 1

DIRECTIONS: Each question or incomplete statement is followed by several suggested answers or completions. Select the one that BEST answers the question or completes the statement. *PRINT THE LETTER OF THE CORRECT ANSWER IN THE SPACE AT THE RIGHT.*

1. A general contractor, on a lump sum building construction job, is required to submit a breakdown of his estimate in order to

   A. prevent collusion in bidding
   B. serve as a guide in checking his monthly estimates for payment
   C. enable designers to prepare budget estimates for proposed work
   D. enable designers to compare it with their estimate of cost of the job

2. Of the following, the index MOST often applied to indicate the strength of sewage is

   A. odor
   B. biochemical oxygen demand
   C. foaming
   D. turbidity

3. Of the following, the MINIMUM amount of cover required for water mains in the city is *primarily* determined by the

   A. traffic shock loads
   B. pressure in the main
   C. depth of rock below street surfaces
   D. depth of frost

4. The one of the following in which an inspector of pile driving has the MOST interest during driving wood piles is

   A. weather conditions
   B. mushrooming of the head
   C. penetration
   D. water table location

5. A bidder on a public job is required to furnish a bid bond to guarantee that he will

   A. sign a contract if awarded the job
   B. complete the job on schedule
   C. pay the mechanics who will work on the job
   D. pay the subcontractors whom he will employ to work on the job

Questions 6-7.

DIRECTIONS: Questions 6 and 7 refer to the following diagram.

A section through a roof appears as shown below.

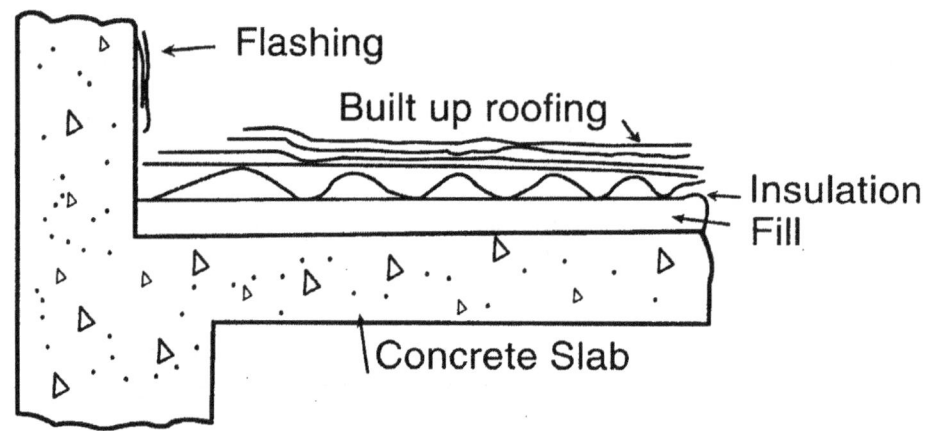

6. Of the following, the MAIN purpose of the fill is to

   A. provide a smooth base for the insulation
   B. reduce sound transmission
   C. absorb impact of roof loads
   D. facilitate drainage

7. Of the following, the material composition of the fill is *most likely*

   A. one-inch cinder block
   B. compacted sand
   C. Wood
   D. lightweight concrete

8. An excavation for a building in the downtown area is kept dry by pumping from a sump. It would be a danger signal to an inspector if

   A. the pumped water is always clear
   B. after a heavy rain, the pumped water is muddy
   C. the pumped water is continually muddy
   D. the rate of pumping decreases materially with time

9. The PRIMARY reason for placing reinforced steel in concrete is that concrete is weak in

   A. torsion   B. tension   C. compression   D. bond

10. Of the following types of construction, the one that would *most likely* be paid for on a lump sum basis would be a new

    A. subway
    B. sewer
    C. street paving and regulating
    D. building

11. Of the following situations, the one in which it is MOST important to have a fire extinguisher on hand is when

    A. welding a broken bracket on a bulldozer
    B. welding a structural steel field connection
    C. burning reinforcing steel in place before a concrete pour
    D. bending reinforced steel at the bar bending machine

12. Wall plaster is composed of

    A. sand, cement, gypsum, water
    B. coarse aggregate, gypsum, water
    C. sand, gypsum, water
    D. lime, gypsum, cement, water

13. Of the following, the LEAST important factor in establishing grades for a new urban street is existing

    A. manholes   B. underground utilities
    C. sewers   D. sidewalks

14. The activated sludge treatment process reduces organic matter in the sewage to inorganic matter PRIMARILY by

    A. electrolysis   B. sedimentation
    C. bacteriological action   D. catalytic action

15. Assume that you are a party chief on a preliminary survey for a major construction project with a four-man party. Two of your men are able to operate the transit. You consider one of these men an expert, while the other is lacking in experience. You have been following a policy of assigning each man to the transit on alternate days. You get a call from the design department to furnish a check on a series of angles as quickly as possible. On this day, it is the inexperienced man's turn at the transit. You should

    A. allow the inexperienced man to run the gun for that is the only way he can become experienced
    B. have the experienced man run the gun and explain the need for speed and accuracy
    C. run the gun yourself to avoid arguments
    D. have the experienced man run the gun and explain to the Inexperienced man that the next time the design department wants a quick check, it would be his turn at the transit

16. A Rockwell test is a test for

    A. water hardness   B. well water purity
    C. hardness of metal   D. rock bearing capacity

17. A slump test is made on a sample of concrete PRIMARILY to measure its

    A. finishing qualities   B. resistance to bleeding
    C. strength   D. workability

18. Of the following, the MOST important factor that the individual must fulfill in order to insure his own safety on a construction job is to

    A. be familiar with the specifications
    B. work slowly
    C. be alert
    D. wear clothing to suit the climatic condition

19. Assume that a civil engineer is assigned as resident engineer on a minor construction contract.
Of the following statements relating to his assignment, the one that is CORRECT is:

   A. It is a good policy for the resident engineer to give orders directly to the contractor's men
   B. In checking for conformance with specifications, the resident engineer should rely on the word of the contractor rather than on the inspector's report
   C. The resident engineer generally should not interfere in matters of dispute between a contractor and his foreman
   D. It is permissible for the resident engineer to make a misrepresentation in order to obtain proof that the contractor failed to comply with the specifications

20. Of the following, the BEST method of dewatering a small deep hole in rock is to

   A. use well points to pump the area
   B. drive steel sheet piling and pump the area dry
   C. drive wood sheet piling and pump the area dry
   D. dig a sump in a low spot and pump the water from it

21. Batter piles are used in a pile foundation when

   A. the forces coming into the foundation are lateral
   B. obstructions in the soil merit their use
   C. the soil consists of material with a low-bearing capacity
   D. the elevation of the bedrock is too high to warrant the driving of normal piles

22. Of the following woods, the one that is NOT considered a hardwood is

   A. oak   B. maple   C. walnut   D. fir

23. The excavating unit which works BEST in soft-to-medium-hard materials, can dig holes extending far below the surface, and can lift the material to a high disposal point is the

   A. power shovel   B. clam shell
   C. orange peel   D. back-hoe

24. The PRIMARY reason for vibrating concrete is to

   A. force a maximum amount of water to the surface
   B. prevent segregation in the concrete
   C. move the concrete more easily into the forms
   D. prevent the formation of air pockets in the concrete

25. The rational method of estimating the rate of storm-water run-off is expressed by the formula $Q = C i A$.
In this formula,

   A. Q is the rate of run-off in cfs
   B. C is the coefficient of run-off in cfs
   C. i is the average intensity of precipitation in acre-inches
   D. A is the area in acre-inches

KEY (CORRECT ANSWERS)

1. B
2. B
3. D
4. C
5. A

6. D
7. D
8. C
9. B
10. D

11. C
12. C
13. A
14. C
15. B

16. C
17. D
18. C
19. C
20. D

21. A
22. D
23. B
24. D
25. A

TEST 2

DIRECTIONS: Each question or incomplete statement is followed by several suggested answers or completions. Select the one that BEST answers the question or completes the statement. *PRINT THE LETTER OF THE CORRECT ANSWER IN THE SPACE AT THE RIGHT.*

1. Of the following, the one which is NOT usually used for primary treatment of sewage is a   1.____
   A. comminutor
   B. grit chamber
   C. trickling filter
   D. skimming

2. Of the following, construction joints in reinforced concrete floor systems should be made at   2.____
   A. the edge of a beam
   B. the edge of a girder
   C. points of maximum shear
   D. points of maximum positive bending moment

3. To prevent objectionable deposits in a sanitary sewer, the MINIMUM average velocity when flowing full should be, in fps,   3.____
   A. 0.5   B. 1.2   C. 2.0   D. 3.0

4. The tool that is GENERALLY used in plaster work to float over freshly rodded brown mortar is   4.____
   A. darby   B. featheredge   C. paddle   D. rod

5. An inferior paint well applied to a thoroughly cleaned and conditioned surface will give many times the protection and decorative effect that will be obtained by the best paint poorly applied to an uncleaned or damp surface.
   Assuming that the above evaluation is correct, an APPROPRIATE instruction for your painting inspector, based on this statement, is   5.____
   A. to make sure that the paint used is equivalent to the approved sample
   B. to allow use of inferior paint provided the surface is clean and dry
   C. that the inspection of cleaning and painting of all surfaces is too casual
   D. to make sure the surface to be painted is clean and free from dampness

6. Of the following, the MOST compressible soil is usually   6.____
   A. sand   B. clay   C. gravel   D. silt

7. Vitrified clay pipe   7.____
   A. can be ordered in lengths from 4 to 16 feet
   B. is easy to cut
   C. is joined by the use of Dresser Couplings
   D. is hard and brittle

8. A *hawk* is a tool USUALLY used in   8.____
   A. plastering
   B. brickwork
   C. roofing
   D. carpentry

9. The specifications for concrete state that the water used for concrete shall be free of organic material.
   Of the following chemicals, the one that is organic is

   A. NaCl B. $C_6H_{12}O_6$ C. HNO_3 D. $CaSO_4 2H_2O$

10. The *Proctor Test* is used in testing

    A. asphalt B. concrete C. soils D. mortar

11. A rectangular reinforced concrete beam is to resist a bending moment of 75,000 pound-feet.
    If the effective depth is 20' and K ($=\frac{1}{2}f_c jk$) is 180, the required width of the beam, in inches, is MOST NEARLY ($M=Kbd^2$)

    A. 12.3 B. 12.5 C. 12.7 D. 12.9

12. Of the following, the Chezy Formula, in reference to the flow of water, is used to compute the

    A. velocity B. viscosity C. pressure D. losses

13. The length of a 20-penny nail is MOST NEARLY _____ inches.

    A. $2\frac{1}{2}$ B. 3 C. $3\frac{1}{2}$ D. 4

14. In the schedule of room finishes on an architectural plan of a building are the headings: Room, Space No., Floor, Base, Wall, Ceiling.
    The Base *most likely* refers to the

    A. wainscot
    B. material beneath the flooring material such as felt or paper
    C. material at the bottom of the wall
    D. structural material supporting the floor

15. Of the following, the STRONGEST and MOST DURABLE of all building stones used to face an exterior wall is

    A. trap B. granite C. limestone D. sandstone

16. The width and thickness of the main plate of a riveted lap joint is 6" and 3/4", respectively. The allowable loads in shear, bearing, and tension are 70,000#, 80,000#, and 60,000#, respectively. The allowable f_s = 20000 psi.
    The efficiency of this joint is MOST NEARLY

    A. 82% B. 55% C. 75% D. 66.7%

17. A post, consisting of a steel pipe whose net cross-sectional area is 40 sq. inches, is subjected to direct compression by a load of 80,000#.
    If the post is 8 ft. high, the reduction in length due to the load is, in inches, MOST NEARLY (E= 30,000,000#/sq. in. and $E = \frac{S}{E}$)

    A. .001 B. .006 C. .011 D. .016

18.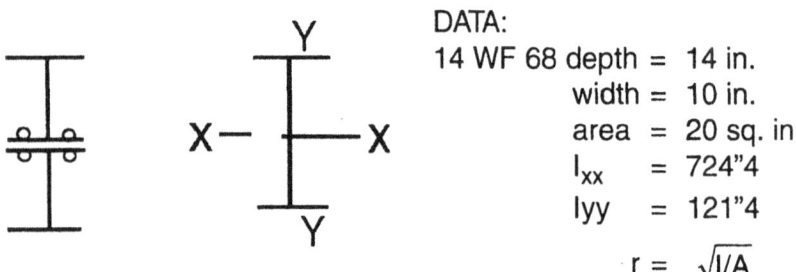

DATA:
14 WF 68 depth = 14 in.
width = 10 in.
area = 20 sq. in
I_{xx} = 724"4
I_{yy} = 121"4
$r = \sqrt{I/A}$

Two WF 68 columns are connected as shown above.
Their LEAST radius of gyration when acting together as a unit is in inches, MOST NEARLY

A. 2.46 B. 4.92 C. 6.02 D. 12.04

19. The PRIMARY physical difference between steel and cast iron is that steel is much

A. *lighter* than cast iron
B. *weaker* in compression
C. *stronger* in tension
D. *weaker* in tension

20. Of the following, the one that is an example of a flexible pavement is a

A. gravel base and a concrete wearing course
B. plain concrete slab
C. gravel base and a bituminous wearing course
D. concrete base and an asphalt wearing course

21. Shutoff valves on 12" water supply lines found in the city streets USUALLY are _____ valves.

A. gate B. globe C. check D. stop

22. An analysis of drinking water shows that the pH is 6.0. The pH may be increased by adding

A. H_2SO_4
B. chlorine
C. caustic soda
D. fluorine

23.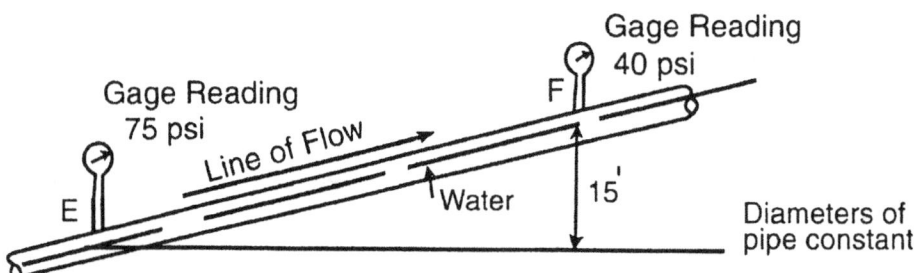

The head loss between E and F is, in feet of water, MOST NEARLY

A. 66 B. 81 C. 90 D. 93

24. A contract for a new building is generally broken into four separate contracts. These contracts are USUALLY:

    A. General Construction, Plumbing & Drainage, Heating and Ventilating, Electrical
    B. Foundation, Superstructure, Electrical, Mechanical
    C. Structural, Mechanical, Electrical, Foundation
    D. General Construction, Plumbing, Drainage, Electrical

25. The terms *shakes, checks, seasoning,* and *preservation* are all likely to be used in specifications for

    A. glass brick
    B. cast iron
    C. plaster
    D. timber

KEY (CORRECT ANSWERS)

1.	C	11.	B
2.	D	12.	A
3.	C	13.	D
4.	A	14.	C
5.	D	15.	B
6.	B	16.	D
7.	D	17.	B
8.	A	18.	A
9.	B	19.	C
10.	C	20.	C

21. A
22. C
23. A
24. A
25. D

EXAMINATION SECTION
TEST 1

DIRECTIONS: Each question or incomplete statement is followed by several suggested answers or completions. Select the one that BEST answers the question or completes the statement. *PRINT THE LETTER OF THE CORRECT ANSWER IN THE SPACE AT THE RIGHT.*

1. Dowels connecting adjacent roadway slabs are used primarily to   1.___

    A. transmit compressive stress to adjacent slabs
    B. reinforce against temperature stress
    C. reinforce against shrinkage stress
    D. prevent differential settlement of slabs

2. Good practice requires that the minimum overhead clearance at the crown for an underpass at the intersection of two highways be MOST NEARLY _____ feet.   2.___

    A. 10 B. 14 C. 17 D. 19

3. A simple beam on an 18'0" span carries a uniformly distributed load including its own weight of 200 pounds per foot.   3.___
   If a jack is placed under the midspan and the midpoint jacked up so it is at the same elevation as the ends, the load on the jack, in pounds, will be

    A. 960   B. 1600
    C. 1800   D. more than 1800

4. Of the following, the one which is NOT the symbol for a standard beam connection is   4.___

    A. A3 B. B3 C. H3 D. T3

5. Of the following items, the one that is NOT important in determining the minimum length of vertical curve required to connect two intersecting grades is   5.___

    A. maximum speed of vehicle
    B. grades of tangents
    C. whether intersection is at a summit or a sag
    D. crown of road

6. For an angle of intersection of 16°30', tables of the functions of a one-degree curve show the middle ordinate to be 59.30 feet.   6.___
   For the same angle of intersection, the middle ordinate for a curve whose radius is 1433 feet is MOST NEARLY

    A. 14.83 B. 24.94 C. 67.35 D. 183.72

7. The *Proctor Test* is used in testing   7.___

    A. asphalt B. concrete C. soils D. mortar

8. Within the cross-section of a WF beam, the horizontal shearing stress is a maximum at the   8.___

11

A. midpoint of the beam
B. outermost fiber of the compression flange
C. outermost fiber of the tension flange
D. point of intersection of web and flange

9. The maximum load allowed on a 3/8" fillet weld, 6" long, when the allowable shearing stress is 13,000 #/sq.in. is MOST NEARLY, in pounds,

A. 20,700 B. 21,900 C. 24,300 D. 26,370

10. A closed level circuit was run starting at BM *A*. The elevation of *A* on closing the circuit was found to be 0.097 lower than at the start.
Of the following, the MOST logical reason for this error, barring mistakes, is the

A. length of the rod was not standard due either to a uniform expansion or contraction
B. level settled after the backsights had been read
C. turning points settled after the foresights had been read
D. line of sight was inclined upward and each foresight distance exceeded the corresponding backsight distance

11. The sensitivity of the bubble tube of an engineer's level can best be measured by

A. measuring the distance between etched lines on the vial
B. taking readings on a rod a known distance away with bubble in two different positions
C. making a two-peg test
D. measuring the curvature of the etched surface of the vial

12. Of the following, the MOST important source of accidental error in ordinary leveling work is

A. change in length of leveling rod due to change in temperature
B. axis of level tube not perpendicular to vertical axis
C. eye piece is not focused accurately
D. failure to wave rod

13. When taking a single measure of the horizontal angle between two points which differ greatly in elevation, the MOST important of the following relationships in the transit is

A. axis of long bubble parallel to line of sight
B. transverse axis perpendicular to vertical axis
C. index correction of vertical arc equal to zero
D. vertical cross-hair in plane perpendicular to transverse axis

14. Of the following factors, the one that is LEAST important in determining the total amount of superelevation required at the edge of pavement on a horizontal curve is

A. speed of vehicle
B. weight of vehicle
C. radius of curve
D. width of pavement

15. If the horizontal circle of a transit is graduated to 20' and 39 divisions on the limb equal 40 civisions on the vernier, then the LEAST count of the vernier is

A. 14" B. 28" C. 30" D. 1'6"

16. The slump test for concrete is used to determine the

   A. strength B. consistency
   C. water ratio D. segregation

17. The following notes are taken from the survey of a closed traverse with five sides:

⌖ at	Deflection Angles
A	R 65° 25'
B	L 45° 14'
C	R 135° 42'
D	R 92° 17'
E	

   The value of the deflection angle at E is MOST NEARLY

   A. 111°22' B. 111°34' C. 111°46' D. 111°50'

18. A Williot-Mohr diagram is used to determine

   A. deflection in trusses
   B. wind stress in framed bents
   C. diagonal shear in beams
   D. uplift pressure on the base of a cam

19. A reinforced concrete beam is 10" wide by 16" effective depth. If fs = 20,000 lb./sq.in., fc = 1350 lb./sq.in. and n = 10, then the value of k is MOST NEARLY

   A. .367 B. .373 C. .403 D. .419

20. Of the following concrete structures, the one in which gunite is MOST likely to be used is

   A. footings B. piles C. walls D. beams

21. For soil sampling in hardpan, the BEST method to use is

   A. jet probing B. wash boring
   C. auger boring D. core boring

22. The bending moment at the ends of a beam fully restrained at both ends which supports a uniform load of w pounds per foot throughout its entire length l is

   A. $\frac{wl^2}{8}$ B. $\frac{wl}{10}$ C. $\frac{wl^2}{10}$ D. $\frac{wl^2}{12}$

23. A reinforced concrete beam 10" wide by 16" effective depth is subjected to an end shear of 15,000 lbs.
   If fs = 20,000 #/sq.in., fc = 2500 #/sq.in., u = 187 #/sq.in., and j = .857, the perimeter of steel required to reinforce against the shear, in inches, is MOST NEARLY

   A. 2.38 B. 3.72 C. 5.85 D. 6.94

24. A precast reinforced concrete beam 20'0" long, weight 50 #/ft. is to be lifted by two slings symmetrically placed.
   For minimum bending stress in the beam, the distance from an end to a point of support, in feet, is MOST NEARLY

A. 3.98   B. 4.15   C. 4.35   D. 5.15

25. For maximum stress in *ab*, the distance the load *P* should be from the wall is MOST NEARLY
    A. 10'7"
    B. 11'9"
    C. 13'3"
    D. 15'0"

KEY (CORRECT ANSWERS)

1. D		11. B	
2. B		12. C	
3. D		13. B	
4. D		14. B	
5. D		15. C	
6. A		16. B	
7. C		17. D	
8. A		18. A	
9. A		19. C	
10. D		20. C	

21. D
22. D
23. C
24. B
25. D

TEST 2

DIRECTIONS: Each question or incomplete statement is followed by several suggested answers or completions. Select the one that BEST answers the question or completes the statement. *PRINT THE LETTER OF THE CORRECT ANSWER IN THE SPACE AT THE RIGHT.*

1. The rod reading at Sta. 100+27 is 4.26. With the same H.I., the rod reading at Sta. 103+16 is 6.34.
   The grade between the two stations is MOST NEARLY

   A. +0.72%   B. +0.79%   C. -0.72%   D. -0.79%

2. In taping a distance known to be 2000 ft. long, the distance is found to be 1900.02 ft. The error is MOST probably caused by

   A. neglecting temperature correction
   B. neglecting to record one tape length
   C. tension on tape not standard
   D. wind blowing tape out of line

3. The sum of the deflection angles for a closed traverse, where *n* equals the number of sides of the traverse, is

   A. (n-2)180°   B. 180°n   C. (n-l)360°   D. 360°

4. When a level rod is *waved,* the correct reading is the

   A. largest reading
   B. smallest reading
   C. average of the largest and the smallest reading
   D. difference between the largest and the smallest reading

5. A topographic map to a scale of 1:2400 has a 5-foot vertical interval. A straight line on the map connecting two adjacent contours is 0.437 inches long.
   The slope of this line is, in percent, MOST NEARLY

   A. 5.6   B. 5.7   C. 5.8   D. 6.0

6. A Philadelphia rod is fully extended and the distance from the 1-foot mark to the 11-foot mark is measured and found to be 10.005.
   In a level circuit, a high-rod reading on this rod is

   A. 0.005 too large
   B. 0.005 too small
   C. considered correct since the errors will balance out
   D. correct if the rod is waved

7. A differential leveling circuit without sideshots was run between two bench marks. The level was set up x times.
   The number of turning points used was

   A. 2x   B. x-2   C. x-1   D. x

8. A closed traverse is usually preferred to an open traverse because

A. more ground can be covered
B. a mathematical check on the work is provided
C. the area can be determined
D. the computations are easier

9. The difference in elevation between two points on the hydraulic gradient of a pipe of uniform diameter is a measure of the loss of _____ head.

A. potential   B. pressure   C. velocity   D. total

10. Of the following values of f in the formula $h = f \dfrac{l}{d}\dfrac{V^2}{2g}$, the one which would MOST probably apply to a smooth pipe is

A. 0.02   B. 0.11   C. 0.31   D. 0.41

11. The required cross-sectional area of a culvert is a function of

A. width of roadway   B. depth of fill
C. drainage area served   D. headwall area

12. The value of k for a particular reinforced concrete beam is 0.400. The value of j for this beam is MOST NEARLY

A. 0.873   B. 0.870   C. 0.867   D. 0.865

13. A steel bar one inch in diameter is imbedded a distance of 30 inches in a mass of concrete.
If the bar is subjected to axial pull of 10,000#, the bond stress is, in pounds per square inch, MOST NEARLY

A. 106   B. 108   C. 112   D. 116

14. The slump test for concrete is a measure of

A. water-cement ratio   B. consistency
C. strength   D. size of aggregate

15. The term *special anchorage* in concrete construction refers to

A. an anchor bolt to tie a beam to a wall
B. tieing the reinforcement to a steel beam
C. a *U*-shaped bar to take care of shearing stresses
D. a hook at the end of a reinforcing bar

16.

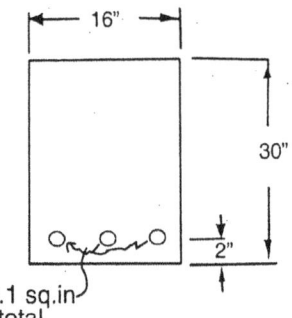

$k = \dfrac{1}{2} f_c k^2 j = 236$

Assuming exactly balanced design, the maximum bending moment that can be carried by the reinforced concrete beam in the accompanying sketch is, in inch pounds, MOST NEARLY

    A. 2,960,000   B. 3,420,370   C. 4,160,500   D. 5,180,600

17. The maximum deflection of a simple beam on a span 1 carrying a uniformly distributed load of w per unit length is $\frac{5}{384}\frac{w}{EI}$ multiplied by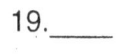

    A. 1^2 B. 1^3 C. 1^4 D. 1^7

18. The section modulus of a beam is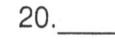

    A. $\int y^2 dA$ B. $\frac{V}{Ib}A\bar{y}$ C. $\frac{\sqrt{I}}{A}$ D. $\frac{I}{c}$

19. A timber beam 3" x 12" (actual dimensions) is simply supported on a clear span of 9'0" and carries a uniform load of 1000 #/ft. throughout its entire length.
The maximum bending stress in the beam is, in lbs./sq.in., MOST NEARLY

    A. 1570   B. 1690   C. 1745   D. 1860

20. A wooden beam 8 inches wide by 12 inches deep (actual dimensions) carries a uniform load of 600 pounds per foot including its own weight on a simple span of 16'0".
The MAXIMUM shear stress intensity in the beam is, in pounds per square inch,

    A. 70   B. 71   C. 72   D. 75

21. The horizontal component of the reaction at joint B in the accompanying diagram is MOST NEARLY

    A. 32^K
    B. 36^K
    C. 40^K
    D. 44^K

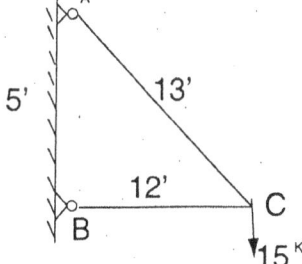

22. The yield point of a ductile metal is that unit stress at which

    A. the stress ceases to be proportional to the strain
    B. there is an increase in deformation with no increase in stress
    C. the material ruptures
    D. the metal ceases to act as an elastic material

Questions 23-27.

DIRECTIONS: Questions 23 through 27 refer to the sketch of the beam and girder connection shown below.

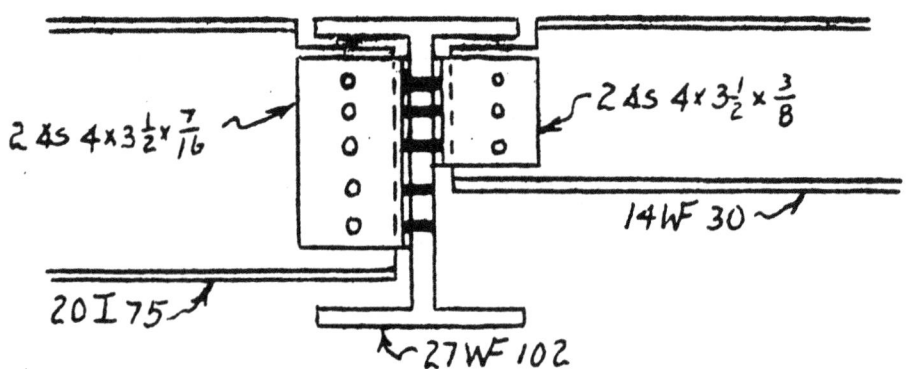

23. The diameter of the rivets used would MOST likely be

    A. 5/8"   B. 7/8"   C. 1 3/16"   D. 1 5/8"

24. Of the following allowable stresses, the only one that would be used in determining the number of rivets connecting the angles to the 20 I 75 is the allowable stress in

    A. single shear
    B. end bearing
    C. web shear
    D. enclosed bearing

25. The allowable load on rivet A is determined by the allowable stress in

    A. double shear
    B. single shear
    C. tension
    D. torsion

26. Both beams shown are

    A. chased   B. blocked   C. squared   D. clipped

27. The number of field rivets required in the connection is

    A. 4   B. 6   C. 9   D. 10

28. The term *batter* in concrete work refers to

    A. bracing of forms
    B. slope of finished surface
    C. consistency of concrete
    D. pressure of wet concrete in forms

29. Of the following items, the one that is LEAST related to the others is

    A. B.O.D.
    B. Imhoff tank
    C. effluent
    D. liquid limit

30. A beam on a simple span of 16'0" carries a concentrated load of 20 kips 5'0" from the left support and a uniform load of 3 kips per foot over the entire span.
    The distance from the left support to the point of maximum moment is, in feet, MOST NEARLY

    A. 5.92   B. 5.97   C. 6.02   D. 6.07

31. A beam has a trapezoidal cross-section which is symmetrical about a vertical axis. The top width is 4 inches, the bottom width 8 inches, and the depth 6 inches.
    The distance from the bottom of the beam to the neutral axis is, in inches,

A. 2.83   B. 2.75   C. 2.67   D. 2.59

32. The ends of a steel bar 1 inch square are set in rigid walls spaced 4'0" in the clear. Another square steel bar 2 inches on a side is set in rigid walls spaced 8'0" in the clear. The ratio of the unit stress in the longer bar to that in the shorter bar due to an increase in temperature is

    A. 3/8   B. 5/8   C. 1   D. 3/2

Questions 33-35.

DIRECTIONS: Questions 33 through 35 refer to the truss shown below.

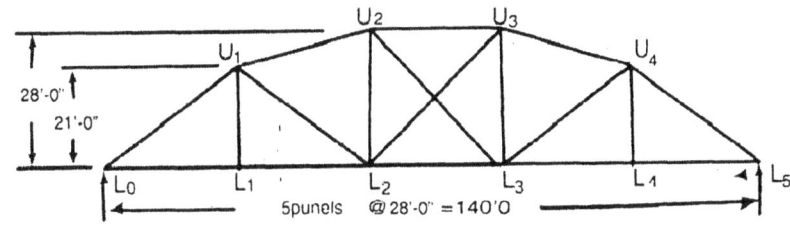

33. To obtain the stress in U_1L_2, the truss should be cut between U_1L_1 and U_2L_2 and moments taken about

    A. U_2
    B. L_1
    C. L_0
    D. a point to the left of L_0

34. The stress in member L_1L_2 for a load of one kip per foot extending over the entire span is, in kips, MOST NEARLY

    A. 74.67   B. 75.33   C. 75.67   D. 76.00

35. The stress in member U_2U_3 for a load of one kip per foot extending over the entire span is, in kips, MOST NEARLY

    A. 83.15   B. 83.30   C. 83.45   D. 84.00

36. In taping a distance on a 6% slope, the slope distance was measured. The correction per hundred feet to be applied to the measured distance is, in feet,

    A. 0.09   B. 0.12   C. 0.15   D. 0.18

37. The linear error of closure of a traverse is computed to be 0.04 feet. The sum of the lengths of the sides is 793.26 ft.
    The precision of the survey should be recorded as

    A. $\dfrac{0.04}{600}$ B. $\dfrac{4}{79326}$ C. $\dfrac{4}{793.26}$ D. $\dfrac{1}{19800}$

38. Errors due to eccentricity in the plates of a transit can be eliminated by
    A. reading the angle twice, once with the telescope normal, the second time with the telescope inverted
    B. using the averaged reading of the A and B verniers
    C. accurate leveling of the transit
    D. using two observers

39. A transit is set up at Sta. B and the deflection angle to Sta. C is measured (backsight on Sta. A) and found to be 22°15' R.
    The value of the angle ABC, measured clockwise from A to C, is

    A. 69°30'   B. 108°45'   C. 144°15'   D. 202°15'

40. The elevations of the P.V.C., P.V.I., and P.V.T. of a symnetrical vertical curve are 100.26, 103.26, and 98.76, respectively.
    The elevation of the midpoint of the vertical curve is MOST NEARLY

    A. 98.63   B. 99.72   C. 101.38   D. 103.17

KEY (CORRECT ANSWERS)

1. C	11. C	21. B	31. C
2. B	12. C	22. B	32. C
3. D	13. A	23. B	33. D
4. B	14. B	24. D	34. A
5. B	15. D	25. B	35. D
6. A	16. A	26. B	36. D
7. C	17. C	27. D	37. D
8. B	18. D	28. B	38. B
9. D	19. B	29. D	39. D
10. A	20. D	30. A	40. C

TEST 3

DIRECTIONS: Each question or incomplete statement is followed by several suggested answers or completions. Select the one that BEST answers the question or completes the statement. *PRINT THE LETTER OF THE CORRECT ANSWER IN THE SPACE AT THE RIGHT.*

1. In highway work, the degree of curve is commonly defined as the angle   1.____

   A. at the center subtended by an arc 100 ft. in length
   B. at the center subtending the entire curve
   C. at which the two tangents to the curve intersect
   D. between a tangent and a chord 100 ft. in length

2. The term *magnetic declination* refers to the   2.____

   A. attraction on a magnetic needle of nearby metallic objects
   B. dip of a magnetic needle
   C. angle between a given line and the meridian
   D. angle between true north and magnetic north

3. The bearings of the sides of a closed quadrilateral are: 3.____

   AB - N12°15'W
   BC - N15°10'E
   CD - S60°20'E
   DA - S18°30'W

   The interior angle CDA of the quadrilateral is

   A. 87°25'   B. 10°110'   C. 126°40'   D. 154°15'

4. In a given triangle, side a = 220 ft. and the angle opposite is 30°00'.   4.____
   If angle B = 45°00', then the side opposite angle B, in feet, is MOST NEARLY

   A. 311   B. 327   C. 346   D. 411

5. Of the following statements, the one that is CORRECT is: 5.____

   A. Blue ink is used when making tracings for blueprint work
   B. If ink lines on a tracing do not dry quickly, they should be blotted
   C. Vertical dimensions should be lettered so that they read from the right side of the sheet
   D. Dimension lines should be of the same weight as lines used in the views

6. A common method of lengthening the life of a wooden pile is by impregnating it with   6.____

   A. white lead   B. red lead
   C. sodium silicate   D. creosote

7. The MOST common unit for measuring excavation is   7.____

   A. cubic yard   B. cubic foot
   C. ton   D. pound

8. The width of each lane in a modern two-lane highway would MOST likely be

   A. 8' B. 12' C. 16' D. 20'

Questions 9-11.

DIRECTIONS: Questions 9 through 11 refer to the figure shown below. (Any trigonomatic computation required is to be done by slide rule.)

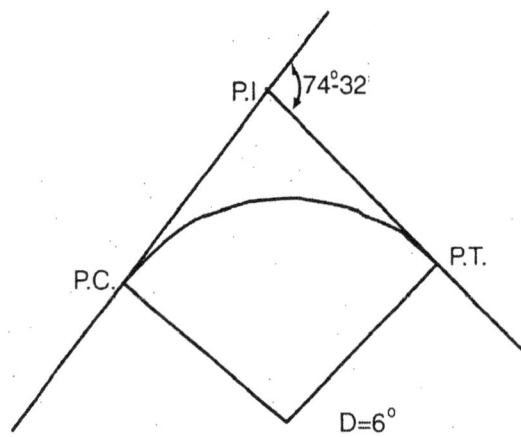

9. The station of the P.C. is 17+57.2.
   The deflection angle from the P.C. to Sta. 19 is MOST NEARLY

   A. 2°39' B. 3°17' C. 4°17' D. 6°17'

10. The radius of the curve is, in feet, MOST NEARLY

    A. 955 B. 960 C. 970 D. 980

11. The station of the P.T. is MOST NEARLY

    A. 29+99.2 B. 29+99.4 C. 29+99.6 D. 30+00.4

12. Two cylindrical tanks with vertical axes lie one above the other. The lower tank is 8'0" in diameter and 8'0" high. The upper tank is 4'0" in diameter and 40'0" high with its base at the level of the top of the lower tank. The lower tank is full of water, and the upper tank is empty.
    The energy, in foot-pounds, required to pump the water from the lower to the upper tank is MOST NEARLY

    A. 502,000 B. 505,000 C. 508,000 D. 511,000

Questions 13-18.

DIRECTIONS: Questions 13 through 18 refer to the sketch of the plate girder shown below.

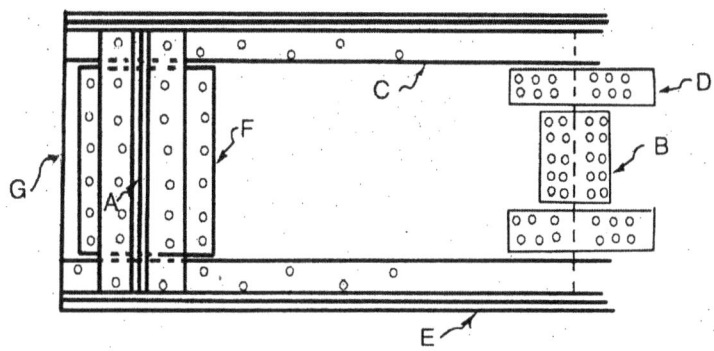

For each of the parts of the plate girder listed below in Questions 13 through 18, select the letter representing that part in the sketch above. For each of questions 13 through 18, the correct answer is

A. A   B. B   C. C   D. D   E. E   F. F   G. G

13. Flange angle

14. Shear splice

15. Stiffener

16. Cover plate

17. Web

18. Filler plate

19. Of the following symbols, the one that represents the ratio of the modulus of elasticity of steel to the modulus of elasticity of concrete in concrete design is

    A. k   B. v   C. p   D. n

20. A rectangular gate 4'0" wide by 6'0" high is submerged in water with the 4'0" side parallel to and 2'0" below the water surface. The gate is in a vertical plane.
    The total pressure on the gate is, in pounds, MOST NEARLY

    A. 7480   B. 7590   C. 7660   D. 7720

21. The distance from the top of the gate to the center of pressure of the water on one side of the gate described in the preceding question is, in feet, MOST NEARLY

    A. 3.60   B. 3.70   C. 3.80   D. 3.90

22. Reservoir A is connected to Reservoir B by two parallel pipes, one 6 inches in diameter, the other 12 inches in diameter. The friction factor, f, is the same for each pipe.
    If the flow in the 12-inch pipe is 6 cubic feet per second, the flow in the 6-inch pipe is, in cubic feet per second, MOST NEARLY

    A. 1.01   B. 1.03   C. 1.05   D. 1.06

23. The hydraulic radius of a rectangular channel 6'0" wide with, a 4'0" depth of water is, in feet, MOST NEARLY

A. 1.71   B. 1.75   C. 1.79   D. 1.83

24. On a transit, the tangent screw is used to

    A. clamp the telescope in either erect or inverted position
    B. adjust the level bubbles
    C. focus the objective lens
    D. rotate the telescope small distances

25. The tangent of angle A is equal to

    A. $\sqrt{1-\cos^2 A}$ B. $\dfrac{\sec A}{\cos A}$ C. $\sin A \cos A$ D. $\dfrac{\sin A}{\cos A}$

26. If two stations on a mass diagram for earthwork have equal ordinates, the

    A. elevations of the two stations are the same
    B. end areas at the two stations are equal
    C. volume of cut equals the volume of fill between the two stations
    D. volume of fill between the two stations may be moved with equal economy to either station

27. The primary cause of parallax in a telescope is

    A. atmospheric disturbances
    B. maladjustment of the cross hairs
    C. improper focusing of the objective
    D. improper focusing of the eyepiece

28. The notes for a three level section for a roadway 20 ft. wide are as follows:

    $$\dfrac{c12}{16} \quad \dfrac{c13}{0} \quad \dfrac{c16}{18}$$

    The side slopes of the embankment are _____ horizontal to _____ vertical.
    A. 1; 2   B. 1; 1   C. 2; 1   D. 2;3

29. Various combinations of the known parts of a triangle are given below. The combination which does NOT describe a unique triangle (i.e., one triangle and one only) is

    A. three sides
    B. two sides and the included angle
    C. one side and two angles
    D. two sides and an acute angle opposite one of the sides

30. To permit easier operation of vehicles, a tangent is MOST frequently connected to a horizontal circular curve by means of a

    A. reversed curve   B. spiral
    C. parabola   D. hyperbola

31. An alidade is MOST commonly used in conjunction with a

    A. transit   B. plane table
    C. barometer   D. tide gauge

32. The increase in length of a 100-foot stool tape due to a temperature rise of 15°F is, in feet, MOST NEARLY 32.____

A. 0.0001 B. 0.0005 C. 0.01 D. 0.05

33. An instrument used to measure the area of a closed traverse, plotted to scale, is a 33.____

A. integraph
B. clinometer
C. planimeter
D. pantograph

Questions 34-35.

DIRECTIONS: Questions 34 and 35 refer to the following diagrams on the following page.

(Diagram for question 34.)

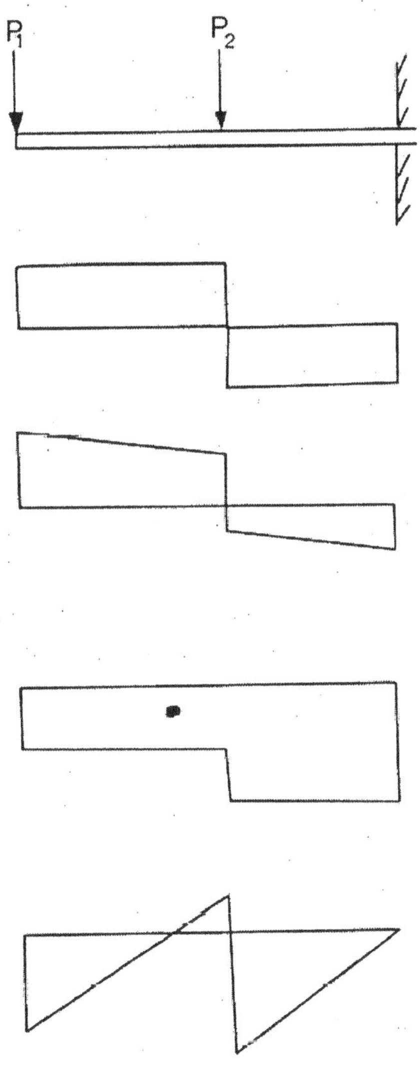

A
B
C
D

(Diagram for question 35.)

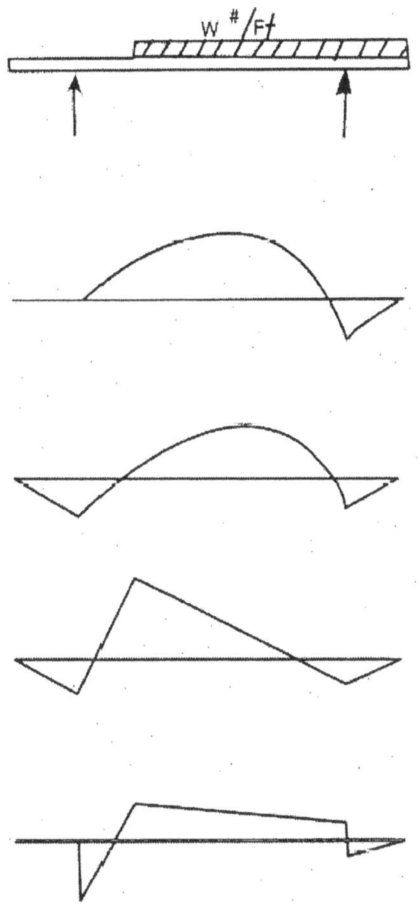

A
B
C
D

34. The shear diagram for the beam shown in the above diagram is (neglecting the weight of the beam) 34.____

A. A B. B C. C D. D

35. The moment diagram for the beam shown in the above diagram is (neglecting the weight of the beam) 35.____

A. A B. B C. C D. D

Questions 36-40.

DIRECTIONS: In Questions 36 through 40, the plan and front elevation of an object are shown on the left, and on the right are shown four figures, one of which, and only one, represents the right side elevation. Print in the space at the right the letter which represents the right side elevation. In the sample shown below, which figure correctly represents the right side elevation?

A. A B. B C. C D. D

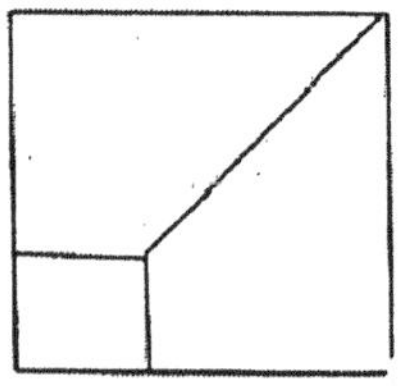

Plan

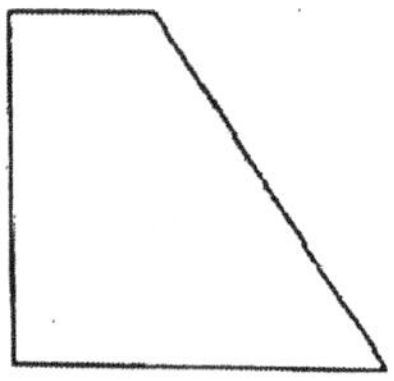

Front Elevation

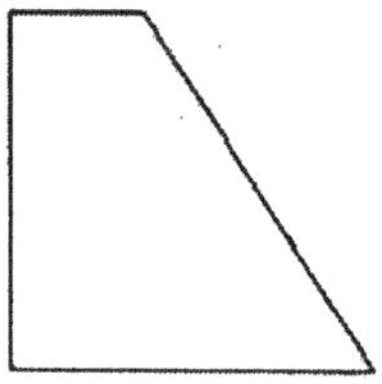

A

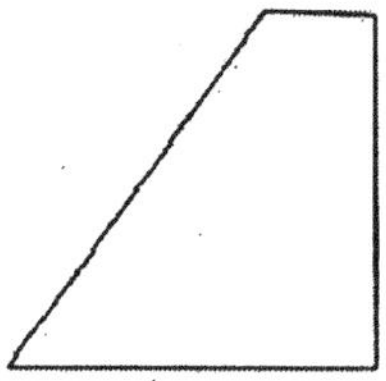

B

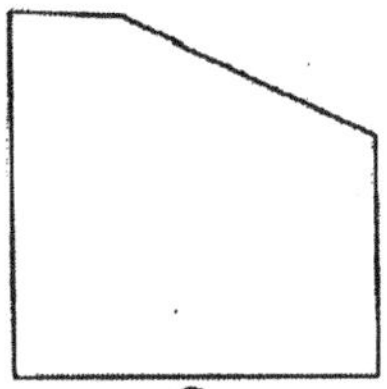

C

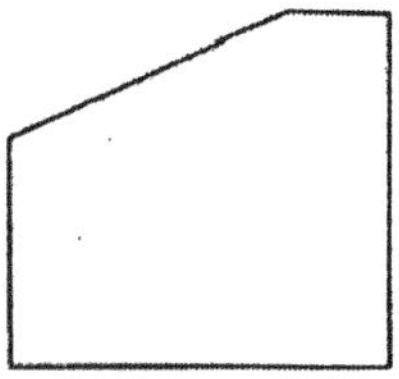

D

The correct answer is A.

In Questions 36 through 40, which figure correctly represents the right side elevation?

A. A B. B C. C D. D

36. 36.____

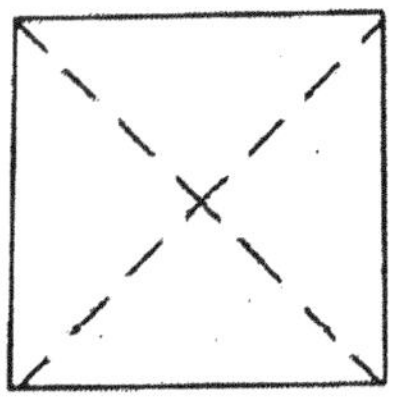

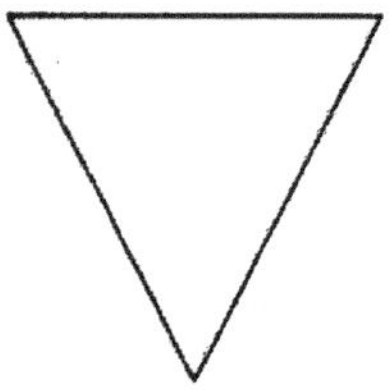

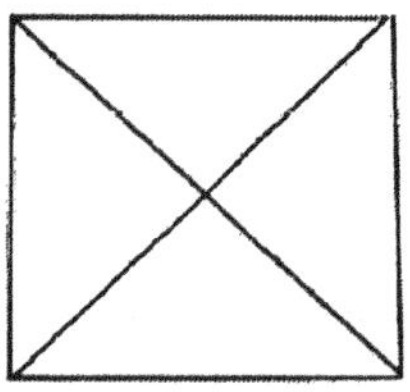

A

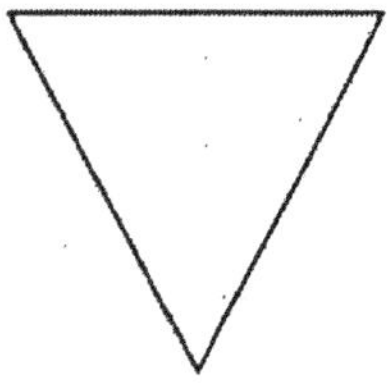

B

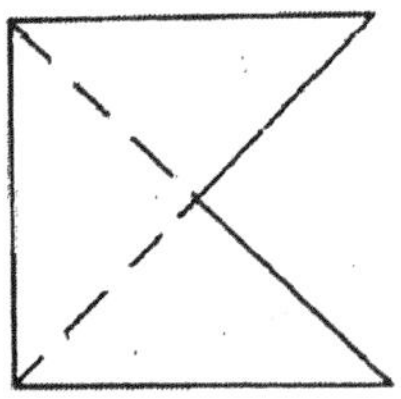

C

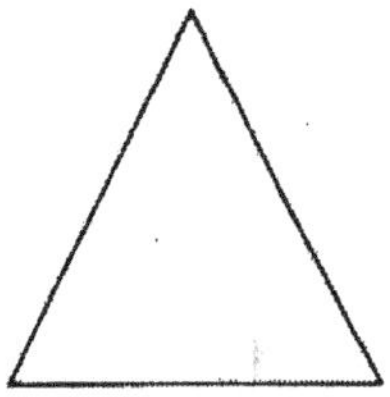

D

37. Questions 37-40.

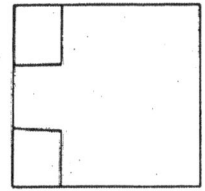

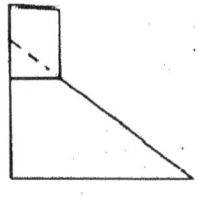 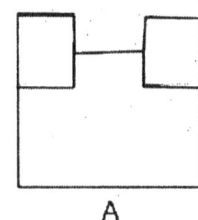 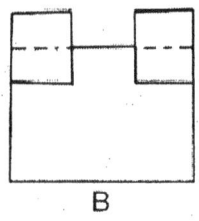 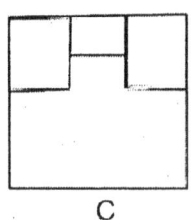 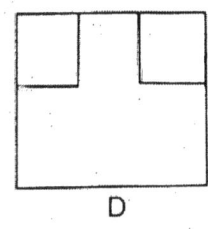
　　　　　　　　A　　　　　　B　　　　　　C　　　　　　D

38.

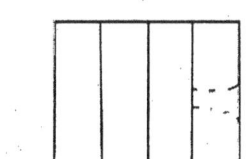

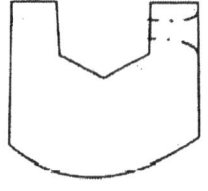 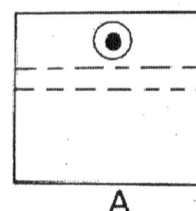 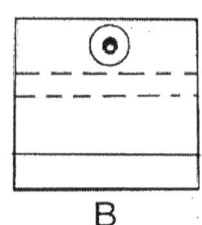 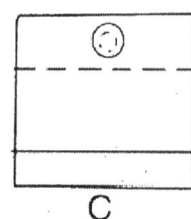 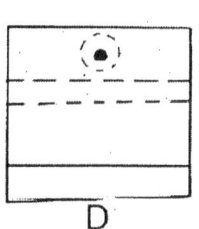
　　　　　　　　A　　　　　　B　　　　　　C　　　　　　D

39.

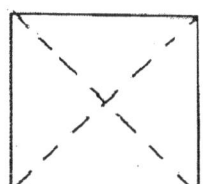

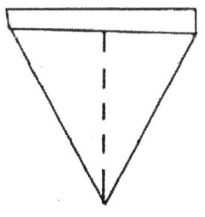 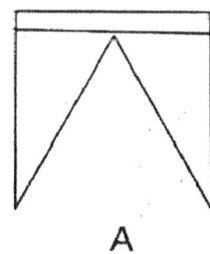 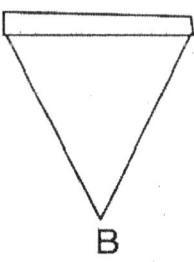 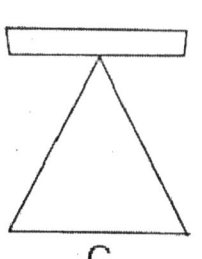 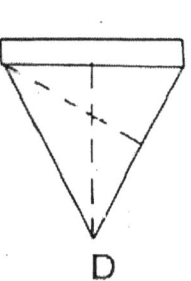
　　　　　　　　A　　　　　　B　　　　　　C　　　　　　D

40.

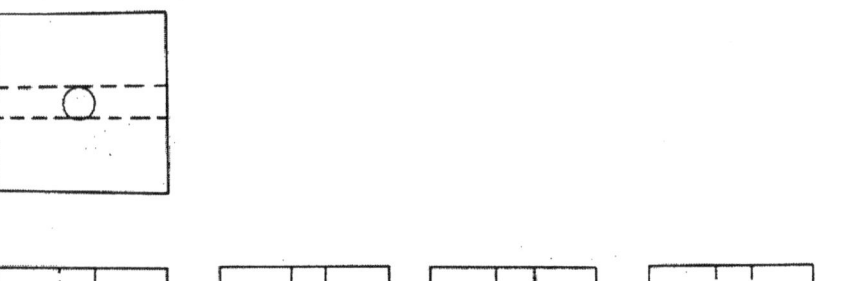

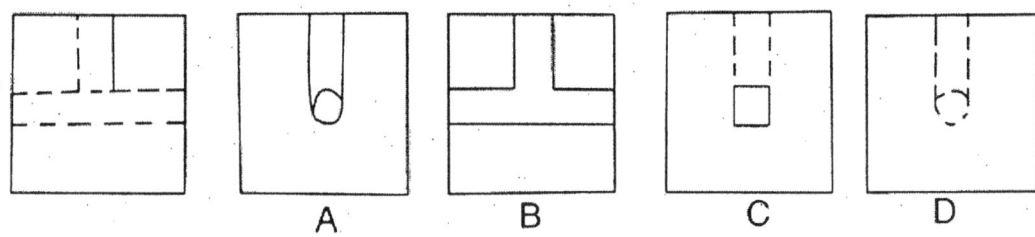

KEY (CORRECT ANSWERS)

1. A	11. B	21. A	31. B
2. D	12. A	22. D	32. C
3. B	13. C	23. A	33. C
4. A	14. B	24. D	34. C
5. C	15. A	25. D	35. A
6. D	16. E	26. C	36. B
7. A	17. G	27. D	37. A
8. B	18. F	28. A	38. B
9. C	19. D	29. D	39. A
10. A	20. A	30. B	40. C

EXAMINATION SECTION
TEST 1

DIRECTIONS: Each question or incomplete statement is followed by several suggested answers or completions. Select the one that BEST answers the question or completes the statement. *PRINT THE LETTER OF THE CORRECT ANSWER IN THE SPACE AT THE RIGHT.*

1. An unbalanced bid is a bidding device used by the contractor. An example of unbalanced bidding is to put

    A. lower unit prices in all unit price items to submit a low bid
    B. lower prices on lump sum items and higher prices on unit price items
    C. lower unit prices on secondary items and higher unit prices on primary items
    D. higher prices on items built early and lower prices on items built later

2. Clearing and grubbing as related to excavation mean cutting trees

    A. so that 1 foot remains above ground
    B. so that 6 inches remains above ground
    C. to ground level
    D. and removing the stumps of the trees

3. The size of a bulldozer is measured by its

    A. weight
    B. flywheel horsepower
    C. ripping capacity
    D. coefficient of traction

4. Of the following, an important use of geotextiles is

    A. as a filter in drainage control
    B. to improve the density of soil
    C. to increase the plasticity of soil
    D. to reduce the CBR of soil

5. A graphical procedure employing a control chart is sometimes used for statistical control in highway construction. After charts of individual tests are prepared, the upper and lower limits are usually _____ standard deviation(s) from a central value.

    A. one   B. two   C. three   D. four

6. On a highway construction job, slope stakes are usually set on both sides of the road at intervals of _____ feet.

    A. 25   B. 50   C. 75   D. 100

7. Earth grade stakes are usually set

    A. when the slope stakes are set
    B. at the center line of the road
    C. after final grading is completed
    D. after rough grading operations have been completed

8. In a borrow pit, measurements for the volume of earth removed are taken usually at _____ foot intervals.

   A. 25   B. 50   C. 75   D. 100

9. In placing surveying stakes for a culvert, a stake is set at the center line of the culvert. A horizontal line on the stake gives the amount of cut or fill to the _____ of the culvert.

   A. top   B. center   C. flow line   D. subgrade

10. Aeolian soils are soils formed by

    A. glacial action
    B. volcanic action
    C. being carried by water
    D. being carried by wind

11. Specific gravity of soils are in the range of

    A. 2.3 to 2.5
    B. 2.4 to 2.6
    C. 2.5 to 2.7
    D. 2.6 to 2.8

12. Of the following soils, the one that is most highly compressible has a _____ plastic limit and _____ liquid limit.

    A. low; high
    B. low; low
    C. high; low
    D. high; high

13. In the present ASSHTO soil classification systems, soils are classified into groups. The number of basic groups are

    A. 6   B. 7   C. 8   D. 9

14. In the present AASHTO soil classification system, granular materials are primarily in Group(s)

    A. A1 *only*
    B. A1 and A2
    C. A1, A2, and A3
    D. A1, A2, A3, and A4

15. The optimum moisture content of a soil occurs when under a given compactive effort, the soil has a maximum

    A. void ratio
    B. plasticity index
    C. elasticity
    D. density

16. The liquid limit that separates an A4 soil from an A5 soil is

    A. 10   B. 20   C. 30   D. 40

17. As part of the soil classification in a given soil is an abbreviation NP. This is an abbreviation for no

    A. permeability
    B. plasticity
    C. peat or other organic materials
    D. porosity

18. For granular materials, the maximum allowable percent passing a Number 200 sieve is

    A. 20   B. 25   C. 30   D. 35

19.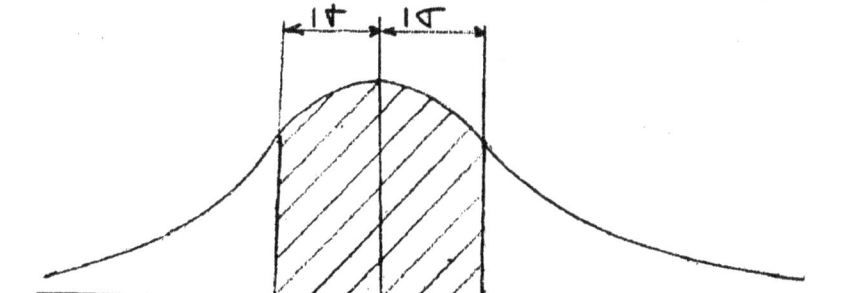

In the normal or Gauss distribution shown above, the shaded area is one standard deviation on either side of the central value covering _____ of the area under the curve.

A. 60% B. 62% C. 65% D. 68%

Questions 20-25.

DIRECTIONS: Questions 20 through 25, inclusive, refer to the diagram below of a vertical curve.

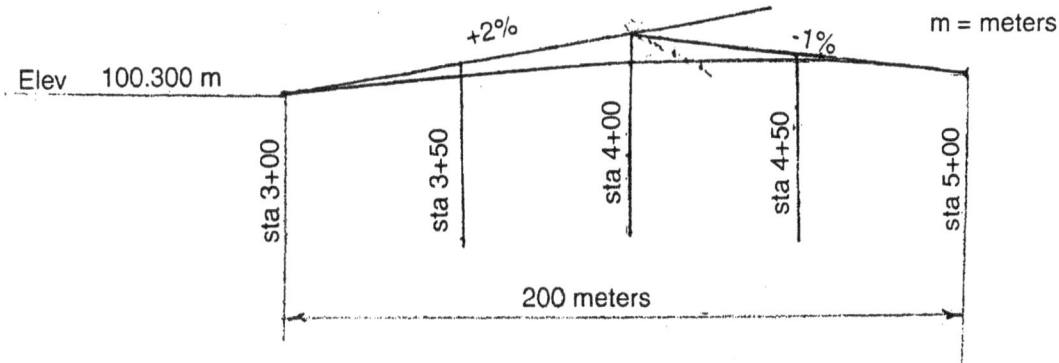

20. The elevation of the curve at Sta4+00 is _____ meters.

   A. 101.250 B. 101.350 C. 101.850 D. 102.150

21. The grade of the curve at Sta4+00 is

   A. +.5% B. +.75% C. +1.00% D. +1.25%

22. The elevation of the curve at Sta3+50 is _____ meters.

   A. 100.992 B. 101.012 C. 101.112 D. 101.212

23. The grade of the curve at Sta3+50 is

   A. 1.75% B. 1.50% C. 1.38% D. 1.25%

24. The station of the high point is

   A. 4+08.333 B. 4+16.667 C. 4+25.000 D. 4+33.333

25. The elevation of the high point is _____ meters.

   A. 101.633 B. 101.750 C. 101.833 D. 101.917

KEY (CORRECT ANSWERS)

1.	D	11.	D
2.	D	12.	A
3.	B	13.	B
4.	A	14.	C
5.	C	15.	D
6.	B	16.	D
7.	D	17.	B
8.	A	18.	D
9.	C	19.	D
10.	D	20.	B

21. A
22. C
23. D
24. D
25. A

———

TEST 2

DIRECTIONS: Each question or incomplete statement is followed by several suggested answers or completions. Select the one that BEST answers the question or completes the statement. *PRINT THE LETTER OF THE CORRECT ANSWER IN THE SPACE AT THE RIGHT.*

Questions 1-3.

DIRECTIONS: Questions 1 through 3 refer to the diagram below.

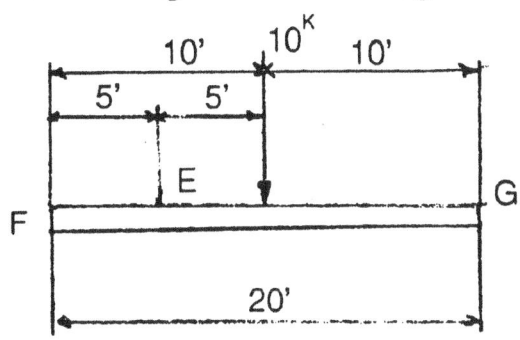

EI is constant

1. The deflection at the center of the beam is   1._____

   A. $-\dfrac{1670^{k^{13}}}{EI}$ B. $-\dfrac{2000^{k^{13}}}{EI}$ C. $-\dfrac{2330^{k^{13}}}{EI}$ D. $-\dfrac{2670^{k^{13}}}{EI}$

2. The slope at F is   2._____

   A. $-\dfrac{200^{k^{12}}}{EI}$ B. $-\dfrac{225^{k^{12}}}{EI}$ C. $-\dfrac{250^{k^{12}}}{EI}$ D. $-\dfrac{275^{k^{12}}}{EI}$

3. The deflection at E is   3._____

   A. $-\dfrac{966^{k^{13}}}{EI}$ B. $-\dfrac{1046^{k^{13}}}{EI}$ C. $-\dfrac{1096^{k^{13}}}{EI}$ D. $-\dfrac{1146^{k^{13}}}{EI}$

Questions 4-7.

DIRECTIONS: Questions 4 through 7, inclusive, refer to the truss below.

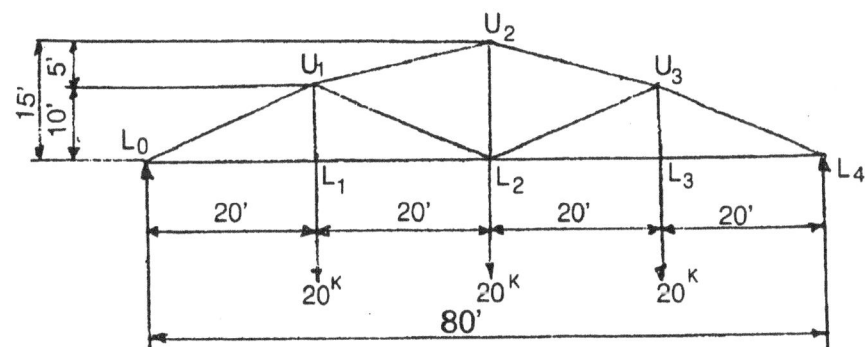

4. The load in member L_1-L_2 is   4.____

   A. $+30^k$ B. $+40^k$ C. $+50^k$ D. $+60^k$

5. The load in member U_1-U_2 is   5.____

   A. -50.9^k B. -52.9^k C. -54.9^k D. -56.9^k

6. The load in member U_1-L_2 is   6.____

   A. -3.4^k B. -5.4^k C. -7.4^k D. -9.4^k

7. The load in member U_2-L_2 is   7.____

   A. $+24.6^k$ B. $+26.6^k$ C. $+28.6^k$ D. $+30.6^k$

Questions 8-11.

DIRECTIONS: Questions 8 through 11, inclusive, refer to the diagram below of a beam with fixed ends.

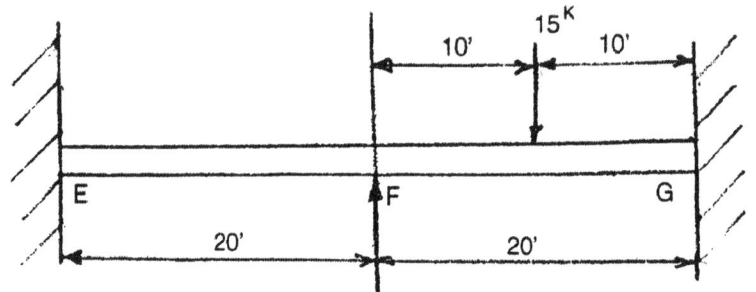

8. The moment in E is   8.____

   A. 9.4^{lk} B. 12.6^{lk} C. 14.8^{lk} D. 17.0^{lk}

9. The moment in G is   9.____

   A. 37.5^{lk} B. 40.0^{lk} C. 43.0^{lk} D. 46.9^{lk}

10. The moment at F is   10.____

    A. 14.4^{lk} B. 18.8^{lk} C. 23.2^{lk} D. 27.6^{lk}

11. The vertical reaction at E is   11.____

    A. -0.4^k B. -1.4^k C. -2.4^k D. -3.4^k

12. The former First Lady of the United States who had legislation enacted to plant wild flowers adjacent to federal highways is   12.____

    A. Rosalyn Carter   B. Barbara Bush
    C. Jackie Kennedy   D. Lady Bird Johnson

13. *Scarification* as used in the specifications means

    A. removing rust from a surface
    B. removing paint from a surface
    C. cleaning equipment
    D. loosening topsoil

    13._____

14. A proposal by the contractor producing a savings to the department without impairing essential functions and characteristics of the facility is termed a(n)

    A. alternative suggestion
    B. design efficiency proposal
    C. value engineering proposal
    D. force account economy

    14._____

15. A cubic meter is MOST NEARLY equal to _____ cubic yards.

    A. 1.31   B. 1.33   C. 1.35   D. 1.37

    15._____

16. One hectare is equal to MOST NEARLY _____ acres.

    A. 2   B. 2.5   C. 3.0   D. 3.5

    16._____

17. One newton is MOST NEARLY equal to _____ pounds.

    A. .12   B. .17   C. .22   D. .29

    17._____

18. A metric ton is _____ pounds.

    A. 2200   B. 2400   C. 2600   D. 2800

    18._____

19. A piezometer is a device that measures

    A. hydraulic pressure
    C. soil grain size
    B. soil compaction
    D. soil grain strength

    19._____

20. Portland cement type 2 is _____ cement.

    A. high early strength
    B. low heat
    C. air entraining
    D. moderate sulfate resisting

    20._____

21. Wire shall have a minimum yield strength of 240 MPa. The MPa is an abbreviation of _____ pascals.

    A. macro   B. micro   C. milli   D. mega

    21._____

22. 7°C is, in degrees Fahrenheit,

    A. 42.6   B. 44.6   C. 46.6   D. 48.6

    22._____

23. In a concrete mix, the absolute ratio of the weight of water to the weight of cement is .44. If a bag of cement weighs 94 pounds and there are 7.48 gallons in a cubic foot, the number of gallons of water per bag of cement for this ratio is MOST NEARLY

    A. 5.0   B. 5.5   C. 5.8   D. 6.1

    23._____

24. The specifications require that when transit mixed concrete is used, approximately 90% of the design water is added followed by mixing the concrete in the drum of the truck. The remainder of the design water may be added

    A. after half the load is emptied
    B. to meet the water cement ratio requirement
    C. if the mix is not uniform
    D. to attain a suitable slump

25. For highways, the minimum median width in a divided highway is _____ feet.

    A. 2   B. 3   C. 4   D. 5

KEY (CORRECT ANSWERS)

1.	A	11.	B
2.	C	12.	D
3.	D	13.	D
4.	D	14.	C
5.	C	15.	A
6.	C	16.	B
7.	B	17.	C
8.	A	18.	A
9.	D	19.	A
10.	B	20.	D

21. D
22. B
23. A
24. D
25. C

EXAMINATION SECTION
TEST 1

DIRECTIONS: Each question or incomplete statement is followed by several suggested answers or completions. Select the one that BEST answers the question or completes the statement. *PRINT THE LETTER OF THE CORRECT ANSWER IN THE SPACE AT THE RIGHT.*

Questions 1-2.

DIRECTIONS: Questions 1 and 2 refer to the formula below.

The formula for stopping sight distance SSD13

$$SSD = 1.47tV + \frac{V^2}{30(f+G)}$$

1. The number 1.47 is a(n)

   A. empirically derived constant
   B. conversion factor
   C. factor based on perception reaction time
   D. factor of safety

2. The term t is usually assumed to be _____ seconds.

   A. 1.5   B. 2.0   C. 2.5   D. 3.0

3. An automobile weighing W is rounding a curve of radius R with a velocity V. Neglecting the friction between the tires and the roadway, if the forces acting on the car are in equilibrium, then

   A. $\sin\theta = \dfrac{V^2}{gR}$

   B. $\cos\theta = \dfrac{V^2}{gR}$

   C. $\tan\theta = \dfrac{V^2}{gR}$

   D. $\cot\theta = \dfrac{V^2}{gR}$

Questions 4-5.

DIRECTIONS: Questions 4 and 5 refer to the horizontal curve below.

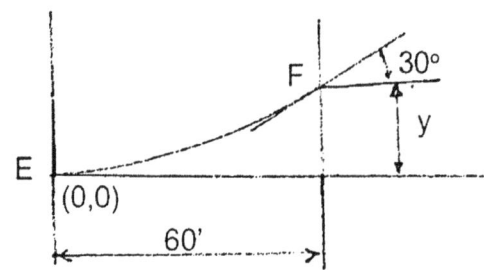

The equation of the curve is $y = kx^3$. The slope of the curve at F is $30°$.

4. The value of k is

   A. .000023   B. .000033   C. .000043   D. .000053

5. The value of y is

   A. 5.0   B. 7.1   C. 9.3   D. 11.5

6. A $4°$ horizontal curve has a radius of _____ feet.

   A. 1232.4   B. 1332.4   C. 1432.4   D. 1532.4

Questions 7-10.

DIRECTIONS: Questions 7 through 10, inclusive, refer to the diagram of a horizontal circular highway curve.

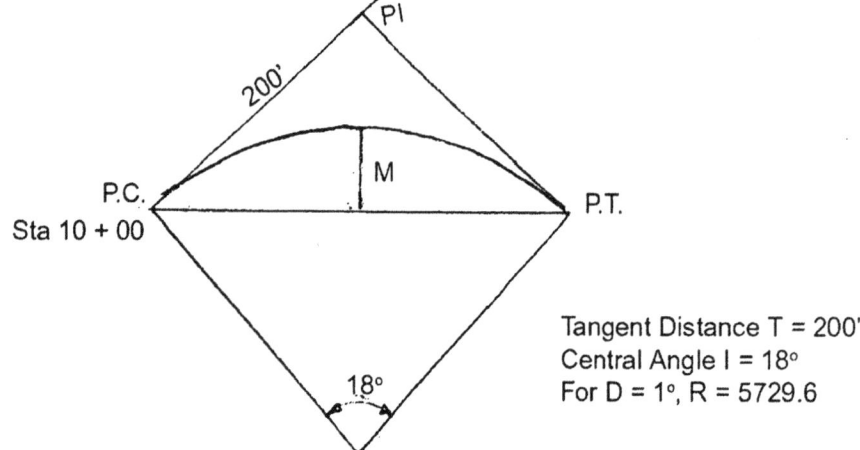

Tangent Distance T = 200'
Central Angle I = 18°
For D = 1°, R = 5729.6

7. The radius of the curve is _____ feet.

   A. 1212.7   B. 1232.7   C. 1262.7   D. 1292.7

8. The length of the arc of the circular curve is MOST NEARLY _____ feet.

   A. 396.7   B. 397.0   C. 397.7   D. 398.0

9. The long chord P.C. to P.T. is MOST NEARLY _____ feet.

   A. 392.06   B. 393.06   C. 394.06   D. 395.06

10. The middle ordinate M is most nearly _____ feet.

    A. 14.95   B. 15.15   C. 15.35   D. 15.55

11.

   The sight distance EF is MOST NEARLY _____ feet.

   A. 324   B. 364   C. 404   D. 444

12. For crest vertical curves, the length of the curve depends on the change in grade and H_e and H_o where H_e is the driver's eye height and H_o is the object height. Their relation is usually

    A. $H_e < H_o$
    B. $H_e = H_o$
    C. $H_e > H_o$
    D. H_e is either greater, equal or less than H_o, depending on the judgment of chief of design

13. The length of a transition curve which connects a tangent to a circular curve should be sufficient to

    A. keep the rate of change of direction small
    B. achieve the superelevation of the road section
    C. prevent disruption of the drainage system
    D. prevent an abrupt change of direction when the circular curve is reached

14. It is desirable to have a minimum road grade of at least 0.3% in order to

    A. follow the land contours
    B. facilitate keeping the shoulders clear of debris
    C. secure adequate drainage for the roadway
    D. prevent drivers becoming drowsy on long stretches of level roadway

Questions 15-16.

DIRECTIONS: Questions 15 and 16 refer to the horizontal highway curve below.

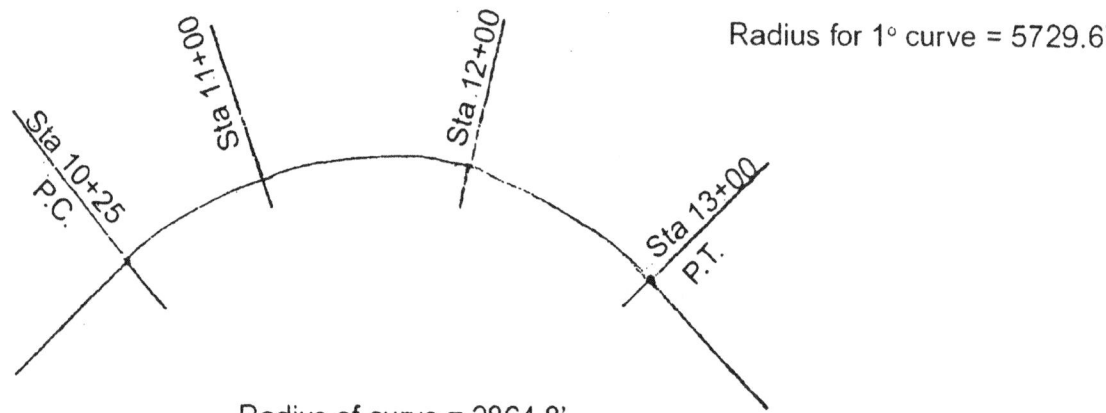

15. The deflection angle from the P.C. to Sta 11+00 is

    A. 0°45'   B. 1°00'   C. 1°15'   D. 1°30'

16. The deflection angle to Sta 13+00 is

    A. 2°00'   B. 2°45'   C. 3°45'   D. 5°30'

17. Air entrained cement is used in air entrained concrete. The acceptable amount of air is generally between _____ percent of the total volume.

    A. 1 and 5   B. 2 and 6   C. 3 and 7   D. 4 and 8

18. Pumping of joints in a concrete roadway slab will occur during frequent occurrence of heavy wheel loads, the presence in the subgrade soil that is susceptible to pumping and

    A. inadequate thickness of the concrete slab
    B. air entrained cement is used in the roadway
    C. surplus water in the subgrade
    D. coarse and fine sand subgrades

19. Distributed steel reinforcing is primarily used to control cracking of a concrete roadway pavement and to maintain the integrity of the slab between transverse joints. Wire fabric or bar mats are used.
    In a concrete roadway section, the steel is usually placed at _____ of the slab.

    A. or near the center
    B. the bottom
    C. the top
    D. the bottom and at the top

20. In slipform paving for a concrete roadway, the slump in the concrete being poured should be _____ inch(es).

    A. 1/2 to 1   B. 1 to 1 1/2   C. 1 1/2 to 2   D. 2 to 2 1/2

21. The collapse of a section of the New England Thruway at Mianus was due primarily to faulty   21.____

    A. steel
    B. design
    C. construction
    D. periodic inspections

22. The coefficient of expansion of concrete due to temperature change is considered   22.____

    A. the same as that for steel
    B. less than that for steel
    C. more than that for steel
    D. more or less than that for steel, depending on the type of steel being used

23. Design hourly volume is a future hourly volume used for design. It is usually taken as the _____ hourly volume of the year.   23.____

    A. 10th   B. 15th   C. 20th   D. 30th

24. Let E be an experiment and S a sample space associated with the experiment. A function X assigned to every element SES a real number X(S) is called a   24.____

    A. relative frequency
    B. likely outcome
    C. random variable
    D. conditional probability

25. The color code brown on a traffic device denotes   25.____

    A. public recreation and scenic guidance
    B. construction and maintenance warning
    C. general warning
    D. motorist service guidance

KEY (CORRECT ANSWERS)

1. B
2. C
3. C
4. D
5. D

6. C
7. C
8. A
9. D
10. D

11. D
12. C
13. B
14. C
15. A

16. B
17. D
18. C
19. A
20. B

21. D
22. A
23. D
24. C
25. A

TEST 2

DIRECTIONS: Each question or incomplete statement is followed by several suggested answers or completions. Select the one that BEST answers the question or completes the statement. *PRINT THE LETTER OF THE CORRECT ANSWER IN THE SPACE AT THE RIGHT.*

1. The minimum headroom clearance for a sign over a roadway, according to the Federal Highway Administration, should be _____ feet.

    A. 15 B. 16 C. 17 D. 18

2. In traffic flow, time mean speed _____ space mean speed.

    A. equals
    B. is less than
    C. is greater than
    D. may be greater or less than

3. Overall speed and running speed are speeds over a relatively long section of street or highway between an origin and a destination. Test vehicles are driven over the test section of the roadway. The driver attempts to float in the traffic stream.
   This means

    A. driving as fast as he can under the speed limit
    B. driving in the middle lane of a three lane road
    C. passing as many vehicles as pass the test vehicle
    D. trying to keep his speed the same as the average speed of the vehicles on the road

4. The difference between overall speed and running speed on a test run between origin and destination is overall speed is the

    A. average of the maximum and minimum speed while running speed is the distance covered divided by the time elapsed
    B. distance traveled divided by the time required while running speed is the distance traveled divided by the time required reduced by time for stop delays
    C. distance traveled divided by the total time required while running speed is the minimum time needed to cover the distance
    D. distance traveled divided by the total time required while running speed is the effort by the driver to stay in the flow of traffic

5. The ductility test on asphalt is considered a measure of the _____ of the asphalt.

    A. impact resistance   B. elasticity
    C. durability   D. cementing power

6. In asphalt paving work, there are three different types of specific gravity: bulk, apparent, and effective. Of the following statements relating to specific gravity, the one that is CORRECT is:

    A. Water absorption is normally not used in determining the quantity of permeable voids in the volume of aggregates
    B. The apparent specific gravity is less than the bulk specific gravity

C. The effective specific gravity is less than the bulk specific gravity
D. The effective specific gravity falls between the bulk specific gravity and the apparent specific gravity

7. The temperature range of asphalt prior to entering the mixer in a batch or continuous plant is usually

   A. 150 to 250° F B. 175 to 275° F
   C. 200 to 300° F D. 225 to 325° F

8. The most likely cause of the various distress types in asphalt concrete pavements is

   A. structural failure B. temperature changes
   C. moisture changes D. faulty construction

9. Bleeding in asphalt concrete pavements is MOST likely caused by

   A. faulty mix composition B. structural failure
   C. temperature changes D. moisture changes

10. Depressions in asphalt concrete pavements is MOST likely caused by

    A. faulty construction B. faulty mix composition
    C. temperature changes D. moisture changes

11. The gradation curve of particle sizes is represented graphically with the ordinate defining the percent by weight passing a given size and the abscissa representing the particle size.
    The ordinate is plotted on a(n) _____ scale and the abscissa is plotted on a(n) _____ scale.

    A. arithmetic; arithmetic
    B. logarithmic; arithmetic
    C. arithmetic; logarithmic
    D. logarithmic; logarithmic

12. The viscosity of a liquid is a measure of its

    A. resistance to flow
    B. volatility
    C. solubility in carbon tetrachloride
    D. elasticity

13. Failures that occur in soil masses as a result of the action of highway loads are primarily _____ failures.

    A. tensile B. torsion C. shear D. buckling

14. Bitumens composed primarily of high molecular weight hydrocarbons are soluble in

    A. toluene B. carbon sulfate
    C. carbon disulfide D. ammonium chloride

15. One pascal-second equals _____ poise(s).

    A. 1 B. 5 C. 10 D. 20

16. RS emulsions are best used

    A. where deep penetration is desired
    B. with coarse aggregates
    C. in warm weather
    D. in spraying applications

17. The specific gravity of bituminous material is generally determined

    A. with a pyenometer   B. with a hygrometer
    C. by displacement   D. with a hydrometer

18. The principal reason for determining the specific gravity of a bituminous material is

    A. converting from volume to weight measurements and vice versa
    B. identifying the type of bituminous material used in a mix
    C. for checking the uniformity of a mix where large quantities are involved
    D. insure that the properties of the mix continue to meet specifications

19. The specific gravity of asphaltic products derived from petroleum vary from

    A. .80 to .84   B. .92 to 1.06
    C. 1.04 to 1.18   D. 1.16 to 1.30

20. The flash point is an indirect measurement of the quality and kind of volatiles present in the asphalt being tested.
    Rapid cure cutback asphalts have a flashpoint of _____ or less.

    A. 100° F   B. 130° F   C. 150° F   D. 180° F

21. Traffic density is defined as the

    A. number of vehicles passing a given point in a given period of time
    B. average number of vehicles occupying a given length of roadway at a given instant
    C. average center to center distance of vehicles on a given stretch of roadway at a given instant
    D. minimum distance center to center of vehicles on a given stretch of roadway at a given instant

22. Of the following, the best distribution that describes the vehicle distribution on a given stretch of highway at a given instant is the _____ distribution.

    A. Poisson   B. Pascal
    C. normal   D. hypergeometric

23. In slipform paving for a concrete roadway, the slump in the concrete being poured should be _____ inch(es).

    A. 1/2 to 1   B. 1 to 1 1/2   C. 1 1/2 to 2   D. 2 to 2 1/2

24. A water-cement ratio of 6 gallons per sack of cement is equal to a water-cement ratio of _____ by weight.

    A. .50   B. .53   C. .56   D. .59

25. One micron is equal to _____ centimeters.   25._____

　　A. 10^{-2}　　　　B. 10^{-3}　　　　C. 10^{-4}　　　　D. 10^{-5}

KEY (CORRECT ANSWERS)

1. C
2. C
3. C
4. B
5. D

6. D
7. D
8. D
9. A
10. A

11. C
12. A
13. C
14. C
15. C

16. D
17. A
18. A
19. B
20. A

21. B
22. A
23. B
24. B
25. C

EXAMINATION SECTION
TEST 1

DIRECTIONS: Each question or incomplete statement is followed by several suggested answers or completions. Select the one that BEST answers the question or completes the statement. *PRINT THE LETTER OF THE CORRECT ANSWER IN THE SPACE AT THE RIGHT.*

1. Reflective cracks in asphalt overlays

    A. are cracks in asphalt overlays that show the crack pattern of the pavement underneath
    B. are cracks that reflect caused by weakness in the base soil
    C. are the result of change in weights and frequency of truck travel in that they are greater than the loads the pavement was designed for
    D. reflect the type of cracks that normally could be expected for this type of pavement

1.____

2. In a guide for the estimation of Pavement Condition Rating for asphalt concrete pavement on a highway is the following classification: *Pavement is in fairly good condition with frequent slight cracking or very slight channeling and a few areas with slight alligatoring. Rideability is fairly good with intermittent rough and uneven sections.*
The maintenance recommendation for this class of pavement condition is

    A. no maintenance required
    B. normal maintenance only
    C. resurface in 3 to 5 years
    D. resurface within 3 years

2.____

3. A major problem in bituminous asphalt plants is

    A. varying water content in the bituminous aggregate
    B. accuracy in the weighing equipment
    C. air pollution caused by plant exhausts
    D. producing a uniform mixture

3.____

4. The primary difference between asphalt concrete and sheet asphalt is asphalt concrete

    A. uses a finer sand than sheet asphalt
    B. uses a lower viscosity asphalt than sheet asphalt
    C. generally has a thinner layer than sheet asphalt
    D. contains coarse aggregate whereas sheet asphalt does not have coarse aggregate

4.____

5. It is common practice to apply a prime coat over untreated and some treated bases before asphalt concrete is placed. Of the following, the reasons for applying a prime coat are to

    A. bind loose particles of the base and minimize heat loss in the applied asphalt concrete
    B. act as a bond between base and pavement and prevent loss of asphalt in the asphalt concrete due to seepage
    C. deter rising moisture from penetrating the pavement and minimize heat loss in the applied asphalt concrete
    D. bind loose particles in the base and deter rising moisture from penetrating the asphalt pavement

5.____

6. The asphalt content of open graded mixes is generally at

   A. the same level as dense graded asphalt
   B. a higher level than dense graded asphalt
   C. a lower level than dense graded asphalt
   D. at a higher or lower level than dense graded asphalt depending on the percent of fine aggregate in the open graded asphalt mix

7. Sheet asphalt was extensively used in the past with a thickness of _____ inch(es).

   A. 1/2   B. 3/4   C. 1   D. 1 1/2

8. The progressive separation of aggregate particles in a pavement from the surface downward or from the edges inward in an asphalt concrete pavement is known as

   A. raveling   B. spalling
   C. scaling   D. reflective cracks

9. A profilometer used on an asphalt concrete road measures the _____ the road.

   A. grade of   B. roughness of
   C. impact resistance of   D. channels in

10. Reinforcing steel is used in a footing. The minimum distance the bottom of the steel is above the subgrade should be _____ inch(es).

    A. 1   B. 2   C. 3   D. 4

11. Loose sand weighs 120 pounds per cubic foot and the specific gravity of sand is 2.65. The absolute volume of a cubic foot of loose sand is, in cubic feet, most nearly

    A. .73   B. .75   C. .77   D. .79

12. The maximum size of coarse aggregate in a concrete mix for a reinforced concrete structure is determined by the size of the concrete section and the

    A. type of cement used
    B. proportion of fine aggregate
    C. minimum distance between reinforcing bars
    D. yield point of the reinforcing steel

13. Cement (High Early Strength) is Type _____ cement.

    A. I   B. II   C. III   D. IV

14. Slunp in concrete is a measure of

    A. strength   B. porosity
    C. permeability   D. workability

15. The cross section area of a #8 bar is _____ square inches.

    A. .60   B. .79   C. 1.00   D. 1.25

16. Construction joints for slabs in a building shall be made

    A. at the supports
    B. within 1/8 of the span of the slab from the supports
    C. from 1/8 to 3/8 of the span of the slab from the supports
    D. near the center of the span

17. Chutes for depositing concrete shall have a slope no greater than

    A. 1 to 1   B. 1½ to 1   C. 2 to 1   D. 2½ to 1

18. Air entrained cement is used in a concrete mix on highways primarily to

    A. make the concrete stronger after 28 days
    B. have a higher early strength
    C. make the surface more resistant to freezing and thawing
    D. make the surface less porous to better resist the impact of trucks

19. Beach sand is unsuitable as a fine aggregate in concrete because it has salt contamination and the sand particles are

    A. smooth   B. rough
    C. uniform in size D. too fine

20. The fineness modulus of sand for concrete is taken on the job to insure

    A. the quality of the sand
    B. that the gradation of the sand does not change
    C. that there is not an excess of fines in the sand
    D. that there is not an excess of oversized particles in the sand

21. The coarse and fine aggregate for concrete are usually tested

    A. at the quarry site
    B. at the job site
    C. by sampling a loaded truck
    D. in the design engineering office

22. The slump in concrete for highway mixtures range from _____ inches.

    A. 1 to 3   B. 2 to 5   C. 3 to 6   D. 4 to 7

23. A bag of cement weighs _____ pounds.

    A. 90   B. 94   C. 97   D. 100

24. The design strength of concrete is to be reached at the end of _____ days.

    A. 7   B. 14   C. 21   D. 28

25. Of the following, water-cement ratio may be defined as _____ of water per _____ of cement.

    A. gallons; bag   B. gallons; 100 pounds
    C. quarts; bag   D. quarts; 100 pounds

KEY (CORRECT ANSWERS)

1. A
2. C
3. C
4. D
5. D

6. B
7. D
8. A
9. B
10. C

11. A
12. C
13. C
14. D
15. B

16. D
17. C
18. C
19. C
20. B

21. A
22. A
23. B
24. D
25. A

TEST 2

DIRECTIONS: Each question or incomplete statement is followed by several suggested answers or completions. Select the one that BEST answers the question or completes the statement. *PRINT THE LETTER OF THE CORRECT ANSWER IN THE SPACE AT THE RIGHT.*

1. The maximum size of coarse aggregate in a concrete mix for a reinforced concrete structure is determined by the size of the section and the 1.____

    A. type of cement used
    B. proportion of fine aggregate
    C. minimum distance between reinforcing bars
    D. the yield point of the reinforcing steel

Questions 2-3.

DIRECTIONS: Questions 2 and 3 refer to concrete mix design.

2. The present and most popular method of rational mixture design is sponsored by ACI committee 211, 1994. In this method, the design using ordinary cement is based on 2.____

    A. slump and water-cement ratio
    B. aggregate size and water-cement ratio
    C. slump, aggregate size, and water-cement ratio
    D. slump and water content

3. In the method of mix design of ACI committee 211, 1994, water content is expressed in 3.____

    A. pounds of water per bag of cement
    B. pounds of water per cubic foot of concrete
    C. gallons of water per cubic yard of concrete
    D. pounds of water per cubic yard of concrete

4. The right to use or control the property of another for designated purposes is the definition of 4.____

    A. property acquisition   B. right-of-way
    C. an air right   D. an easement

5. A 24 inch circular drainage pipe is shown on a profile drawing of a highway as an ellipse with the major axis vertical. The reason for this is 5.____

    A. the horizontal and vertical scales of the profile drawing are different
    B. the pipe is not perpendicular to the center line of the roadway
    C. to emphasize the height of the pipe
    D. the slope of the pipe is taken into account

6. On a highway plan is a note for #4 wire game fence reading Lt Sta 2970 + 00 to 2979 + 85, Rt Sta 2970 + 00 to 2980 + 70. The total number of linear feet of new #4 wire game fence is, in feet, most nearly 6.____

    A. 1955   B. 2005   C. 2055   D. 2105

7. The superelevation of a curve is .075 feet. The superelevation, in inches, is most nearly

   A. 9 B. 5/8 C. 3/4 D. 7/8

8. On a plan for a highway is a note $\dfrac{\text{S.C.}}{\text{Sta } 2968 + 56.50}$ The S.C. is an abbreviation for

   A. slope at curve
   B. spiral to circular curve
   C. superelevated curve
   D. separation at center

9. Of the following methods of soil stabilization for the base of a highway pavement, the one that is most effective is

   A. a cement admixture
   B. a lime admixture
   C. an emulsified asphalt treated soil
   D. mechanical soil stabilization

10. An asphalt pavement mixture having a brownish dull appearance and lacking a shiny black luster

    A. is normal for an asphalt mixture
    B. contains too little aggregate
    C. is too cold
    D. contains too little asphalt

11. Steam rising from an asphalt mix when it is dumped into a hopper indicates

    A. there is excessive moisture in the aggregate
    B. the mix is overheated
    C. emulsification is taking place
    D. the mixture has not been adequately mixed

12. The disadvantage of excessive fine aggregate in an asphalt mix is

    A. it is difficult to get a uniform mix
    B. it will require an excessive amount of asphalt
    C. it is difficult to apply because of the grittiness of the mix
    D. the final surface will tend to be rough

13. On highways where heavy trucks are permitted, the percent of total traffic that are heavy trucks is, in percent, MOST NEARLY

    A. 4 B. 11 C. 18 D. 25

14. A single axle 80 kN load is equal to _____ pounds per axle.

    A. 12,000 B. 14,000 C. 16,000 D. 18,000

15. Normal traffic growth in the United States is _____ percent per year.

    A. 1-2 B. 3-5 C. 5-7 D. 7-9

16. EAL is an abbreviation for _____ axle load

    A. equal
    B. equivalent
    C. effective
    D. estimated

17. A roughometer is a single-wheeled trailer instrumented to measure the roughness of a pavement surface. The measure is in inches per   17.____

    A. foot   B. yard   C. hundred yards   D. mile

18. The Atterberg Limit is a test on   18.____

    A. coarse aggregate   B. asphalt
    C. soil   D. Portland cement

19. Of the following, the one that is a high strength bolt is designated   19.____

    A. A7   B. A36   C. A180   D. A325

20. Construction contracts in a broad sense fall into two categories - fixed price and   20.____

    A. cost-plus   B. fixed price plus overhead and profit
    C. negotiated price   D. arbitrated price

21. A punch list on a construction job is usually made by the inspector   21.____

    A. weekly
    B. monthly
    C. continuously during the last half of the job
    D. near the end of the job

22. When an accident occurs on a construction job in which someone is injured, an accident report is usually made out by the   22.____

    A. insurance carrier   B. contractor
    C. inspector   D. inspector's superior

23. The inspector and the contractor share common goals. The one of the goals listed below that is NOT shared by the contractor and the inspector is   23.____

    A. get a good job done
    B. see that the contractor makes a reasonable profit
    C. get the job done as speedily as possible
    D. have the job done at as low a cost as possible

24. A crack relief layer is placed over an existing Portland cement concrete pavement followed by a well-graded intermediate course, then a dense graded surface course. The crack relief layer consists of an open graded   24.____

    A. mix of 100% crushed material with 25-35% interconnected voids
    B. crushed material heavily compacted with no binder
    C. hot mix made up of 80% crushed material with 20% shredded rubber
    D. dense crushed material with voids filled by asphalt

25. Most of the major work performed on the nation's bridges involves   25.____

    A. painting the bridges
    B. upgrading the bridges to carry heavier loads
    C. replacing the concrete decks
    D. replacing the suspenders on cable supported bridges

KEY (CORRECT ANSWERS)

1. C
2. C
3. D
4. D
5. A

6. C
7. D
8. B
9. A
10. D

11. A
12. B
13. B
14. D
15. B

16. B
17. D
18. C
19. D
20. A

21. D
22. B
23. B
24. A
25. C

EXAMINATION SECTION
TEST 1

DIRECTIONS: Each question or incomplete statement is followed by several suggested answers or completions. Select the one that BEST answers the question or completes the statement. *PRINT THE LETTER OF THE CORRECT ANSWER IN THE SPACE AT THE RIGHT.*

1. In pouring concrete for a large footing, the vibrator is used to move concrete into place. This is

   A. *good* practice as it moves the concrete quickly into place
   B. *good* practice as it eliminates air pockets
   C. *poor* practice as it promotes segregation
   D. *poor* practice as it increases pressure against the forms

2. For successful winter work in placing ordinary concrete, adequate protection against the cold should be provided.
   Special protection is NOT required when the temperature is over _____ and is required when the temperature is below _____.

   A. 50° F; 50° F
   B. 40° F; 40° F
   C. 30° F; 30° F
   D. 20° F; 20° F

3. The MAIN reason for curing concrete is to

   A. prevent segregation of the concrete
   B. prevent the formation of air pockets in the concrete
   C. keep the concrete surface moist
   D. minimize bleeding in the poured concrete

4. Of the following, the concrete mix that uses the greatest amount of cement per cubic yard of concrete is

   A. 1:2:4   B. 1:2:3 1/2   C. 1:2 1/2:5   D. 1:2 1/2:3 1/2

5. The volume of concrete in a sidewalk 6 ft. x 30 ft. x 4 inches is, in cubic feet, MOST NEARLY

   A. 45   B. 50   C. 55   D. 60

6. Of the following, the chemical compound that is added to a concrete mix to accelerate setting in cold weather is

   A. potassium chloride
   B. calcium chloride
   C. sodium nitrate
   D. calcium nitrate

7. The compressive strength of concrete

   A. reaches a maximum after 28 days
   B. reaches a maximum after 90 days
   C. reaches a maximum after 180 days
   D. increases after 180 days

8. The smallest size of coarse aggregate for concrete is, in inches, MOST NEARLY

   A. 1/4 B. 3/8 C. 1/2 D. 5/8

9. Of the following, the most practical way to determine that the water used in a concrete mix is satisfactory is

   A. send a sample to the laboratory
   B. taste the water
   C. the water is also used for drinking
   D. take a sample and let it stand for a while; and if no sediment at the bottom of the sample, it is satisfactory

10. Grout is

    A. cement, sand with water added so that it will flow readily
    B. cement with water added so that it is fluid
    C. cement and lime with water added so that it will flow readily
    D. gravel, sand, and lime with water added so that it will flow readily

11. Wire fabric has a designation 4 x 12 6/10. Of the following, the statement that is correct is the _____ center to enter and are _____.

    A. longitudinal wires are 12"; 10 gage
    B. longitudinal wires are 4"; 6 gage
    C. transverse wires are 4"; 6 gage
    D. transverse wires are 12; 6 gage

12. The volume of a bag of cement is _____ cubic foot(feet).

    A. 1 B. 1 1/2 C. 2 D. 2 1/2

13. The specifications state: *Forms for slabs shall be set with a camber of 1/4 inch for each 10 feet of span.* The purpose of this requirement is to

    A. compensate for deflection
    B. allow for small errors in setting the formwork
    C. allow for shrinkage of the concrete
    D. compensate for settlement of the supports for the formwork

14. When an inspector goes out to inspect the reinforcing steel before placing of the concrete, the most important drawings he should have with him are the _____ drawings.

    A. structural steel   B. reinforcing steel detail
    C. formwork   D. erection

15. A reinforcing bar has hooks at each end as shown at the right. The detail drawing of the bar will show dimension

    A. A
    B. B
    C. C
    D. D

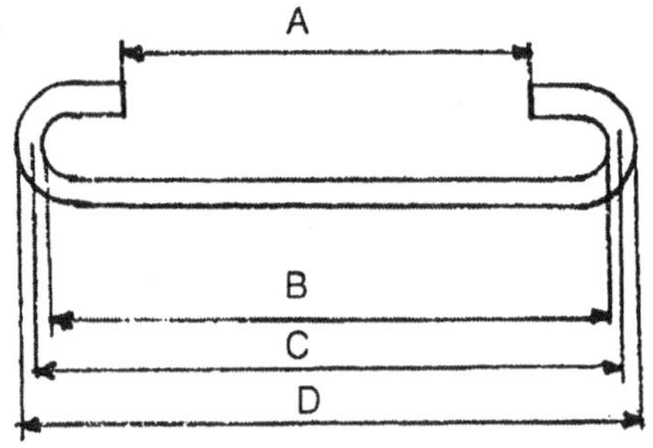

16. Concrete sidewalks are usually finished with a   16._____

    A. screed   B. steel float
    C. wood float   D. darby

17. A new manhole consists of a concrete base made with ordinary cement and a brick   17._____
    superstructure. The minimum time that is usually required after the pouring of the con-
    crete base to start the brickwork is _____ hours.

    A. 24   B. 48   C. 72   D. 96

18. In a new manhole, the slump in the concrete used in the base should be _____ inches.   18._____

    A. 2 to 3   B. 3 to 4   C. 4 to 5   D. 5 to 6

19. The dimensions of a cylinder used for testing the strength of concrete is _____ inch   19._____
    diameter and _____ inches high.

    A. 6; 9   B. 6; 12   C. 8; 9   D. 8; 12

20. The specification for the mixing time required for a concrete mix in a Ready-Mix truck is   20._____
    one minute for a one cubic yard batch and a quarter of a minute for every additional cubic
    yard. The minimum mixing time for a ten cubic yard batch is _____ minutes.

    A. 2 3/4   B. 3   C. 3 1/4   D. 3 1/2

21. The subgrade for a concrete footing is wetted down before concrete is poured into the   21._____
    footing.
    This is

    A. *poor* practice as the water-cement ratio of the concrete will be increased
    B. *poor* practice as it will leave a pocket on the underside of the footing
    C. *good* practice as the water-cement ratio of the concrete will be decreased
    D. *good* practice as the soil will not withdraw water from the concrete

22. Concrete should not be poured too rapidly into the formwork for thin walls primarily   22._____
    because

    A. segregation will result
    B. air pockets will form in the wall
    C. there will be excessive pressure on the formwork
    D. there will be seepage of water through the formwork.

23. The FIRST step in finishing the surface of a concrete pavement is   23._____

    A. darbying   B. floating   C. screeding   D. tamping

24. The grade of a reinforcing steel is 40. The 40 represents the _____ of the steel.   24._____

    A. tensile strength   B. ultimate strength
    C. yield point   D. elastic limit

25. In reinforced concrete work, stirrups would MOST likely be found in   25._____

    A. beams   B. columns   C. walls   D. footings

KEY (CORRECT ANSWERS)

1.	C		11.	B
2.	B		12.	A
3.	C		13.	A
4.	B		14.	B
5.	D		15.	D
6.	B		16.	C
7.	D		17.	A
8.	B		18.	A
9.	C		19.	B
10.	A		20.	C

21. D
22. C
23. C
24. C
25. A

TEST 2

DIRECTIONS: Each question or incomplete statement is followed by several suggested answers or completions. Select the one that BEST answers the question or completes the statement. *PRINT THE LETTER OF THE CORRECT ANSWER IN THE SPACE AT THE RIGHT.*

Questions 1-6.

DIRECTIONS: Questions 1 through 6, inclusive, refer to the following retaining wall.

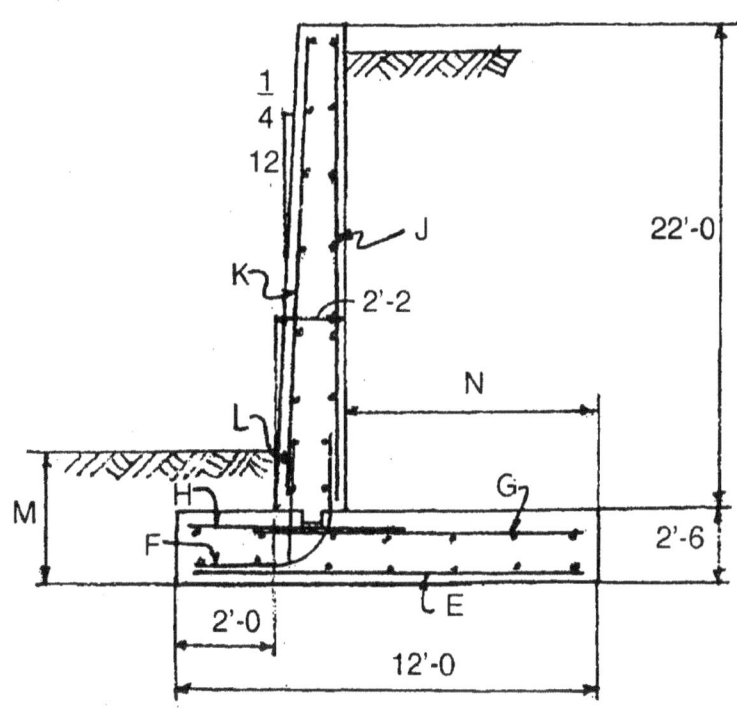

1. The largest size steel bars are most likely to be 1.____
   A. H, K, L   B. E, F, J   C. F, G, H   D. F, G, J

2. Distance M is USUALLY at least 2.____
   A. 2'6"   B. 3'0"   C. 3'6"   D. 4'0"

3. Dimension N is 3.____
   A. 7'6"   B. 7'8"   C. 7'10"   D. 8'0"

4. The width of the wall at the top of the wall is 4.____
   A. 1'8"   B. 1'8 1/2"   C. 1'9"   D. 1'9 1/2"

5. The volume of one foot of wall, in cubic feet, is most nearly (neglect the key at the bottom of the wall) 5.____
   A. 41.2   B. 41.7   C. 42.2   D. 42.6

6. The number of cubic yards of concrete in the footing fifty feet long is, in cubic yards, most nearly (neglect the key at the bottom of the wall)

   A. 54.6
   B. 55.6
   C. 56.6
   D. 57.6

Questions 7-9.

DIRECTIONS: Questions 7 through 9, inclusive, refer to the markings on a reinforcing bar. The end of a reinforcing bar is marked H6N60.

7. The H in H6N60 indicates the

   A. method of treatment of the reinforcing bar
   B. hardness of the reinforcing steel bar
   C. initial of the steel mill
   D. type of steel in the reinforcing bar

8. The N in the reinforcing steel bar means

   A. new billet steel
   B. normalized reinforcing steel
   C. the area in which the steel has been produced (north east)
   D. the initial of the manufacturer

9. The 60 represents the

   A. ultimate strength of the steel
   B. diameter of the steel in millimeters
   C. allowable unit stress in the steel
   D. grade of the steel

10. The plywood industry produces a special product intended for concrete forming called

    A. structure ply
    B. plyform
    C. formply
    D. plycoat

11. Lumber that has been inspected and sorted will carry a grade stamp. The item LEAST likely to be found on the grade stamp is

    A. state of origin
    B. grade
    C. species
    D. condition of seasoning

12. In dimensioned lumber, wane indicates

    A. a lack of lumber
    B. narrow annular rings
    C. undersized width or length of lumber
    D. improper seasoning

13. A sidewalk slab is required to be 4" thick. Measuring down from a nail in the side form that represents the top of the slab, the distance is 4 1/2 inches. Of the following, the BEST action to take is

    A. have the contractor fill the subgrade with a half inch of sand
    B. have the contractor fill the subgrade with a half inch of grout

C. take no action as the contract requirement is met
D. point out the discrepancy to the contractor and ask him to take appropriate action

14. If high visibility is necessary on the job, a vest _____ colored should be worn. 14.____

   A. red   B. orange   C. yellow   D. green

15. Emulsified asphalt tack coats are preferred to using cut back asphalts PRIMARILY because 15.____

   A. cut-back asphalts present environmental problems
   B. cut-back asphalts are slower drying than emulsified asphalts
   C. cut-back asphalts are faster drying than emulsified asphalts
   D. emulsified asphalts are easier to place than cut-back asphalts

16. Spread footings are footings that 16.____

   A. cover a large area
   B. have an irregular shape
   C. are sometimes called strap footings
   D. transmit their loads through a combination of piles and soil

17. An excavation for a footing is over-excavated and the subgrade is well below the design elevation. Of the following, the BEST action for the contractor to take is 17.____

   A. fill the excavation with well compacted soil until it reaches the design elevation of the bottom of the footing
   B. fill the subgrade with gravel to reach the bottom elevation of the footing
   C. lower the elevation of the footing but retain its thickness
   D. change the footing to a pile supported footing

18. The inspector should be aware of the items in the contract that are unit price so that he can 18.____

   A. make the proper inspection of these items
   B. keep a record of when they are delivered to the job site
   C. make measurements and compute quantities that may be necessary
   D. record the dates of installation of these items

19. The attitudes that an inspector should adopt in dealing with the contractor are to be 19.____

   A. understanding and flexible
   B. helpful and cautious
   C. cautious and skeptical
   D. firm and fair

20. Among the provisions for the safety of workers on the job, the most basic and general one is 20.____

   A. workmen should work slowly
   B. keep alcohol off the job
   C. good housekeeping
   D. wear suitable clothing for extreme weather conditions

21. Ladders should extend a minimum of _____ above the level to which they lead. 21.____

    A. six feet B. knee-high
    C. waist-high D. five feet

22. An inspector notices a worker working in an unsafe manner. Of the following, the BEST 22.____
    action the inspector can take is to

    A. tell the worker the correct way to work
    B. tell the worker's supervisor of the unsafe behavior of the worker
    C. record the incident in your log book
    D. notify the contractor so that the unsafe practice will cease

23. In making the daily report, personal remarks by the inspector should not be included. Of 23.____
    the following, the best reason for this exclusion is

    A. it may raise questions as to the accuracy of the report
    B. the wrong people may read the daily report
    C. the inspector should have no opinions
    D. it may indicate bias on the part of the inspector

24. The major difference between a softwood and a hardwood in forestry terms is 24.____

    A. the softwoods are from the south and the hardwoods are from the north
    B. the softwoods are evergreens and the hardwoods are deciduous
    C. the softwoods are soft and the hardwoods are hard
    D. there is one grading method for softwoods and another grading method for hard-
       woods

25. Lumber is considered unseasoned if it has a moisture content of not less than _____ 25.____
    percent in weight of water.

    A. 17 B. 20 C. 23 D. 26

KEY (CORRECT ANSWERS)

1. D
2. D
3. C
4. B
5. D

6. B
7. C
8. A
9. D
10. B

11. A
12. A
13. C
14. B
15. A

16. A
17. A
18. C
19. D
20. C

21. C
22. B
23. D
24. B
25. B

EXAMINATION SECTION
TEST 1

DIRECTIONS: Each question or incomplete statement is followed by several suggested answers or completions. Select the one that BEST answers the question or completes the statement. *PRINT THE LETTER OF THE CORRECT ANSWER IN THE SPACE AT THE RIGHT.*

1. Management by exception (MBE) is

    A. designed to locate bottlenecks
    B. designed to pinpoint superior performance
    C. a form of index locating
    D. a form of variance reporting

2. In managerial terms, gap analysis is useful primarily in

    A. problem solving
    B. setting standards
    C. inventory control
    D. locating bottlenecks

3. ABC analysis involves

    A. problem solving
    B. indexing
    C. brainstorming
    D. inventory control

4. The Federal Discrimination in Employment Act as amended in 1978 prohibits job discrimination based on age for persons between the ages of

    A. 35 and 60   B. 40 and 65   C. 45 and 65   D. 40 and 70

5. Inspectors should be familiar with the contractor's CPM charts for a construction job primarily to determine if

    A. the job is on schedule
    B. the contractor is using the charts correctly
    C. material is on hand to keep the job on schedule
    D. there is a potential source of delay

6. The value engineering approach is frequently found in public works contracts. Value engineering is

    A. an effort to cut down or eliminate extra work payments
    B. a team approach to optimize the cost of the project
    C. to insure that material and equipment will perform as specified
    D. to insure that insurance costs on the project can be minimized

7. Historically, most costly claims have been either for

    A. unreasonable inspection requirements or unforeseen weather conditions
    B. unreasonable specification requirements or unreasonable completion time for the contract
    C. added costs due to inflation or unavailability of material
    D. delays or alleged changed conditions

8. A claim is a

   A. dispute that cannot be resolved
   B. dispute arising from ambiguity in the specifications
   C. dispute arising from the quality of the work
   D. recognition that the courts are the sole arbiters of a dispute

9. Disputes arising between a contractor and the owning agency are

   A. the result of inflexibility of either or both parties to the dispute
   B. mainly the result of shortcomings in the design
   C. the result of shortcomings in the specifications
   D. inevitable

Questions 10-13.

DIRECTIONS: Questions 10 through 13, inclusive, refers to the array of numbers listed below.

16, 7, 9, 5, 10, 8, 5, 1, 2

10. The mean of the numbers is

    A. 2   B. 5   C. 7   D. 8

11. The median of the numbers is

    A. 2   B. 5   C. 7   D. 8

12. The mode of the numbers is

    A. 2   B. 5   C. 7   D. 8

13. In statistical measurements, a subgroup that is representative of the entire group is a

    A. commutative group   B. sample
    C. central index   D. Abelian group

14. Productivity is the ratio of

    A. $\dfrac{\text{product costs}}{\text{labor costs}}$

    B. $\dfrac{\text{cost of final product}}{\text{cost of materials}}$

    C. $\dfrac{\text{outputs}}{\text{inputs}}$

    D. $\dfrac{\text{outputs cost}}{\text{time needed to product the output}}$

15. Downtime is the time a piece of equipment is

    A. idle waiting for other equipment to become available
    B. not being used for the purpose it was intended

C. being used inefficiently
D. unavailable for use

16. Index numbers 16.____

    A. relates to the cost of a product as material costs vary
    B. allows the user to find the variation from the norm
    C. are a way of comparing costs of different approaches to a problem
    D. a way of measuring and comparing changes over a period of time

17. The underlying idea behind Management by Objectives is to provide a mechanism for managers to 17.____

    A. coordinate personal and departmental plans with organizational goals
    B. motivate employees by having them participate in job decisions
    C. motivate employees by training them for the next higher position
    D. set objectives that are reasonable for the employees to attain, thus improving self-esteem among the employees

18. The ultimate objective of the project manager in planning and scheduling a project is to 18.____

    A. meet the completion dates of the project
    B. use the least amount of labor on the project
    C. use the least amount of material on the project
    D. prevent interference between the different trades

19. Scheduling with respect to the critical path method usually does not involve 19.____

    A. cost allocation
    B. starting and finishing time
    C. float for each activity
    D. project duration

20. When CPM is used on a construction project, updates are most commonly made 20.____

    A. weekly   B. every two weeks
    C. monthly   D. every two months

Questions 21-24.

DIRECTIONS: Questions 21 through 24 refer to the following network.

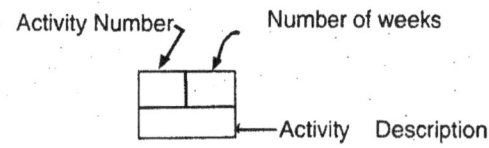

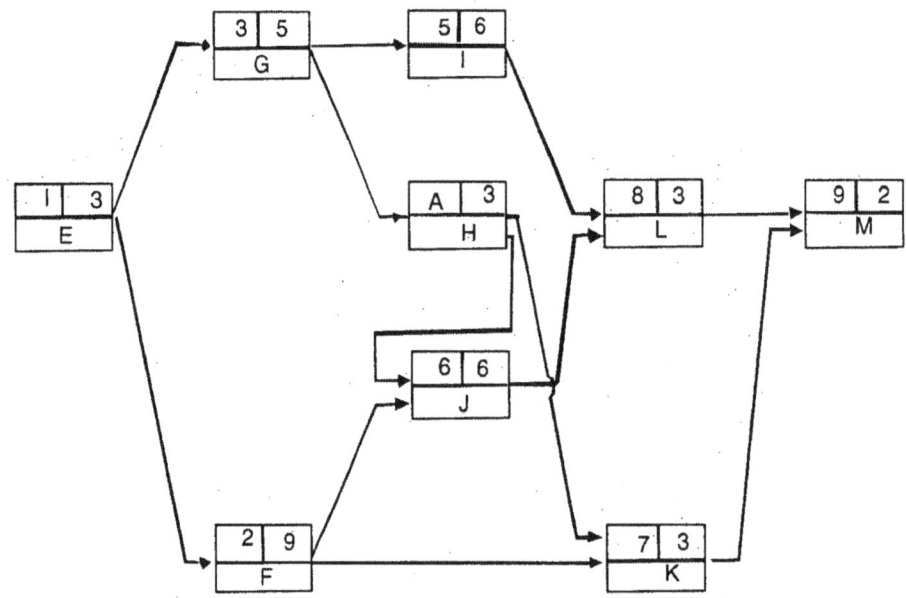

Activity Number	Activity Description	Duration in Weeks	Early Start	Early Finish	Late Start	Late Finish	Total Slack
1	E	3					
2	F	9					
3	G	5					
4	H	3					
5	I	6					
6	J	6					
7	K	3					
8	L	3					
9	M	2					

21. The critical path is

    A. E G H J L M   B. E G I L M
    C. E F J L M   D. E G H K M

21.____

22. The minimum time needed to complete the job is, in weeks,

    A. 19   B. 21   C. 22   D. 23

22.____

23. The slack time in J is, in weeks,

    A. 0   B. 1   C. 2   D. 3

23.____

24. The slack time in K is, in weeks,

    A. 4   B. 5   C. 6   D. 7

24.____

25. Of the following, the primary objective of CPM is to 25.____
    A. eliminate duplication of work
    B. overcome obstacles such as bad weather
    C. spot potential bottlenecks
    D. save on the cost of material

KEY (CORRECT ANSWERS)

1.	D	11.	C
2.	A	12.	B
3.	D	13.	B
4.	D	14.	C
5.	A	15.	D
6.	B	16.	D
7.	D	17.	A
8.	A	18.	A
9.	D	19.	A
10.	C	20.	C

21.	C
22.	D
23.	A
24.	C
25.	C

TEST 2

DIRECTIONS: Each question or incomplete statement is followed by several suggested answers or completions. Select the one that BEST answers the question or completes the statement. *PRINT THE LETTER OF THE CORRECT ANSWER IN THE SPACE AT THE RIGHT.*

1. Gantt refers to   1.____
   A. bar charts B. milestone charts
   C. PERT networks D. Management by Objectives

2. PERT is an abbreviation for   2.____
   A. Progress Evaluation in Real Time
   B. Preliminary Evaluation of Running Time
   C. Program Evaluation Review Techniques
   D. Program Estimation and Repair Times

3. In project management terms, slack is equivalent to   3.____
   A. tare B. off time C. delay D. float

4. The FIRST step in planning and programming a roadway pavement management system is to evaluate   4.____
   A. priorities for the work to be done
   B. the condition of your equipment
   C. the condition of the roads in the system
   D. the storage and maintenance facilities

5. Managers accomplish their work in an ever changing environment by integrating three time-tested approaches. The one of the following that is NOT a time-tested approach is   5.____
   A. scientific adaptation B. scientific management
   C. behavior management D. management sciences

6. The most effective managers manage for optimum results. This means that the manager is seeking to _____ a given situation.   6.____
   A. get the maximum results from
   B. get the most favorable results from
   C. get the most reasonable results from
   D. satisfy the conflicting interests in

7. If a manager believes that an employee is irresponsible, the employee, in subtle response to the manager's assessment, will in fact prove to be irresponsible. This is an example of a(n)   7.____
   A. conditioned reflex B. self-fulfilling prophesy
   C. Freudian response D. automatic reaction

8. Perhaps nothing distinguishes the younger generation from the older so much as the value placed on work. The older generation was generally raised to believe in the Protestant work ethic.   8.____
   This ethic holds primarily that

A. people should try to get the highest salary possible
B. work should help people to advance
C. work should be well done if it is interesting
D. work is valuable in itself and the person who does it focuses on his work

9. The standard method currently in use in inspecting bituminous paving is to inspect each activity in detail as the paving work is being installed. In recent years some agencies use a different method of inspection known as a(n)

   A. as-built quality control method
   B. statistically controlled quality assurance method
   C. data based history of previous contracts of this type
   D. performance evaluation of the completed paving contract

9.____

10. Aggregates for use in bituminous pavements should be tested for grading,

    A. abrasion, soundness, and specific gravity
    B. type of rock, abrasion, and specific gravity
    C. abrasion, soundness, and deleterious material
    D. specific gravity, chemical composition of the aggregate, and deleterious material

10.____

11. Of the following, the one that is LEAST likely to be a test for asphalt is

    A. specific gravity   B. flashpoint
    C. viscosity   D. penetration

11.____

12. According to the AASHO, for bituminous pavements PSI is an abbreviation for _____ Index.

    A. Present Serviceability   B. Pavement Smoothness
    C. Pavement Serviceability   D. Present Smoothness

12.____

13. According to the AASHO, a bituminous pavement that is in extremely poor condition will have a PSI

    A. above 5.5   B. above 3.5
    C. below 3.5   D. below 1.5

13.____

14. The U.S. Federal Highway Administration defines asphalt maintenance as including work designed primarily for rejuvenation or protection of existing surfaces less than _____ inch minimum thickness.

    A. 1/4   B. 1/2   C. 3/4   D. 1

14.____

15. The maintenance phase of a highway management system includes the establishment of a program and schedule of work based largely on budget considerations, the actual operations of crack filling, patching, etc. and

    A. inspection of completed work
    B. planning of future operations
    C. upgrading existing pavements
    D. acquisition and processing of data

15.____

16. In a bituminous asphalt pavement, the progressive separation of aggregate particles in a pavement from the surface downward or from the edges inward is the definition of

    A. alligatoring
    B. raveling
    C. scaling
    D. disintegration

17. The bituminous pavement condition for the purpose of overlay design includes ride quality, structural capacity, skid resistance, and

    A. durability
    B. age of the pavement
    C. CBR value
    D. surface distress

18. An asphalt mix is being transferred from an asphalt truck to the hopper of the paving machine. Blue smoke rises from the material being emptied into the hopper of the paving machine.
    Your conclusion should be that

    A. this is normal and is to be expected
    B. the mix is overheated
    C. the mix is too cold
    D. the mix is being transferred too rapidly

19. Polished aggregate in an asphalt pavement are aggregate particles that have been rounded and polished smooth by traffic. This is a

    A. *good* condition as it allows a smooth ride
    B. *good* condition as it preserves tires
    C. *poor* condition as it promotes skidding
    D. *poor* condition as it tends to break the bond between the asphalt and the aggregate

20. A slippery asphalt surface requires a skid-resistant surfacing material. Of the following, the cover that would be most appropriate is a(n)

    A. asphalt tack coat
    B. fog seal
    C. layer of sand rolled into the asphalt surface
    D. asphalt emulsion slurry seal

21. The maximum size of aggregate in a hot mix asphalt concrete surfacing and bases allowed by the Federal Highway Administration Grading A is _____ inch(es).

    A. 3/4   B. 1   C. 1 1/4   D. 1 1/2

22. Wet sand weighs 132 pounds per cubic foot and contains 8% noisture. The dry weight of a cubic foot of sand is _____ pounds.

    A. 122.2   B. 122.0   C. 121.7   D. 121.4

23. A very light spray application of 551h emulsified asphalt diluted with water is used on existing pavement as a seal to riinimize raveling and to enrich the surface of a dried-out pavement is known as a(n)

    A. prime coat
    B. tack coat
    C. fog seal
    D. emulsion seal

24. 90 kilometers per hour is equivalent to _____ miles per hour. 24.____

    A. 49	B. 54	C. 59	D. 64

25. In a table of pavement distress manifestations is a column broadly titled *Density of Pavement Distress*. 25.____
    This is equivalent to _____ of the defects.

    A. average depth
    B. average area
    C. extent of occurrence
    D. seriousness

KEY (CORRECT ANSWERS)

1. A
2. A
3. D
4. C
5. A

6. B
7. B
8. D
9. B
10. C

11. A
12. A
13. D
14. C
15. D

16. B
17. D
18. B
19. C
20. D

21. D
22. A
23. C
24. B
25. C

COMMUNICATION

EXAMINATION SECTION
TEST 1

DIRECTIONS: Each question or incomplete statement is followed by several suggested answers or completions. Select the one that BEST answers the question or completes the statement. *PRINT THE LETTER OF THE CORRECT ANSWER IN THE SPACE AT THE RIGHT.*

1. In some agencies the counsel to the agency head is given the right to bypass the chain of command and issue orders directly to the staff concerning matters that involve certain specific processes and practices.
 This situation MOST nearly illustrates the principle of _____ authority.
 A. the acceptance theory of
 B. multiple-linear
 C. splintered
 D. functional

 1._____

2. It is commonly understood that communication is an important part of the administrative process.
 Which of the following is NOT a valid principle of the communication process in administration?
 A. The channels of communication should be spontaneous.
 B. The lines of communication should be as direct and as short as possible.
 C. Communications should be authenticated.
 D. The persons serving in communications centers should be competent.

 2._____

3. Of the following, the one factor which is generally considered LEAST essential to successful committee operations is
 A. stating a clear definition of the authority and scope of the committee
 B. selecting the committee chairman carefully
 C. limiting the size of the committee to four persons
 D. limiting the subject matter to that which can be handled in group discussion

 3._____

4. Of the following, the failure by line managers to accept and appreciate the benefits and limitations of a new program or system VERY FREQUENTLY can be traced to the
 A. budgetary problems involved
 B. resultant need to reduce staff
 C. lack of controls it engenders
 D. failure of top management to support its implementation

 4._____

5. If a manager were thinking about using a committee of subordinates to solve an operating problem, which of the following would generally NOT be an advantage of such use of the committee approach?
 A. Improved coordination
 B. Low cost
 C. Increased motivation
 D. Integrated judgment

 5._____

6. Every supervisor has many occasions to lead a conference or participate in a conference of some sort.
Of the following statements that pertain to conferences and conference leadership, which is generally considered to be MOST valid?
   A. Since World War II, the trend has been toward fewer shared decisions and more conferences.
   B. The most important part of a conference leader's job is to direct discussion.
   C. In providing opportunities for group interaction, management should avoid consideration of its past management philosophy.
   D. A good administrator cannot lead a good conference if he is a poor public speaker.

7. Of the following, it is usually LEAST desirable for a conference leader to
   A. call the name of a person after asking a question
   B. summarize proceedings periodically
   C. make a practice of repeating questions
   D. ask a question without indicating who is to reply

8. Assume that, in a certain organization, a situation has developed in which there is little difference in status or authority between individuals.
Which of the following would be the MOST likely result with regard to communication in this organization?
   A. Both the accuracy and flow of communication will be improved.
   B. Both the accuracy and flow of communication will substantially decrease.
   C. Employees will seek more formal lines of communication.
   D. Neither the flow nor the accuracy of communication will be improved over the former hierarchical structure.

9. The main function of many agency administrative officers is "information management." Information that is received by an administrative officer may be classified as active or passive, depending upon whether or not it requires the recipient to take some action.
Of the following, the item received which is clearly the MOST active information is
   A. an appointment of a new staff member
   B. a payment voucher for a new desk
   C. a press release concerning a past event
   D. the minutes of a staff meeting

10. Of the following, the one LEAST considered to be a communication barrier is
    A. group feedback   B. charged words
    C. selective perception   D. symbolic meanings

11. Management studies support the hypothesis that, in spite of the tendency of employees to censor the information communicated to their supervisor, subordinates are more likely to communicate problem-oriented information UPWARD when they have a
    A. long period of service in the organization
    B. high degree of trust in the supervisor
    C. high educational level
    D. low status on the organizational ladder

11._____

12. Electronic data processing equipment can produce more information faster than can be generated by any other means.
    In view of this, the MOST important problem faced by management at present is to
    A. keep computers fully occupied
    B. find enough computer personnel
    C. assimilate and properly evaluate the information
    D. obtain funds to establish appropriate information systems

12._____

13. A well-designed management information system essentially provides each executive and manager the information he needs for
    A. determining computer time requirements
    B. planning and measuring results
    C. drawing a new organization chart
    D. developing a new office layout

13._____

14. It is generally agreed that management policies should be periodically reappraised and restated in accordance with current conditions.
    Of the following, the approach which would be MOST effective in determining whether a policy should be revised is to
    A. conduct interviews with staff members at all levels in order to ascertain the relationship between the policy and actual practice
    B. make proposed revisions in the policy and apply it to current problems
    C. make up hypothetical situations using both the old policy and a revised version in order to make comparisons
    D. call a meeting of top level staff in order to discuss ways of revising the policy

14._____

15. Your superior has asked you to notify division employees of an important change in one of the operating procedures described in the division manual. Every employee presently has a copy of this manual.
    Which of the following is normally the MOST practical way to get the employees to understand such a change?
    A. Notify each employee individually of the change and answer any questions he might have
    B. Send a written notice to key personnel, directing them to inform the people under them

15._____

C. Call a general meeting, distribute a corrected page for the manual, and discuss the change
D. Send a memo to employees describing the change in general terms and asking them to make the necessary corrections in their copies of the manual

16. Assume that the work in your department involves the use of any technical terms.
In such a situation, when you are answering inquiries from the general public, it would usually be BEST to
    A. use simple language and avoid the technical terms
    B. employ the technical terms whenever possible
    C. bandy technical terms freely, but explain each term in parentheses
    D. apologize if you are forced to use a technical term

17. Suppose that you receive a telephone call from someone identifying himself as an employee in another city department who asks to be given information which your own department regards as confidential.
Which of the following is the BEST way of handling such a request?
    A. Give the information requested, since your caller as official standing
    B. Grant the request, provided the caller gives you a signed receipt
    C. Refuse the request, because you have no way of knowing whether the caller is really who he claims to be
    D. Explain that the information is confidential and inform the caller of the channels he must go through to have the information released to him

18. Studies show that office employees place high importance on the social and human aspects of the organization. What office employees like best about their jobs is the kind of people with whom they work. So strive hard to group people who are most likely to get along well together.
Based on this information, it is MOST reasonable to assume that office workers are most pleased to work in a group which
    A. is congenial   B. has high productivity
    C. allows individual creativity D. is unlike other groups

19. A certain supervisor does not compliment members of his staff when they come up with good ideas. He feels that coming up with good ideas is part of the job and does not merit special attention.
This supervisor's practice is
    A. *poor*, because recognition for good ideas is a good motivator
    B. *poor*, because the staff will suspect that the supervisor has no good ideas of his own
    C. *good*, because it is reasonable to assume that employees will tell their supervisor of ways to improve office practice
    D. *good*, because the other members of the staff are not made to seem inferior by comparison

5 (#1)

20. Some employees of a department have sent an anonymous letter containing many complaints to the department head.
Of the following, what is this MOST likely to show about the department?
    A. It is probably a good place to work.
    B. Communications are probably poor.
    C. The complaints are probably unjustified.
    D. These employees are probably untrustworthy.

20._____

21. Which of the following actions would usually be MOST appropriate for a supervisor to take after receiving an instruction sheet from his superior explaining a new procedure which is to be followed?
    A. Put the instruction sheet aside temporarily until he determines what is wrong with the old procedure.
    B. Call his superior and ask whether the procedure is one he must implement immediately.
    C. Write a memorandum to the superior asking for more details.
    D. Try the new procedure and advise the superior of any problems or possible improvements.

21._____

22. Of the following, which one is considered the PRIMARY advantage of using a committee to resolved a problem in an organization?
    A. No one person will be held accountable for the decision since a group of people was involved.
    B. People with different backgrounds give attention to the problem.
    C. The decision will take considerable time so there is unlikely to be a decision that will later be regretted.
    D. One person cannot dominate the decision-making process.

22._____

23. Employees in a certain office come to their supervisor with all their complaints about the office and the work. Almost every employee has had at least one minor complaint at some time.
The situation with respect to complaints in this office may BEST be described as probably
    A. *good*; employees who complain care about their jobs and work hard
    B. *good*; grievances brought out into the open can be corrected
    C. *bad*; only serious complaints should be discussed
    D. *bad*; it indicates the staff does not have confidence in the administration

23._____

24. The administrator who allows his staff to suggest ways to do their work will usually find that
    A. this practice contributes to high productivity
    B. the administrator's ideas produce greater output
    C. clerical employees suggest inefficient work methods
    D. subordinate employees resent performing a management function

24._____

25. The MAIN purpose for a supervisor's questioning the employees at a conference he is holding is to
    A. stress those areas of information covered but not understood by the participants
    B. encourage participants to think through the problem under discussion
    C. catch those subordinates who are not paying attention
    D. permit the more knowledgeable participants to display their grasp of the problems being discussed

KEY (CORRECT ANSWERS)

1.	D		11.	B
2.	A		12.	C
3.	C		13.	B
4.	D		14.	A
5.	B		15.	C
6.	B		16.	A
7.	C		17.	D
8.	D		18.	A
9.	A		19.	A
10.	A		20.	B

21.	D
22.	B
23.	B
24.	A
25.	B

TEST 2

DIRECTIONS: Each question or incomplete statement is followed by several suggested answers or completions. Select the one that BEST answers the question or completes the statement. *PRINT THE LETTER OF THE CORRECT ANSWER IN THE SPACE AT THE RIGHT.*

1. For a superior to use *consultative supervision* with his subordinates effectively, it is ESSENTIAL that he
   A. accept the fact that his formal authority will be weakened by the procedure
   B. admit that he does not know more than all his men together and that his ideas are not always best
   C. utilize a committee system so that the procedure is orderly
   D. make sure that all subordinates are consulted so that no one feels left out

   1.____

2. The *grapevine* is an informal means of communication in an organization. The attitude of a supervisor with respect to the grapevine should be to
   A. ignore it since it deals mainly with rumors and sensational information
   B. regard it as a serious danger which should be eliminated
   C. accept it as a real line of communication which should be listened to
   D. utilize it for most purposes instead of the official line of communication

   2.____

3. The supervisor of an office that must deal with the public should realize that planning in this type of work situation
   A. is useless because he does not know how many people will request service or what service they will request
   B. must be done at a higher level but that he should be ready to implement the results of such planning
   C. is useful primarily for those activities that are not concerned with public contact
   D. is useful for all the activities of the office, including those that relate to public contact

   3.____

4. Assume that it is your job to receive incoming telephone calls. Those calls which you cannot handle yourself have to be transferred to the appropriate office.
   If you receive an outside call for an extension line which is busy, the one of the following which you should do FIRST is to
   A. interrupt the person speaking on the extension and tell him a call is waiting
   B. tell the caller the line is busy and let him know every thirty seconds whether or not it is free
   C. leave the caller on "hold" until the extension is free
   D. tell the caller the line is busy and ask him if he wishes to wait

   4.____

5. Your superior has subscribed to several publications directly related to your division's work, and he has asked you to see to it that the publications are circulated among the supervisory personnel in the division. There are eight supervisors involved.
   The BEST method of insuring that all eight see these publications is to
   A. place the publication in the division's general reference library as soon as it arrives
   B. inform each supervisor whenever a publication arrives and remind all of them that they are responsible for reading it
   C. prepare a standard slip that can be stapled to each publication, listing the eight supervisors and saying, "Please read, initial your name, and pass along"
   D. send a memo to the eight supervisors saying that they may wish to purchase individual subscriptions in their own names if they are interested in seeing each issue

5.____

6. Your superior has telephoned a number of key officials in your agency to ask whether they can meet at a certain time next month. He has found that they can all make it, and he has asked you to confirm the meeting.
   Which of the following is the BEST way to confirm such a meeting?
   A. Note the meeting on your superior's calendar.
   B. Post a notice of the meeting on the agency bulletin board.
   C. Call the officials on the day of the meeting to remind them of the meeting.
   D. Write a memo to each official involved, repeating the time and place of the meeting.

6.____

7. Assume that a new city regulation requires that certain kinds of private organizations file information forms with your department. You have been asked to write the short explanatory message that will be printed on the front cover of the pamphlet containing the forms and instructions.
   Which of the following would be the MOST appropriate way of beginning this message?
   A. Get the readers' attention by emphasizing immediately that there are legal penalties for organizations that fail to file before a certain date.
   B. Briefly state the nature of the enclosed forms and the types of organizations that must file.
   C. Say that your department is very sorry to have to put organizations to such an inconvenience.
   D. Quote the entire regulation adopted by the city, even if it is quite long and is expressed din complicated legal language.

7.____

8. Suppose that you have been told to make up the vacation schedule for the 18 employees in a particular unit. In order for the unit to operate effectively, only a few employees can be on vacation at the same time.
   Which of the following is the MOST advisable approach in making up the schedule?
   A. Draw up a schedule assigning vacations in alphabetical order
   B. Find out when the supervisors want to take their vacations, and randomly assign whatever periods are left to the non-supervisory personnel

8.____

C. Assign the most desirable times to employees of longest standing and the least desirable times to the newest employees
D. Have all employees state their own preference, and then work out any conflicts in consultation with the people involved

9. Assume that you have been asked to prepare job descriptions for various positions in your department.
Which of the following are the basic points that should be covered in a *job description*?
   A. General duties and responsibilities of the position, with examples of day-to-day tasks
   B. Comments on the performances of present employees
   C. Estimates of the number of openings that may be available in each category during the coming year
   D. Instructions for carrying out the specific tasks assigned to your department

9._____

10. Of the following, the biggest DISADVANTAGE in allowing a free flow of communications in an agency is that such a free flow
    A. decreases creativity
    B. increases the use of the *grapevine*
    C. lengthens the chain of command
    D. reduces the executive's power to direct the flow of information

10._____

11. A downward flow of authority in an organization is one example of _____ communication.
    A. horizontal   B. informal   C. circular   D. vertical

11._____

12. Of the following, the one that would MOST likely block effective communication is
    A. concentration only on the issues at hand
    B. lack of interest or commitment
    C. use of written reports
    D. use of charts and graphs

12._____

13. An ADVANTAGE of the *lecture* as a teaching tool is that it
    A. enables a person to present his ideas to a large number of people
    B. allows the audience to retain a maximum of the information given
    C. holds the attention of the audience for the longest time
    D. enables the audience member to easily recall the main points

13._____

14. An ADVANTAGE of the *small-group* discussion as a teaching tool is that
    A. it always focuses attention on one person as the leader
    B. it places collective responsibility on the group as a whole
    C. its members gain experience by summarizing the ideas of others
    D. each member of the group acts as a member of a team

14._____

15. The one of the following that is an ADVANTAGE of a *large-group* discussion, when compared to a small-group discussion, is that the large-group discussion
    A. moves along more quickly than a small-group discussion
    B. allows its participants to feel more at ease, and speak out more freely
    C. gives the whole group a chance to exchange ideas on a certain subject at the same occasion
    D. allows its members to feel a greater sense of personal responsibility

15._____

KEY (CORRECT ANSWERS)

1.	D	6.	D	11.	D
2.	C	7.	B	12.	B
3.	D	8.	D	13.	A
4.	D	9.	A	14.	D
5.	C	10.	D	15.	C

EXAMINATION SECTION

TEST 1

DIRECTIONS: Each question or incomplete statement is followed by several suggested answers or completions. Select the one that BEST answers the question or completes the statement. *PRINT THE LETTER OF THE CORRECT ANSWER IN THE SPACE AT THE RIGHT.*

1. Of the following, the one MOST important quality required of a good supervisor is
   A. ambition   B. leadership   C. friendliness   D. popularity

   1.____

2. It is often said that a supervisor can delegate authority but never responsibility. This means MOST NEARLY that
   A. a supervisor must do his own work if he expects it to be done properly
   B. a supervisor can assign someone else to do his work, but in the last analysis, the supervisor himself must take the blame for any actions followed
   C. authority and responsibility are two separate things that cannot be borne by the same person
   D. it is better for a supervisor never to delegate his authority

   2.____

3. One of your men who is a habitual complainer asks you to grant him a minor privilege.
   Before granting or denying such a request, you should consider
   A. the merits of the case
   B. that it is good for group morale to grant a request of this nature
   C. the man's seniority
   D. that to deny such a request will lower your standing with the men

   3.____

4. A supervisory practice on the part of a foreman which is MOST likely to lead to confusion and inefficiency is for him to
   A. give orders verbally directly to the man assigned to the job
   B. issue orders only in writing
   C. follow up his orders after issuing them
   D. relay his orders to the men through co-workers

   4.____

5. It would be POOR supervision on a foreman's part if he
   A. asked an experienced maintainer for his opinion on the method of doing a special job
   B. make it a policy to avoid criticizing a man in front of his co-workers
   C. consulted his assistant supervisor on unusual problems
   D. allowed a cooling-off period of several days before giving one of his men a deserved reprimand

   5.____

6. Of the following behavior characteristics of a supervisor, the one that is MOST likely to lower the morale of the men he supervises is
   A. diligence
   B. favoritism
   C. punctuality
   D. thoroughness

7. Of the following, the BEST method of getting an employee who is not working up to his capacity to produce more work is to
   A. have another employee criticize his production
   B. privately criticize his production but encourage him to produce more
   C. criticize his production before his associates
   D. criticize his production and threaten to fire him

8. Of the following, the BEST thing for a supervisor to do when a subordinate has done a very good job is to
   A. tell him to take it easy
   B. praise his work
   C. reduce his workload
   D. say nothing because he may become conceited

9. Your orders to your crew are MOST likely to be followed if you
   A. explain the reasons for these orders
   B. warn that all violators will be punished
   C. promise easy assignments to those who follow these orders best
   D. say that they are for the good of the department

10. In order to be a good supervisor, you should
    A. impress upon your men that you demand perfection in their work at all times
    B. avoid being blamed for your crew's mistakes
    C. impress your superior with your ability
    D. see to it that your men get what they are entitled to

11. In giving instructions to a crew, you should
    A. speak in as loud a tone as possible
    B. speak in a coaxing, persuasive manner
    C. speak quietly, clearly, and courteously
    D. always use the word *please* when giving instructions

12. Of the following factors, the one which is LEAST important in evaluating an employee and his work is his
    A. dependability
    B. quantity of work done
    C. quality of work done
    D. education and training

13. When a District Superintendent first assumes his command, it is LEAST important for him at the beginning to observe
    A. how his equipment is designed and its adaptability
    B. how to reorganize the district for greater efficiency
    C. the capabilities of the men in the district
    D. the methods of operation being employed

14. When making an inspection of one of the buildings under your supervision, the BEST procedure to follow in making a record of the inspection is to
    A. return immediately to the office and write a report from memory
    B. write down all the important facts during or as soon as you complete the inspection
    C. fix in your mind all important facts so that you can repeat them from memory if necessary
    D. fix in your mind all important facts so that you can make out your report at the end of the day

15. Assume that your superior has directed you to make certain changes in your established procedure. After using this modified procedure on several occasions, you find that the original procedure was distinctly superior and you wish to return to it.
    You should
    A. let your superior find this out for himself
    B. simply change back to the original procedure
    C. compile definite data and information to prove your case to your superior
    D. persuade one of the more experienced workers to take this matter up with your superior

16. An inspector visited a large building under construction. He inspected the soil lines at 9 A.M., water lines at 10 A.M., fixtures at 11 A.M., and did his office work in the afternoon. He followed the same pattern daily for weeks.
    This procedure was
    A. *good*, because it was methodical and he did not miss anything
    B. *good*, because it gave equal time to all phases of the plumbing
    C. *bad*, because not enough time was devoted to fixtures
    D. *bad*, because the tradesmen knew when the inspection would occur

17. Assume that one of the foremen in a training course, which you are conducting, proposes a poor solution for a maintenance problem.
    Of the following, the BEST course of action for you to take is to
    A. accept the solution tentatively and correct it during the next class meeting
    B. point out all the defects of this proposed solution and wait until somebody thinks of a better solution
    C. try to get the class to reject this proposed solution and develop a better solution
    D. let the matter pass since somebody will present a better solution as the class work proceeds

18. As a supervisor, you should be seeking ways to improve the efficiency of shop operations by means such as changing established work procedures.
    The following are offered as possible actions that you should consider in changing established work procedures:
    I. Make changes only when your foremen agree to them
    II. Discuss changes with your supervisor before putting them into practice

III. Standardize any operation which is performed on a continuing basis
IV. Make changes quickly and quietly in order to avoid dissent
V. Secure expert guidance before instituting unfamiliar procedures
Of the following suggested answers, the one that describes the actions to be taken to change established work procedures is
    A. I, IV, V   B. II, III, V   C. III, IV, V   D. All of the above

19. A supervisor determined that a foreman, without informing his superior, delegated responsibility for checking time cards to a member of his gang. The supervisor then called the foreman into his office where he reprimanded the foreman.
This action of the supervisor in reprimanding the foreman was
    A. *proper*, because the checking of time cards is the foreman's responsibility and should not be delegated
    B. *proper*, because the foreman did not ask the supervisor for permission to delegate responsibility
    C. *improper*, because the foreman may no longer take the initiative in solving future problems
    D. *improper*, because the supervisor is interfering in a function which is not his responsibility

20. A capable supervisor should check all operations under his control.
Of the following, the LEAST important reason for doing this is to make sure that
    A. operations are being performed as scheduled
    B. he personally observes all operations at all times
    C. all the operations are still needed
    D. his manpower is being utilized efficiently

21. A supervisor makes it a practice to apply fair and firm discipline in all cases of rule infractions, including those of a minor nature.
This practice should PRIMARILY be considered
    A. *bad*, since applying discipline for minor violations is a waste of time
    B. *good*, because not applying discipline for minor infractions can lead to a more serious erosion of discipline
    C. *bad*, because employees do not like to be disciplined for minor violations of the rules
    D. *good*, because violating any rule can cause a dangerous situation to occur

22. A maintainer would PROPERLY consider it poor supervisory practice for a foreman to consult with him on
    A. which of several repair jobs should be scheduled first
    B. how to cope with personal problems at home
    C. whether the neatness of his headquarters can be improved
    D. how to express a suggestion which the maintainer plans to submit formally

23. Assume that you have determined that the work of one of your foremen and the men he supervises is consistently behind schedule. When you discuss this situation with the foreman, he tells you that his men are poor workers and then complains that he must spend all of his time checking on their work.
The following actions are offered for your consideration as possible ways of solving the problem of poor performance of the foreman and his men:
I. Review the work standards with the foreman and determine whether they are realistic.
II. Tell the foreman that you will recommend him for the foreman's training course for retraining.
III. Ask the foreman for the names of the maintainers and then replace them as soon as possible.
IV. Tell the foreman that you expect him to meet a satisfactory level of performance.
V. Tell the foreman to insist that his men work overtime to catch up to the schedule.
VI. Tell the foreman to review the type and amount of training he has given the maintainers.
VII. Tell the foreman that he will be out of a job if he does not produce on schedule.
VIII. Avoid all criticism of the foreman and his methods.
Which of the following suggested answers CORRECTLY lists the proper actions to be taken to solve the problem of poor performance of the foreman and his men?
   A. I, II, IV, VI   B. I, III, V, VII   C. II, III, VI, VIII   D. IV, V, VI, VIII

23.____

24. When a conference or a group discussion is tending to turn into a *bull session* without constructive purpose, the BEST action to take is to
   A. reprimand the leader of the bull session
   B. redirect the discussion to the business at hand
   C. dismiss the meeting and reschedule it for another day
   D. allow the bull session to continue

24.____

25. Assume that you have been assigned responsibility for a program in which a high production rate is mandatory. From past experience, you know that your foremen do not perform equally well in the various types of jobs given to them. Which of the following methods should you use in selecting foremen for the specific types of work involved in the program?
   A. Leave the method of selecting foremen to your supervisor
   B. Assign each foreman to the work he does best
   C. Allow each foreman to choose his own job
   D. Assign each foreman to a job which will permit him to improve his own abilities

25.____

KEY (CORRECT ANSWERS)

1.	B	11.	C
2.	B	12.	D
3.	A	13.	B
4.	D	14.	B
5.	D	15.	C
6.	B	16.	D
7.	B	17.	C
8.	B	18.	B
9.	A	19.	A
10.	D	20.	B

21. B
22. A
23. A
24. B
25. B

TEST 2

DIRECTIONS: Each question or incomplete statement is followed by several suggested answers or completions. Select the one that BEST answers the question or completes the statement. *PRINT THE LETTER OF THE CORRECT ANSWER IN THE SPACE AT THE RIGHT.*

1. A foreman who is familiar with modern management principles should know that the one of the following requirements of an administrator which is LEAST important is his ability to
   A. coordinate work
   B. plan, organize, and direct the work under his control
   C. cooperate with others
   D. perform the duties of the employees under his jurisdiction

   1.____

2. When subordinates request his advice in solving problems encountered in their work, a certain chief occasionally answers the request by first asking the subordinate what he thinks should be done.
   This action by the chief is, on the whole,
   A. *desirable*, because it stimulates subordinates to give more thought to the solution of problems encountered
   B. *undesirable*, because it discourages subordinates from asking questions
   C. *desirable*, because it discourages subordinates from asking questions
   D. *undesirable*, because it undermines the confidence of subordinates in the ability of their supervisor

   2.____

3. Of the following factors that may be considered by a unit head in dealing with the tardy subordinate, the one which should be given LEAST consideration is the
   A. frequency with which the employee is tardy
   B. effect of the employee's tardiness upon the work of other employees
   C. willingness of the employee to work overtime when necessary
   D. cause of the employee's tardiness

   3.____

4. The MOST important requirement of a good inspectional report is that it should be
   A. properly addressed   B. lengthy
   C. clear and brief   D. spelled correctly

   4.____

5. Building superintendents frequently inquire about departmental inspectional procedures.
   Of the following, it is BEST to
   A. advise them to write to the department for an official reply
   B. refuse as the inspectional procedure is a restricted matter
   C. briefly explain the procedure to them
   D. avoid the inquiry by changing the subject

   5.____

6. Reprimanding a crew member before other workers is a
    A. *good* practice; the reprimand serves as a warning to the other workers
    B. *bad* practice; people usually resent criticism made in public
    C. *good* practice; the other workers will realize that the supervisor is fair
    D. *bad* practice; the other workers will take sides in the dispute

7. Of the following actions, the one which is LEAST likely to promote good work is for the group leader to
    A. praise workers for doing a good job
    B. call attention to the opportunities for promotion for better workers
    C. threaten to recommend discharge of workers who are below standard
    D. put into practice any good suggestion made by crew members

8. A supervisor notices that a member of his crew has skipped a routine step in his job.
   Of the following, the BEST action for the supervisor to take is to
    A. promptly question the worker about the incident
    B. immediately assign another man to complete the job
    C. bring up the incident the next time the worker asks for a favor
    D. say nothing about the incident but watch the worker carefully in the future

9. Assume you have been told to show a new worker how to operate a piece of equipment.
   Your FIRST step should be to
    A. ask the worker if he has any questions about the equipment
    B. permit the worker to operate the equipment himself while you carefully watch to prevent damage
    C. demonstrate the operation of the equipment for the worker
    D. have the worker read an instruction booklet on the maintenance of the equipment

10. Whenever a new man was assigned to his crew, the supervisor would introduce him to all other crew members, take him on a tour of the plant, tell him about bus schedules and places to eat.
    This practice is
    A. *good*; the new man is made to feel welcome
    B. *bad*; supervisors should not interfere in personal matters
    C. *good*; the new man knows that he can bring his personal problems to the supervisor
    D. *bad*; work time should not be spent on personal matters

11. The MOST important factor in successful leadership is the ability to
    A. obtain instant obedience to all orders
    B. establish friendly personal relations with crew members
    C. avoid disciplining crew members
    D. make crew members want to do what should be done

12. Explaining the reasons for departmental procedure to workers tends to
    A. waste time which should be used for productive purposes
    B. increase their interest in their work
    C. make them more critical of departmental procedures
    D. confuse them

13. If you want a job done well do it yourself.
    For a supervisor to follow this advice would be
    A. *good*; a supervisor is responsible for the work of his crew
    B. *bad*; a supervisor should train his men, not do their work
    C. *good*; a supervisor should be skilled in all jobs assigned to his crew
    D. *bad*; a supervisor loses respect when he works with his hands

14. When a supervisor discovers a mistake in one of the jobs for which his crew is responsible, it is MOST important for him to find out
    A. whether anybody else knows about the mistake
    B. who was to blame for the mistake
    C. how to prevent similar mistakes in the future
    D. whether similar mistakes occurred in the past

15. A supervisor who has to explain a new procedure to his crew should realize that questions from the crew USUALLY show that they
    A. are opposed to the new practice
    B. are completely confused by the explanation
    C. need more training in the new procedure
    D. are interested in the explanation

16. A good way for a supervisor to retain the confidence of his or her employees is to
    A. say as little as possible
    B. check work frequently
    C. make no promises unless they will be fulfilled
    D. never hesitate in giving an answer to any question

17. Good supervision is ESSENTIALLY a matter of
    A. patience in supervising workers   B. care in selecting workers
    C. skill in human relations   D. fairness in disciplining workers

18. It is MOST important for an employee who has been assigned a monotonous task to
    A. perform this task before doing other work
    B. ask another employee to help
    C. perform this task only after all other work has been completed
    D. take measures to prevent mistakes in performing the task

19. One of your employees has violated a minor agency regulation.
The FIRST thing you should do is
    A. warn the employee that you will have to take disciplinary action if it should happen again
    B. ask the employee to explain his or her actions
    C. inform your supervisor and wait for advice
    D. write a memo describing the incident and place it in the employee's personnel file

19.____

20. One of your employees tells you that he feels you give him much more work than the other employees, and he is having trouble meeting your deadlines.
You should
    A. ask if he has been under a lot of non-work related stress lately
    B. review his recent assignments to determine if he is correct
    C. explain that this is a busy time, but you are dividing the work equally
    D. tell him that he is the most competent employee and that is why he receives more work

20.____

21. A supervisor assigns one of his crew to complete a portion of a job. A short time later, the supervisor notices that the portion has not been completed.
Of the following, the BEST way for the supervisor to handle this is to
    A. ask the crew member why he has not completed the assignment
    B. reprimand the crew member for not obeying orders
    C. assign another crew member to complete the assignment
    D. complete the assignment himself

21.____

22. Supposes that a member of your crew complains that you are *playing favorites* in assigning work.
Of the following, the BEST method of handling the complaint is to
    A. deny it and refuse to discuss the matter with the worker
    B. take the opportunity to tell the worker what is wrong with his work
    C. ask the worker for examples to prove his point and try to clear up any misunderstanding
    D. promise to be more careful in making assignments in the future

22.____

23. A member of your crew comes to you with a complaint. After discussing the matter with him, it is clear that you have convinced him that his complaint was not justified.
At this point, you should
    A. permit him to drop the matter
    B. make him admit his error
    C. pretend to see some justification in his complaint
    D. warn him against making unjustified complaints

23.____

24. Suppose that a supervisor has in his crew an older man who works rather slowly. In other respects, this man is a good worker; he is seldom absent, works carefully, never loafs, and is cooperative.

24.____

The BEST way for the supervisor to handle this worker is to
  A. try to get him to work faster and less carefully
  B. give him the most disagreeable job
  C. request that he be given special training
  D. permit him to work at his own speed

25. Suppose that a member of your crew comes to you with a suggestion he thinks will save time in doing a job. You realize immediately that it won't work.
Under these circumstances, your BEST action would be to
  A. thank the worker for the suggestion and forget about it
  B. explain to the worker why you think it won't work
  C. tell the worker to put the suggestion in writing
  D. ask the other members of your crew to criticize the suggestion

25.____

KEY (CORRECT ANSWERS)

1.	D		11.	D
2.	A		12.	B
3.	C		13.	B
4.	C		14.	C
5.	C		15.	D
6.	B		16.	C
7.	C		17.	C
8.	A		18.	D
9.	C		19.	B
10.	A		20.	B

21.	A
22.	C
23.	A
24.	D
25.	B

PHILOSOPHY, PRINCIPLES, PRACTICES, AND TECHNICS OF SUPERVISION, ADMINISTRATION, MANAGEMENT, AND ORGANIZATION

TABLE OF CONTENTS

	Page
MEANING OF SUPERVISION	1
THE OLD AND THE NEW SUPERVISION	1
THE EIGHT (8) BASIC PRINCIPLES OF THE NEW SUPERVISION	1
I. Principle of Responsibility	1
II. Principle of Authority	2
III. Principle of Self-Growth	2
IV. Principle of Individual Worth	2
V. Principle of Creative Leadership	2
VI. Principle of Success and Failure	2
VII. Principle of Science	3
VIII. Principle of Cooperation	3
WHAT IS ADMINISTRATION?	3
I. Practices Commonly Classed as "Supervisory"	3
II. Practices Commonly Classed as "Administrative"	3
III. Practices Commonly Classed as Both "Supervisory" and "Administrative"	4
RESPONSIBILITIES OF THE SUPERVISOR	4
COMPETENCIES OF THE SUPERVISOR	4
THE PROFESSIONAL SUPERVISOR-EMPLOYEE RELATIONSHIP	4
MINI-TEXT IN SUPERVISION, ADMINISTRATION, MANAGEMENT, AND ORGANIZATION	5
I. Brief Highlights	5
A. Levels of Management	6
B. What the Supervisor Must Learn	6
C. A Definition of Supervision	6
D. Elements of the Team Concept	6
E. Principles of Organization	6
F. The Four Important Parts of Every Job	7
G. Principles of Delegation	7
H. Principles of Effective Communications	7
I. Principles of Work Improvement	7
J. Areas of Job Improvement	7
K. Seven Key Points in Making Improvements	8

	L.	Corrective Techniques for Job Improvement	8
	M.	A Planning Checklist	8
	N.	Five Characteristics of Good Directions	9
	O.	Types of Directions	9
	P.	Controls	9
	Q.	Orienting the New Employee	9
	R.	Checklist for Orienting New Employees	9
	S.	Principles of Learning	10
	T.	Causes of Poor Performance	10
	U.	Four Major Steps in On-the-Job Instructions	10
	V.	Employees Want Five Things	10
	W.	Some Don'ts in Regard to Praise	11
	X.	How to Gain Your Workers' Confidence	11
	Y.	Sources of Employee Problems	11
	Z.	The Supervisor's Key to Discipline	11
	AA.	Five Important Processes of Management	12
	BB.	When the Supervisor Fails to Plan	12
	CC.	Fourteen General Principles of Management	12
	DD.	Change	12

II. Brief Topical Summaries — 13
- A. Who/What is the Supervisor? — 13
- B. The Sociology of Work — 13
- C. Principles and Practices of Supervision — 14
- D. Dynamic Leadership — 14
- E. Processes for Solving Problems — 15
- F. Training for Results — 15
- G. Health, Safety, and Accident Prevention — 16
- H. Equal Employment Opportunity — 16
- I. Improving Communications — 16
- J. Self-Development — 17
- K. Teaching and Training — 17
  1. The Teaching Process — 17
     - a. Preparation — 17
     - b. Presentation — 18
     - c. Summary — 18
     - d. Application — 18
     - e. Evaluation — 18
  2. Teaching Methods — 18
     - a. Lecture — 18
     - b. Discussion — 18
     - c. Demonstration — 19
     - d. Performance — 19
     - e. Which Method to Use — 19

PHILOSOPHY, PRINCIPLES, PRACTICES, AND TECHNICS
OF
SUPERVISION, ADMINISTRATION, MANAGEMENT, AND ORGANIZATION

MEANING OF SUPERVISION

The extension of the democratic philosophy has been accompanied by an extension in the scope of supervision. Modern leaders and supervisors no longer think of supervision in the narrow sense of being confined chiefly to visiting employees, supplying materials, or rating the staff. They regard supervision as being intimately related to all the concerned agencies of society, they speak of the supervisor's function in terms of "growth," rather than the "improvement" of employees.

This modern concept of supervision may be defined as follows: Supervision is leadership and the development of leadership within groups which are cooperatively engaged in inspection, research, training, guidance, and evaluation.

THE OLD AND THE NEW SUPERVISION

TRADITIONAL
1. Inspection
2. Focused on the employee
3. Visitation
4. Random and haphazard
5. Imposed and authoritarian
6. One person usually

MODERN
1. Study and analysis
2. Focused on aims, materials, methods, supervisors, employees, environment
3. Demonstrations, intervisitation, workshops, directed reading, bulletins, etc.
4. Definitely organized and planned (scientific)
5. Cooperative and democratic
6. Many persons involved (creative)

THE EIGHT (8) BASIC PRINCIPLES OF THE NEW SUPERVISION

I. Principle of Responsibility
   Authority to act and responsibility for acting must be joined.
   A. If you give responsibility, give authority.
   B. Define employee duties clearly.
   C. Protect employees from criticism by others.
   D. Recognize the rights as well as obligations of employees.
   E. Achieve the aims of a democratic society insofar as it is possible within the area of your work.
   F. Establish a situation favorable to training and learning.
   G. Accept ultimate responsibility for everything done in your section, unit, office, division, department.
   H. Good administration and good supervision are inseparable.

II. Principle of Authority
The success of the supervisor is measured by the extent to which the power of authority is not used.
   A. Exercise simplicity and informality in supervision
   B. Use the simplest machinery of supervision
   C. If it is good for the organization as a whole, it is probably justified.
   D. Seldom be arbitrary or authoritative.
   E. Do not base your work on the power of position or of personality.
   F. Permit and encourage the free expression of opinions.

III. Principle of Self-Growth
The success of the supervisor is measured by the extent to which, and the speed with which, he is no longer needed.
   A. Base criticism on principles, not on specifics.
   B. Point out higher activities to employees.
   C. Train for self-thinking by employees to meet new situations.
   D. Stimulate initiative, self-reliance, and individual responsibility
   E. Concentrate on stimulating the growth of employees rather than on removing defects.

IV. Principle of Individual Worth
Respect for the individual is a paramount consideration in supervision.
   A. Be human and sympathetic in dealing with employees.
   B. Don't nag about things to be done.
   C. Recognize the individual differences among employees and seek opportunities to permit best expression of each personality.

V. Principle of Creative Leadership
The best supervision is that which is not apparent to the employee.
   A. Stimulate, don't drive employees to creative action.
   B. Emphasize doing good things.
   C. Encourage employees to do what they do best.
   D. Do not be too greatly concerned with details of subject or method.
   E. Do not be concerned exclusively with immediate problems and activities.
   F. Reveal higher activities and make them both desired and maximally possible.
   G. Determine procedures in the light of each situation but see that these are derived from a sound basic philosophy.
   H. Aid, inspire, and lead so as to liberate the creative spirit latent in all good employees.

VI. Principle of Success and Failure
There are no unsuccessful employees, only unsuccessful supervisors who have failed to give proper leadership.
   A. Adapt suggestions to the capacities, attitudes, and prejudices of employees.
   B. Be gradual, be progressive, be persistent.
   C. Help the employee find the general principle; have the employee apply his own problem to the general principle.
   D. Give adequate appreciation for good work and honest effort.
   E. Anticipate employee difficulties and help to prevent them.
   F. Encourage employees to do the desirable things they will do anyway.
   G. Judge your supervision by the results it secures.

VII. Principle of Science
Successful supervision is scientific, objective, and experimental. It is based on facts, not on prejudices.
   A. Be cumulative in results.
   B. Never divorce your suggestions from the goals of training.
   C. Don't be impatient of results.
   D. Keep all matters on a professional, not a personal, level.
   E. Do not be concerned exclusively with immediate problems and activities.
   F. Use objective means of determining achievement and rating where possible.

VIII. Principle of Cooperation
Supervision is a cooperative enterprise between supervisor and employee.
   A. Begin with conditions as they are.
   B. Ask opinions of all involved when formulating policies.
   C. Organization is as good as its weakest link.
   D. Let employees help to determine policies and department programs.
   E. Be approachable and accessible—physically and mentally.
   F. Develop pleasant social relationships.

WHAT IS ADMINISTRATION

Administration is concerned with providing the environment, the material facilities, and the operational procedures that will promote the maximum growth and development of supervisors and employees. (Organization is an aspect and a concomitant of administration.)

There is no sharp line of demarcation between supervision and administration; these functions are intimately interrelated and, often, overlapping. They are complementary activities.

I. Practices Commonly Classed as "Supervisory"
   A. Conducting employees' conferences
   B. Visiting sections, units, offices, divisions, departments
   C. Arranging for demonstrations
   D. Examining plans
   E. Suggesting professional reading
   F. Interpreting bulletins
   G. Recommending in-service training courses
   H. Encouraging experimentation
   I. Appraising employee morale
   J. Providing for intervisitation

II. Practices Commonly Classified as "Administrative"
   A. Management of the office
   B. Arrangement of schedules for extra duties
   C. Assignment of rooms or areas
   D. Distribution of supplies
   E. Keeping records and reports
   F. Care of audio-visual materials
   G. Keeping inventory records
   H. Checking record cards and books

    I. Programming special activities
    J. Checking on the attendance and punctuality of employees

III. Practices Commonly Classified as Both "Supervisory" and "Administrative"
    A. Program construction
    B. Testing or evaluating outcomes
    C. Personnel accounting
    D. Ordering instructional materials

RESPONSIBILITIES OF THE SUPERVISOR

A person employed in a supervisory capacity must constantly be able to improve his own efficiency and ability. He represent the employer to the employees and only continuous self-examination can make him a capable supervisor.

Leadership and training are the supervisor's responsibility. An efficient working unit is one in which the employees work with the supervisor. It is his job to bring out the best in his employees. He must always be relaxed, courteous, and calm in his association with his employees. Their feelings are important, and a harsh attitude does not develop the most efficient employees.

COMPETENCES OF THE SUPERVISOR

    I.   Complete knowledge of the duties and responsibilities of his position.
    II.   To be able to organize a job, plan ahead, and carry through.
    III. To have self-confidence and initiative.
    IV.   To be able to handle the unexpected situation and make quick decisions.
    V.   To be able to properly train subordinates in the positions they are best suited for.
    VI.   To be able to keep good human relations among his subordinates.
    VII. To be able to keep good human relations between his subordinates and himself and to earn their respect and trust.

THE PROFESSIONAL SUPERVISOR-EMPLOYEE RELATIONSHIP

There are two kinds of efficiency: one kind is only apparent and is produced in organizations through the exercise of mere discipline; this is but a simulation of the second, or true, efficiency which springs from spontaneous cooperation. If you are a manager, no matter how great or small your responsibility, it is your job, in the final analysis, to create and develop this involuntary cooperation among the people whom you supervise. For, no matter how powerful a combination of money, machines, and materials a company may have, this is a dead and sterile thing without a team of willing, thinking, and articulate people to guide it.

The following 21 points are presented as indicative of the exemplary basic relationship that should exist between supervisor and employee:

1. Each person wants to be liked and respected by his fellow employee and wants to be treated with consideration and respect by his superior.
2. The most competent employee will make an error. However, in a unit where good relations exist between the supervisor and his employees, tenseness and fear do not exist. Thus, errors are not hidden or covered up, and the efficiency of a unit is not impaired.

3. Subordinates resent rules, regulations, or orders that are unreasonable or unexplained.
4. Subordinates are quick to resent unfairness, harshness, injustices, and favoritism.
5. An employee will accept responsibility if he knows that he will be complimented for a job well done, and not too harshly chastised for failure; that his supervisor will check the cause of the failure, and, if it was the supervisor's fault, he will assume the blame therefore. If it was the employee's fault, his supervisor will explain the correct method or means of handling the responsibility.
6. An employee wants to receive credit for a suggestion he has made, that is used. If a suggestion cannot be used, the employee is entitled to an explanation. The supervisor should not say "no" and close the subject.
7. Fear and worry slow up a worker's ability. Poor working environment can impair his physical and mental health. A good supervisor avoids forceful methods, threats, and arguments to get a job done.
8. A forceful supervisor is able to train his employees individually and as a team, and is able to motivate them in the proper channels.
9. A mature supervisor is able to properly evaluate his subordinates and to keep them happy and satisfied.
10. A sensitive supervisor will never patronize his subordinates.
11. A worthy supervisor will respect his employees' confidences.
12. Definite and clear-cut responsibilities should be assigned to each executive.
13. Responsibility should always be coupled with corresponding authority.
14. No change should be made in the scope or responsibilities of a position without a definite understanding to that effect on the part of all persons concerned.
15. No executive or employee, occupying a single position in the organization, should be subject to definite orders from more than one source.
16. Orders should never be given to subordinates over the head of a responsible executive. Rather than do this, the officer in question should be supplanted.
17. Criticisms of subordinates should, whoever possible, be made privately, and in no case should a subordinate be criticized in the presence of executives or employees of equal or lower rank.
18. No dispute or difference between executives or employees as to authority or responsibilities should be considered too trivial for prompt and careful adjudication.
19. Promotions, wage changes, and disciplinary action should always be approved by the executive immediately superior to the one directly responsible.
20. No executive or employee should ever be required, or expected, to be at the same time an assistant to, and critic of, another.
21. Any executive whose work is subject to regular inspection should, wherever practicable, be given the assistance and facilities necessary to enable him to maintain an independent check of the quality of his work.

MINI-TEXT IN SUPERVISION, ADMINISTRATION, MANAGEMENT, AND ORGANIZATION

I. Brief Highlights

Listed concisely and sequentially are major headings and important data in the field for quick recall and review.

A. Levels of Management
Any organization of some size has several levels of management. In terms of a ladder, the levels are:

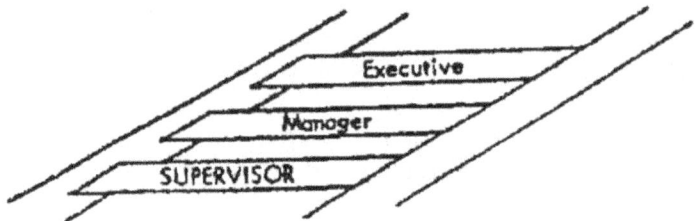

The first level is very important because it is the beginning point of management leadership.

B. What the Supervisor Must Learn
A supervisor must learn to:
1. Deal with people and their differences
2. Get the job done through people
3. Recognize the problems when they exist
4. Overcome obstacles to good performance
5. Evaluate the performance of people
6. Check his own performance in terms of accomplishment

C. A Definition of Supervisor
The term supervisor means any individual having authority, in the interests of the employer, to hire, transfer, suspend, lay-off, recall, promote, discharge, assign, reward, or discipline other employees or responsibility to direct them, or to adjust their grievances, or effectively to recommend such action, if, in connection with the foregoing, exercise of such authority is not of a merely routine or clerical nature but requires the use of independent judgment.

D. Elements of the Team Concept
What is involved in teamwork? The component parts are:
1. Members
2. A leader
3. Goals
4. Plans
5. Cooperation
6. Spirit

E. Principles of Organization
1. A team member must know what his job is.
2. Be sure that the nature and scope of a job are understood.
3. Authority and responsibility should be carefully spelled out.
4. A supervisor should be permitted to make the maximum number of decisions affecting his employees.
5. Employees should report to only one supervisor.
6. A supervisor should direct only as many employees as he can handle effectively.
7. An organization plan should be flexible.

8. Inspection and performance of work should be separate.
9. Organizational problems should receive immediate attention.
10. Assign work in line with ability and experience.

F. The Four Important Parts of Every Job
1. Inherent in every job is the *accountability* for results.
2. A second set of factors in every job is *responsibilities*.
3. Along with duties and responsibilities one must have the *authority* to act within certain limits without obtaining permission to proceed.
4. No job exists in a vacuum. The supervisor is surrounded by key *relationships*.

G. Principles of Delegation
Where work is delegated for the first time, the supervisor should think in terms of these questions:
1. Who is best qualified to do this?
2. Can an employee improve his abilities by doing this?
3. How long should an employee spend on this?
4. Are there any special problems for which he will need guidance?
5. How broad a delegation can I make?

H. Principles of Effective Communications
1. Determine the media.
2. To whom directed?
3. Identification and source authority.
4. Is communication understood?

I. Principles of Work Improvement
1. Most people usually do only the work which is assigned to them.
2. Workers are likely to fit assigned work into the time available to perform it.
3. A good workload usually stimulates output.
4. People usually do their best work when they know that results will be reviewed or inspected.
5. Employees usually feel that someone else is responsible for conditions of work, workplace layout, job methods, type of tools/equipment, and other such factors.
6. Employees are usually defensive about their job security.
7. Employees have natural resistance to change.
8. Employees can support or destroy a supervisor.
9. A supervisor usually earns the respect of his people through his personal example of diligence and efficiency.

J. Areas of Job Improvement
The areas of job improvement are quite numerous, but the most common ones which a supervisor can identify and utilize are:
1. Departmental layout
2. Flow of work
3. Workplace layout
4. Utilization of manpower
5. Work methods
6. Materials handling

7. Utilization
8. Motion economy

K. Seven Key Points in Making Improvements
1. Select the job to be improved
2. Study how it is being done now
3. Question the present method
4. Determine actions to be taken
5. Chart proposed method
6. Get approval and apply
7. Solicit worker participation

l. Corrective Techniques of Job Improvement
Specific Problems
1. Size of workload
2. Inability to meet schedules
3. Strain and fatigue
4. Improper use of men and skills
5. Waste, poor quality, unsafe conditions
6. Bottleneck conditions that hinder output
7. Poor utilization of equipment and machine
8. Efficiency and productivity of labor

General Improvement
1. Departmental layout
2. Flow of work
3. Work plan layout
4. Utilization of manpower
5. Work methods
6. Materials handling
7. Utilization of equipment
8. Motion economy

Corrective Techniques
1. Study with scale model
2. Flow chart study
3. Motion analysis
4. Comparison of units produced to standard allowance
5. Methods analysis
6. Flow chart and equipment study
7. Down time vs. running time
8. Motion analysis

M. A Planning Checklist
1. Objectives
2. Controls
3. Delegations
4. Communications
5. Resources
6. Manpower

7. Equipment
8. Supplies and materials
9. Utilization of time
10. Safety
11. Money
12. Work
13. Timing of improvements

N. Five Characteristics of Good Directions
In order to get results, directions must be:
1. Possible of accomplishment
2. Agreeable with worker interests
3. Related to mission
4. Planned and complete
5. Unmistakably clear

O. Types of Directions
1. Demands or direct orders
2. Requests
3. Suggestion or implication
4. volunteering

P. Controls
A typical listing of the overall areas in which the supervisor should establish controls might be:
1. Manpower
2. Materials
3. Quality of work
4. Quantity of work
5. Time
6. Space
7. Money
8. Methods

Q. Orienting the New Employee
1. Prepare for him
2. Welcome the new employee
3. Orientation for the job
4. Follow-up

R. Checklist for Orienting New Employees Yes No
1. Do you appreciate the feelings of new employees when they first report for work? ___ ___
2. Are you aware of the fact that the new employee must make a big adjustment to his job? ___ ___
3. Have you given him good reasons for liking the job and the organization? ___ ___
4. Have you prepared for his first day on the job? ___ ___
5. Did you welcome him cordially and make him feel needed? ___ ___

		Yes	No
6.	Did you establish rapport with him so that he feels free to talk and discuss matters with you?	___	___
7.	Did you explain his job to him and his relationship to you?	___	___
8.	Does he know that his work will be evaluated periodically on a basis that is fair and objective?	___	___
9.	Did you introduce him to his fellow workers in such a way that they are likely to accept him?	___	___
10.	Does he know what employee benefits he will receive?	___	___
11.	Does he understand the importance of being on the job and what to do if he must leave his duty station?	___	___
12.	Has he been impressed with the importance of accident prevention and safe practice?	___	___
13.	Does he generally know his way around the department?	___	___
14.	Is he under the guidance of a sponsor who will teach the right way of doing things?	___	___
15.	Do you plan to follow-up so that he will continue to adjust successfully to his job?	___	___

S. Principles of Learning
1. Motivation
2. Demonstration or explanation
3. Practice

T. Causes of Poor Performance
1. Improper training for job
2. Wrong tools
3. Inadequate directions
4. Lack of supervisory follow-up
5. Poor communications
6. Lack of standards of performance
7. Wrong work habits
8. Low morale
9. Other

U. Four Major Steps in On-The-Job Instruction
1. Prepare the worker
2. Present the operation
3. Tryout performance
4. Follow-up

V. Employees Want Five Things
1. Security
2. Opportunity
3. Recognition
4. Inclusion
5. Expression

W. Some Don'ts in Regard to Praise
1. Don't praise a person for something he hasn't done.
2. Don't praise a person unless you can be sincere.
3. Don't be sparing in praise just because your superior withholds it from you.
4. Don't let too much time elapse between good performance and recognition of it

X. How to Gain Your Workers' Confidence
Methods of developing confidence include such things as:
1. Knowing the interests, habits, hobbies of employees
2. Admitting your own inadequacies
3. Sharing and telling of confidence in others
4. Supporting people when they are in trouble
5. Delegating matters that can be well handled
6. Being frank and straightforward about problems and working conditions
7. Encouraging others to bring their problems to you
8. Taking action on problems which impede worker progress

Y. Sources of Employee Problems
On-the-job causes might be such things as:
1. A feeling that favoritism is exercised in assignments
2. Assignment of overtime
3. An undue amount of supervision
4. Changing methods or systems
5. Stealing of ideas or trade secrets
6. Lack of interest in job
7. Threat of reduction in force
8. Ignorance or lack of communications
9. Poor equipment
10. Lack of knowing how supervisor feels toward employee
11. Shift assignments

Off-the-job problems might have to do with:
1. Health
2. Finances
3. Housing
4. Family

Z. The Supervisor's Key to Discipline
There are several key points about discipline which the supervisor should keep in mind:
1. Job discipline is one of the disciplines of life and is directed by the supervisor.
2. It is more important to correct an employee fault than to fix blame for it.
3. Employee performance is affected by problems both on the job and off.
4. Sudden or abrupt changes in behavior can be indications of important employee problems.
5. Problems should be dealt with as soon as possible after they are identified.
6. The attitude of the supervisor may have more to do with solving problems than the techniques of problem solving.
7. Correction of employee behavior should be resorted to only after the supervisor is sure that training or counseling will not be helpful.

8. Be sure to document your disciplinary actions.
9. Make sure that you are disciplining on the basis of facts rather than personal feelings.
10. Take each disciplinary step in order, being careful not to make snap judgments, or decisions based on impatience.

AA. Five Important Processes of Management
1. Planning
2. Organizing
3. Scheduling
4. Controlling
5. Motivating

BB. When the Supervisor Fails to Plan
1. Supervisor creates impression of not knowing his job
2. May lead to excessive overtime
3. Job runs itself—supervisor lacks control
4. Deadlines and appointments missed
5. Parts of the work go undone
6. Work interrupted by emergencies
7. Sets a bad example
8. Uneven workload creates peaks and valleys
9. Too much time on minor details at expense of more important tasks

CC. Fourteen General Principles of Management
1. Division of work
2. Authority and responsibility
3. Discipline
4. Unity of command
5. Unity of direction
6. Subordination of individual interest to general interest
7. Remuneration of personnel
8. Centralization
9. Scalar chain
10. Order
11. Equity
12. Stability of tenure of personnel
13. Initiative
14. Esprit de corps

DD. Change

Bringing about change is perhaps attempted more often, and yet less well understood, than anything else the supervisor does. How do people generally react to change? (People tend to resist change that is imposed upon them by other individuals or circumstances.

Change is characteristic of every situation. It is a part of every real endeavor where the efforts of people are concerned.

1. Why do people resist change?
   People may resist change because of:
   a. Fear of the unknown
   b. Implied criticism
   c. Unpleasant experiences in the past
   d. Fear of loss of status
   e. Threat to the ego
   f. Fear of loss of economic stability

2. How can we best overcome the resistance to change?
   In initiating change, take these steps:
   a. Get ready to sell
   b. Identify sources of help
   c. Anticipate objections
   d. Sell benefits
   e. Listen in depth
   f. Follow up

II. Brief Topical Summaries

   A. Who/What is the Supervisor?
      1. The supervisor is often called the "highest level employee and the lowest level manager."
      2. A supervisor is a member of both management and the work group. He acts as a bridge between the two.
      3. Most problems in supervision are in the area of human relations, or people problems.
      4. Employees expect: Respect, opportunity to learn and to advance, and a sense of belonging, and so forth.
      5. Supervisors are responsible for directing people and organizing work. Planning is of paramount importance.
      6. A position description is a set of duties and responsibilities inherent to a given position.
      7. It is important to keep the position description up-to-date and to provide each employee with his own copy.

   B. The Sociology of Work
      1. People are alike in many ways; however, each individual is unique.
      2. The supervisor is challenged in getting to know employee differences. Acquiring skills in evaluating individuals is an asset.
      3. Maintaining meaningful working relationships in the organization is of great importance.
      4. The supervisor has an obligation to help individuals to develop to their fullest potential.
      5. Job rotation on a planned basis helps to build versatility and to maintain interest and enthusiasm in work groups.
      6. Cross training (job rotation) provides backup skills.

7. The supervisor can help reduce tension by maintaining a sense of humor, providing guidance to employees, and by making reasonable and timely decisions. Employees respond favorably to working under reasonably predictable circumstances.
8. Change is characteristic of all managerial behavior. The supervisor must adjust to changes in procedures, new methods, technological changes, and to a number of new and sometimes challenging situations.
9. To overcome the natural tendency for people to resist change, the supervisor should become more skillful in initiating change.

C. Principles and Practices of Supervision
1. Employees should be required to answer to only one superior.
2. A supervisor can effectively direct only a limited number of employees, depending upon the complexity, variety, and proximity of the jobs involved.
3. The organizational chart presents the organization in graphic form. It reflects lines of authority and responsibility as well as interrelationships of units within the organization.
4. Distribution of work can be improved through an analysis using the "Work Distribution Chart."
5. The "Work Distribution Chart" reflects the division of work within a unit in understandable form.
6. When related tasks are given to an employee, he has a better chance of increasing his skills through training.
7. The individual who is given the responsibility for tasks must also be given the appropriate authority to insure adequate results.
8. The supervisor should delegate repetitive, routine work. Preparation of recurring reports, maintaining leave and attendance records are some examples.
9. Good discipline is essential to good task performance. Discipline is reflected in the actions of employees on the job in the absence of supervision.
10. Disciplinary action may have to be taken when the positive aspects of discipline have failed. Reprimand, warning, and suspension are examples of disciplinary action.
11. If a situation calls for a reprimand, be sure it is deserved and remember it is to be done in private.

D. Dynamic Leadership
1. A style is a personal method or manner of exerting influence.
2. Authoritarian leaders often see themselves as the source of power and authority.
3. The democratic leader often perceives the group as the source of authority and power.
4. Supervisors tend to do better when using the pattern of leadership that is most natural for them.
5. Social scientists suggest that the effective supervisor use the leadership style that best fits the problem or circumstances involved.
6. All four styles—telling, selling, consulting, joining—have their place. Using one does not preclude using the other at another time.

7. The theory X point of view assumes that the average person dislikes work, will avoid it whenever possible, and must be coerced to achieve organizational objectives.
8. The theory Y point of view assumes that the average person considers work to be a natural as play, and, when the individual is committed, he requires little supervision or direction to accomplish desired objectives.
9. The leader's basic assumptions concerning human behavior and human nature affect his actions, decisions, and other managerial practices.
10. Dissatisfaction among employees is often present, but difficult to isolate. The supervisor should seek to weaken dissatisfaction by keeping promises, being sincere and considerate, keeping employees informed, and so forth.
11. Constructive suggestions should be encouraged during the natural progress of the work.

E. Processes for Solving Problems
1. People find their daily tasks more meaningful and satisfying when they can improve them.
2. The causes of problems, or the key factors, are often hidden in the background. Ability to solve problems often involves the ability to isolate them from their backgrounds. There is some substance to the cliché that some persons "can't see the forest for the trees."
3. New procedures are often developed from old ones. Problems should be broken down into manageable parts. New ideas can be adapted from old one.
4. People think differently in problem-solving situations. Using a logical, patterned approach is often useful. One approach found to be useful includes these steps:
   a. Define the problem
   b. Establish objectives
   c. Get the facts
   d. Weigh and decide
   e. Take action
   f. Evaluate action

F. Training for Results
1. Participants respond best when they feel training is important to them.
2. The supervisor has responsibility for the training and development of those who report to him.
3. When training is delegated to others, great care must be exercised to insure the trainer has knowledge, aptitude, and interest for his work as a trainer.
4. Training (learning) of some type goes on continually. The most successful supervisor makes certain the learning contributes in a productive manner to operational goals.
5. New employees are particularly susceptible to training. Older employees facing new job situations require specific training, as well as having need for development and growth opportunities.
6. Training needs require continuous monitoring.
7. The training officer of an agency is a professional with a responsibility to assist supervisors in solving training problems.

8. Many of the self-development steps important to the supervisor's own growth are equally important to the development of peers and subordinates. Knowledge of these is important when the supervisor consults with others on development and growth opportunities.

G. Health, Safety, and Accident Prevention
1. Management-minded supervisors take appropriate measures to assist employees in maintaining health and in assuring safe practices in the work environment.
2. Effective safety training and practices help to avoid injury and accidents.
3. Safety should be a management goal. All infractions of safety which are observed should be corrected without exception.
4. Employees' safety attitude, training and instruction, provision of safe tools and equipment, supervision, and leadership are considered highly important factors which contribute to safety and which can be influenced directly by supervisors.
5. When accidents do occur, they should be investigated promptly for very important reasons, including the fact that information which is gained can be used to prevent accidents in the future.

H. Equal Employment Opportunity
1. The supervisor should endeavor to treat all employees fairly, without regard to religion, race, sex, or national origin.
2. Groups tend to reflect the attitude of the leader. Prejudice can be detected even in very subtle form. Supervisors must strive to create a feeling of mutual respect and confidence in every employee.
3. Complete utilization of all human resources is a national goal. Equitable consideration should be accorded women in the work force, minority-group members, the physically and mentally handicapped, and the older employee. The important question is: "Who can do the job?"
4. Training opportunities, recognition for performance, overtime assignments, promotional opportunities, and all other personnel actions are to be handled on an equitable basis.

I. Improving Communications
1. Communications is achieving understanding between the sender and the receiver of a message. It also means sharing information—the creation of understanding.
2. Communication is basic to all human activity. Words are means of conveying meanings; however, real meanings are in people.
3. There are very practical differences in the effectiveness of one-way, impersonal, and two-way communications. Words spoken face-to-face are better understood. Telephone conversations are effective, but lack the rapport of person-to-person exchanges. The whole person communicates.
4. Cooperation and communication in an organization go hand in hand. When there is a mutual respect between people, spelling out rules and procedures for communicating is unnecessary.
5. There are several barriers to effective communications. These include failure to listen with respect and understanding, lack of skill in feedback, and misinterpreting the meanings of words used by the speaker. It is also common

practice to listen to what we want to hear, and tune out things we do not want to hear.
6. Communication is management's chief problem. The supervisor should accept the challenge to communicate more effectively and to improve interagency and intra-agency communications.
7. The supervisor may often plan for and conduct meetings. The planning phase is critical and may determine the success or the failure of a meeting.
8. Speaking before groups usually requires extra effort. Stage fright may never disappear completely, but it can be controlled.

J. Self-Development
1. Every employee is responsible for his own self-development.
2. Toastmaster and toastmistress clubs offer opportunities to improve skills in oral communications.
3. Planning for one's own self-development is of vital importance. Supervisors know their own strengths and limitations better than anyone else.
4. Many opportunities are open to aid the supervisor in his developmental efforts, including job assignments; training opportunities, both governmental and non-governmental—to include universities and professional conferences and seminars.
5. Programmed instruction offers a means of studying at one's own rate.
6. Where difficulties may arise from a supervisor's being away from his work for training, he may participate in televised home study or correspondence courses to meet his self-development needs.

K. Teaching and Training
1. The Teaching Process
Teaching is encouraging and guiding the learning activities of students toward established goals. In most cases this process consists of five steps: preparation, presentation, summarization, evaluation, and application.

   a. Preparation
   Preparation is two-fold in nature; that of the supervisor and the employee. Preparation by the supervisor is absolutely essential to success. He must know what, when, where, how, and whom he will teach. Some of the factors that should be considered are:
   1) The objectives
   2) The materials needed
   3) The methods to be used
   4) Employee participation
   5) Employee interest
   6) Training aids
   7) Evaluation
   8) Summarization

   Employee preparation consists in preparing the employee to receive the material. Probably the most important single factor in the preparation of the employee is arousing and maintaining his interest. He must know the objectives of the training, why he is there, how the material can be used, and its importance to him.

b. Presentation
In presentation, have a carefully designed plan and follow it. The plan should be accurate and complete, yet flexible enough to meet situations as they arise. The method of presentation will be determined by the particular situation and objectives.

c. Summary
A summary should be made at the end of every training unit and program. In addition, there may be internal summaries depending on the nature of the material being taught. The important thing is that the trainee must always be able to understand how each part of the new material relates to the whole.

d. Application
The supervisor must arrange work so the employee will be given a chance to apply new knowledge or skills while the material is still clear in his mind and interest is high. The trainee does not really know whether he has learned the material until he has been given a chance to apply it. If the material is not applied, it loses most of its value.

e. Evaluation
The purpose of all training is to promote learning. To determine whether the training has been a success or failure, the supervisor must evaluate this learning.
In the broadest sense, evaluation includes all the devices, methods, skills, and techniques used by the supervisor to keep himself and the employees informed as to their progress toward the objectives they are pursuing. The extent to which the employee has mastered the knowledge, skills, and abilities, or changed his attitudes, as determined by the program objectives, is the extent to which instruction has succeeded or failed.
Evaluation should not be confined to the end of the lesson, day, or program but should be used continuously. We shall note later the way this relates to the rest of the teaching process.

2. Teaching Methods
A teaching method is a pattern of identifiable student and instructor activity used in presenting training material.
All supervisors are faced with the problem of deciding which method should be used at a given time.

a. Lecture
The lecture is direct oral presentation of material by the supervisor. The present trend is to place less emphasis on the trainer's activity and more on that of the trainee.

b. Discussion
Teaching by discussion or conference involves using questions and other techniques to arouse interest and focus attention upon certain areas, and by doing so creating a learning situation. This can be one of the most

valuable methods because it gives the employees an opportunity to express their ideas and pool their knowledge.

    c. Demonstration
The demonstration is used to teach how something works or how to do something. It can be used to show a principle or what the results of a series of actions will be. A well-staged demonstration is particularly effective because it shows proper methods of performance in a realistic manner.

    d. Performance
Performance is one of the most fundamental of all learning techniques or teaching methods. The trainee may be able to tell how a specific operation should be performed but he cannot be sure he knows how to perform the operation until he has done so.
As with all methods, there are certain advantages and disadvantages to each method.

    e. Which Method to Use
Moreover, there are other methods and techniques of teaching. It is difficult to use any method without other methods entering into it. In any learning situation, a combination of methods is usually more effective than any one method alone.

Finally, evaluation must be integrated into the other aspects of the teaching-learning process.

It must be used in the motivation of the trainees; it must be used to assist in developing understanding during the training; and it must be related to employee application of the results of training.

This is distinctly the role of the supervisor.

TRAFFIC ENGINEERING

BASIC FUNDAMENTALS OF TRAFFIC PLANNING

CONTENTS

	Page
CHAPTER 1 – CONCEPT	1-1
CHAPTER 2 – ORGANIZATION	2-1
CHAPTER 3 – PROCESS	3-1

Basic Fundamentals of Traffic Planning

CONCEPT

THOROUGHFARE PLANNING is a method of identifying travel needs and filling them — to make road travel safe, economical, convenient, free-flowing, and environmentally acceptable. Thoroughfare planners insure that roadways will accommodate traffic demands, maximize the use of roadways, and solve traffic problems.

PLANNING IS A STEP-BY-STEP PROCESS

THOROUGHFARE PLANNING provides not only for modifications to existing roadways to meet current traffic demands; it provides also for the identification of land areas that should be reserved for roadway expansion to meet future traffic demands. Planners, working toward established goals, may recommend that a particular street be retained or redesigned as necessary to perform a specific function. **Effective thoroughfare planning can reap savings in construction and maintenance costs, protect housing areas, and control travel and land-use patterns.**

The **planning process** is a method to:

Identify problems and establish goals and objectives.

Conduct traffic surveys, analyze the survey data, and estimate future traffic volumes and patterns.

Develop alternate solutions and test them against the goals and objectives, then select and implement a final plan.

Review and evaluate the plan on a continuing basis and adjust it as necessary to attain desired goals and objectives.

1-2

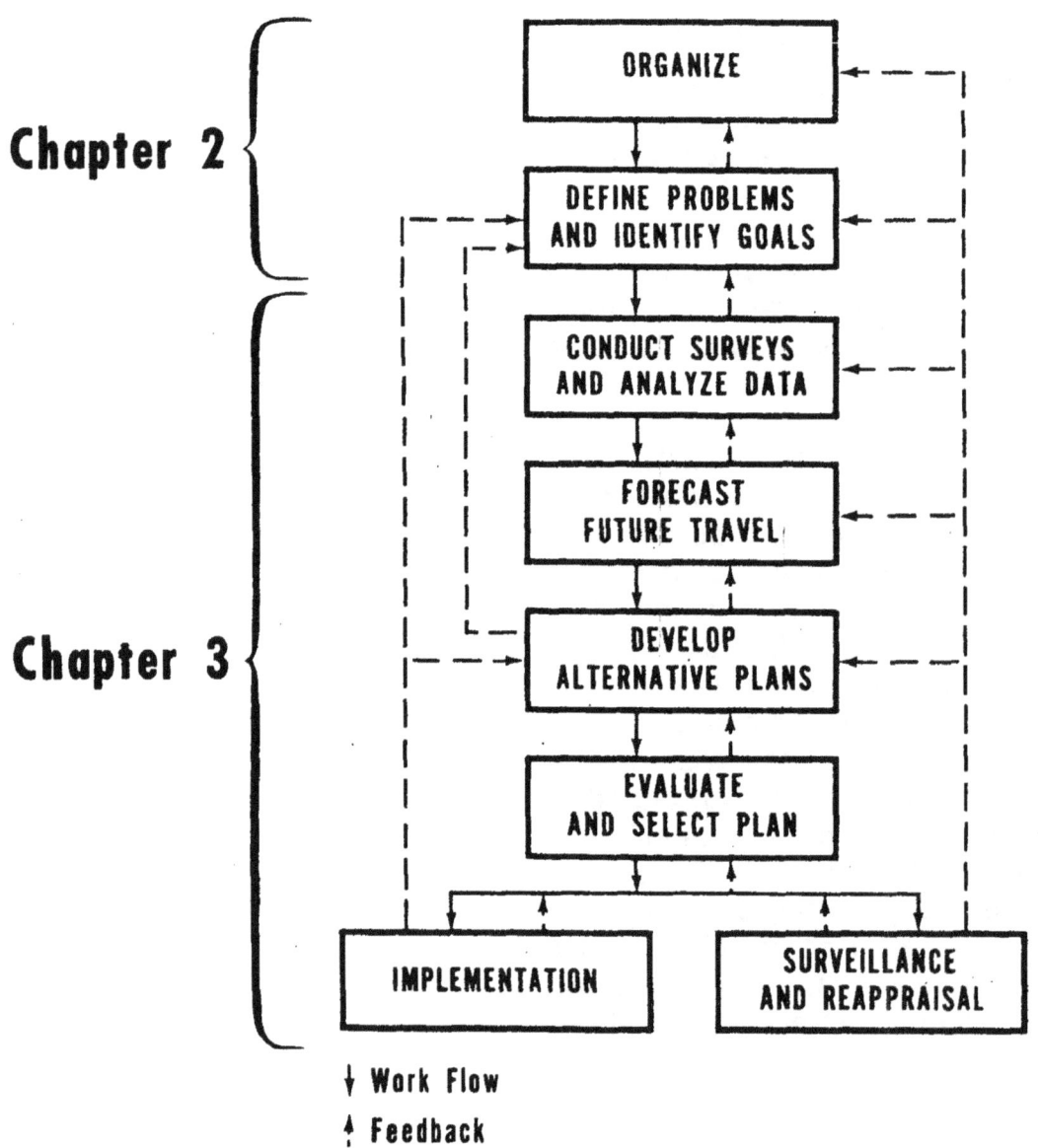

A step-by-step discussion of the planning process is presented in Chapters 2 and 3. Chapter 2 discusses the prerequisites to effective and continuing planning — that is, the formation of a planning committee, the identification of problems, and the establishment of goals. Chapter 3 summarizes the remaining steps to be taken to develop alternative plans for evaluation, selection, and implementation.

ORGANIZATION

PLANNING COMMITTEE

PROBLEM DEFINITION AND GOAL IDENTIFICATION

TRAFFIC PLANNING GOALS must be **determined by the installation decisionmakers,** with the **assistance of technical experts.** Technical experts should provide direction for the decisionmakers *through rational analysis of installation needs and policies.* With this information, **decisionmakers** can effectively select goals and a planning program that will insure an end product that is both workable and desirable.

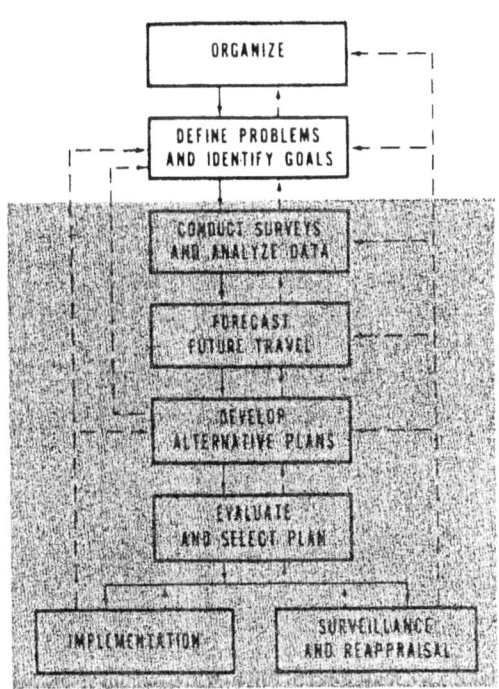

PLANNING COMMITTEE

EFFECTIVE THOROUGHFARE PLANNING *requires concerted effort among policymakers and the technical and administrative staffs of the installation under study.* Each step of the planning process must be based on a simple framework in which the installation's decisionmakers can clearly understand not only the traffic problems, but also the solution to those problems. Committee members usually should be selected to represent the installation's diverse disciplines and viewpoints. For example, an individual representing each of the groups shown below would be desirable.

DECISIONMAKERS MUST

- Identify Traffic Problems
- Establish Goals to Reduce Problems
- Select Thoroughfare Plan
- Gain Support for Plan

TECHNICAL STAFF MUST

- Conduct Traffic Studies
- Estimate Future Travel
- Develop Alternate Plans
- Implement Plan

PROBLEM DEFINITION AND GOAL IDENTIFICATION

THE FIRST STEP IN THOROUGHFARE PLANNING is to **clearly identify all traffic problems of the installation** being studied.

The term *"traffic problem"* is defined as *any situation that impairs the safe and efficient flow of traffic.*

In identifying traffic problems, relativity must be considered; that is, traffic problems vary among different areas of the country. For example, a 5-minute delay in New York City is considered as negligible, while the same delay in Timbuktu would be extremely frustrating to motorists. Therefore, it must be remembered that **traffic problems are relative to the installation being studied.**

FOR EVERY TRAFFIC PROBLEM, THERE IS A POSITIVE GOAL

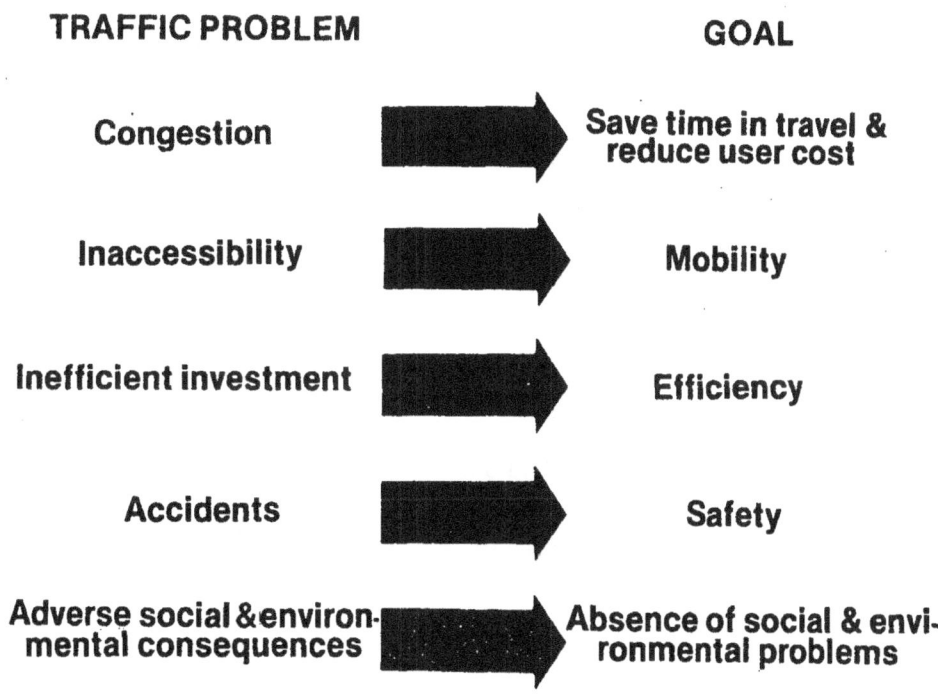

TRAFFIC PROBLEM	GOAL
Congestion	Save time in travel & reduce user cost
Inaccessibility	Mobility
Inefficient investment	Efficiency
Accidents	Safety
Adverse social & environmental consequences	Absence of social & environmental problems

PROBLEM:

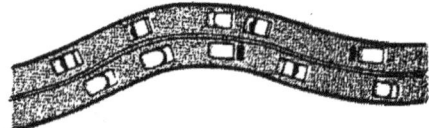

CONGESTION wastes time and increases operating costs.

CONGESTION — Motorists dislike traffic congestion primarily because of wasted time and the resulting increased operating costs. Excessive operating costs can be measured with a fair degree of precision. For example, on a 1-mile free-flowing roadway of 30 miles-per-hour speed, three stops of 30-seconds duration each will result in an increase of approximately 90 percent in total running cost of the car. Measuring the value of a motorist's time is far more difficult. However, evidence shows that, given a choice, motorists will forfeit operating economy to save time.

GOAL: TO PROVIDE EFFICIENT TRAFFIC FLOW

ADEQUATE CAPACITY saves time and reduces operating cost.

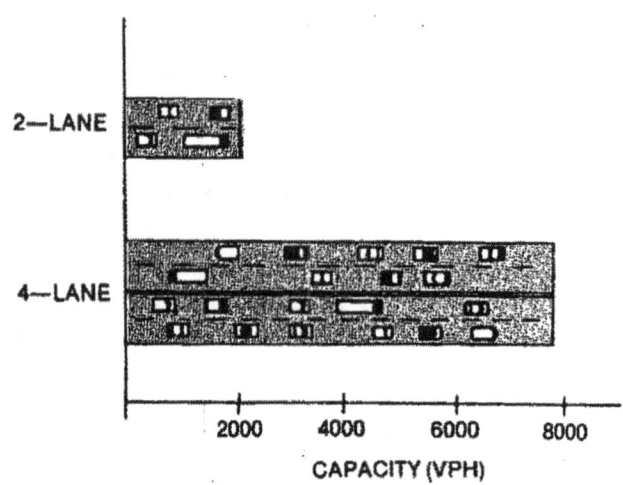

OBJECTIVE	INDICATOR
Cut travel time	Peak period travel time
Minimize congestion	Peak period volume
Reduce user cost	Vehicle user cost

PROBLEM:

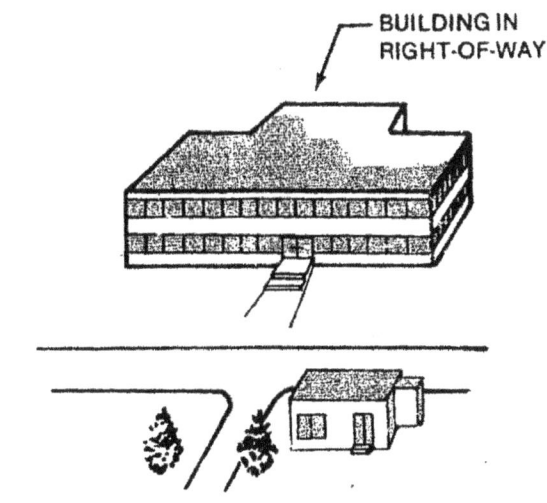

INACCESSIBILITY — Most people like to have the freedom to get where they want to go, when they want to go. High productivity is closely related to proximity in time. Without access, land cannot be developed and people cannot move to jobs, schools, hospitals, and so forth.

GOAL: TO IMPROVE MOBILITY OF POPULATION

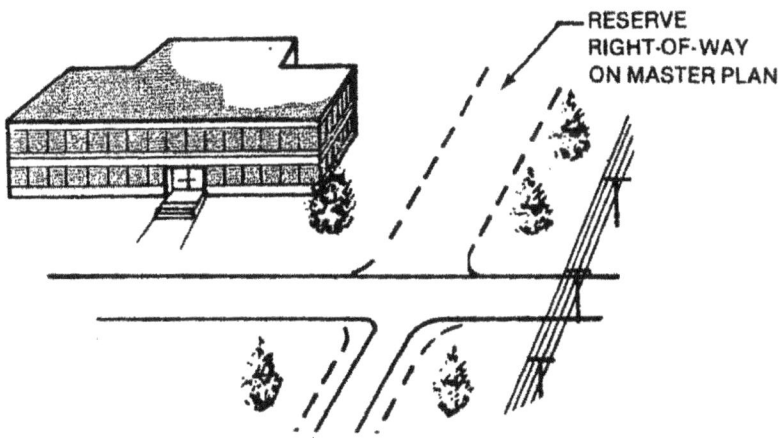

OBJECTIVE	INDICATOR
Reduce travel distance	Distance between point A and point B
Increase productivity of land and people	Changes in access caused by land development

PROBLEM:

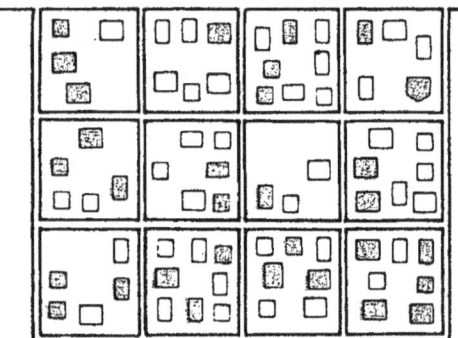

Where width of street, size of house, or size of lot is squeezed to a so-called "efficient minimum" — this is false economy.

INEFFICIENT INVESTMENT — Another universally condemned action is waste of public funds. The case of building unusable traffic facilities or misappropriating public funds is quite rare. However, the more frequent and important waste is that of false economy in traffic facilities. For example, decisions on expenditure are generally based on their budget appeal, not on their adequacy, such as patchwork improvements. The question of whether improvements may solve any particular problem is usually overlooked or avoided; example, a street-widening may prove inadequate the day it is completed and require immediate improvements. Another type of false economy results from so-called "efficient" planning, which creates waste. For example, in housing areas where the width of a street or the size of a house or the lot it occupies has been reduced to a so-called "efficient minimum" — this is false economy. EFFICIENT PLANNING IS MORE THAN AN OBSESSION TO SAVE; IT IS A METHOD TO IMPROVE.

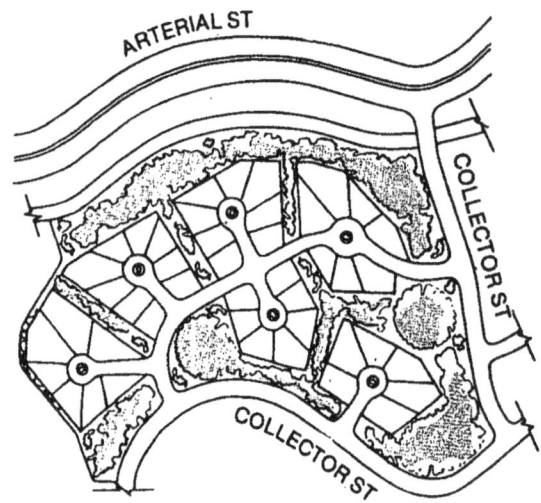

A modern residential street design preserves the neighborhood.

GOAL: TO ELIMINATE WASTE OF PUBLIC FUNDS AND PROTECT LIFE STYLE PATTERNS.

OBJECTIVE	INDICATOR
Decide expenditures based on adequacy, NOT budget appeal	Existing and desirable life-style patterns

PROBLEM:

ACCIDENTS — Accidents are the most significant of all traffic problems. In 1975 alone, approximately 58,800 motor vehicle accidents occurred on military installations, and resulted in an estimated cost of $70,000,000 to DOD and its personnel. Recent surveys of military installations revealed that the yearly accident rate ranged from 1 to over 40 per 1,000 people. This wide range indicates that the accident rate of an installation can be reduced through better traffic facilities.

ACCIDENT COST TO DOD
FATALITY — $287,175 per accident
PERSONAL INJURY — $8,085 per accident
PROPERTY DAMAGE — $520 per accident

GOAL: TO PROVIDE SAFE TRAVEL ROAD

FOUR-LANE UNDIVIDED — 4.09 accidents per million vehicle miles

VERSUS

FOUR-LANE DIVIDED — 2.91 accidents per million vehicle miles

The reduction of accidents on a four-lane divided highway is 29% over the undivided highway

OBJECTIVE	INDICATOR
Reduce accidents and fatalities	Number of accidents and fatalities

PROBLEM:

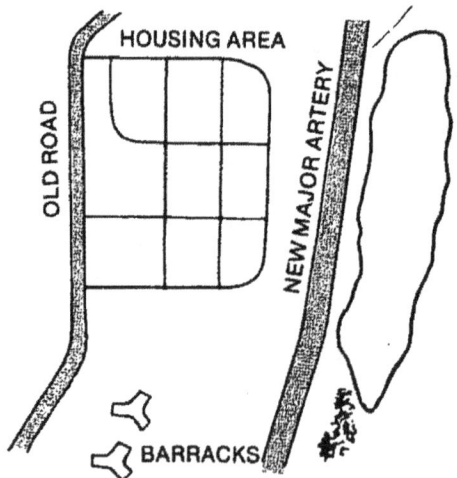

Noise Pollution.

SOCIAL AND ENVIRONMENTAL IMPACT — Ugliness, air pollution, strain, discomfort, noise, and nuisance are all components of the increasingly social nature of transportation problems. All of these problems are difficult to measure. Furthermore, problems such as ugliness are visual images that vary markedly among people, and hence it is difficult to obtain a consensus. The best way to consider these problems is in final plan selection.

GOAL: TO ENHANCE ENVIRONMENT

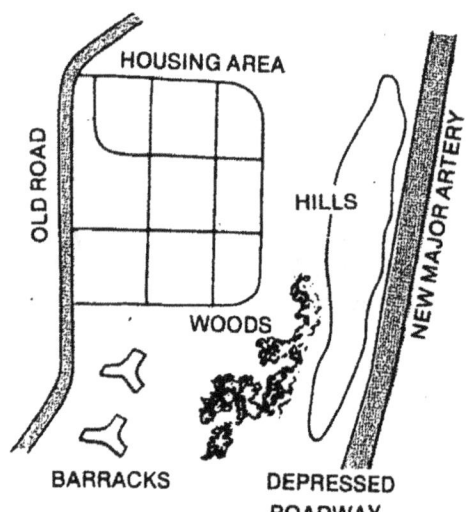

Built-In Noise Protection and Abatement

OBJECTIVE	INDICATOR
Minimize air/noise pollution	Exposure to pollution
Preserve open space	Recreational land available
Reduce travel on residential streets	Traffic volume on streets
Enhance views	Subjective judgment

BE AWARE OF CONFLICTS BETWEEN GOALS

Simply having an agreed set of goals and objectives is not enough because of the conflicts between goals. For example, the least expensive, initially, is to do nothing; whereas, the safest could very likely be the most expensive. Basically, goals should be listed and then screened to eliminate all but the most relevant. The goals selected should then be related to each other, so that losses toward one goal could be offset by gains toward another. Finally, these goals should be related to minimizing the total transportation costs.

III. PROCESS

SURVEYS

FORECAST

DEVELOPMENT

EVALUATION

IMPLEMENTATION

SURVEILLANCE AND REAPPRAISAL

THE ESTABLISHMENT OF A PLANNING PROCEDURE *is necessary in drafting a thoroughfare plan.* The process begins with **a review of existing facilities and travel characteristics. Data for present conditions** are then projected to the design year, and future deficiencies are noted. Based on these projections, **alternative improvements to present conditions** are evaluated, **a general thoroughfare plan** is selected, and **a priority schedule** is developed for implementation. The previous steps are continually reevaluated in view of the data developed at each succeeding step.

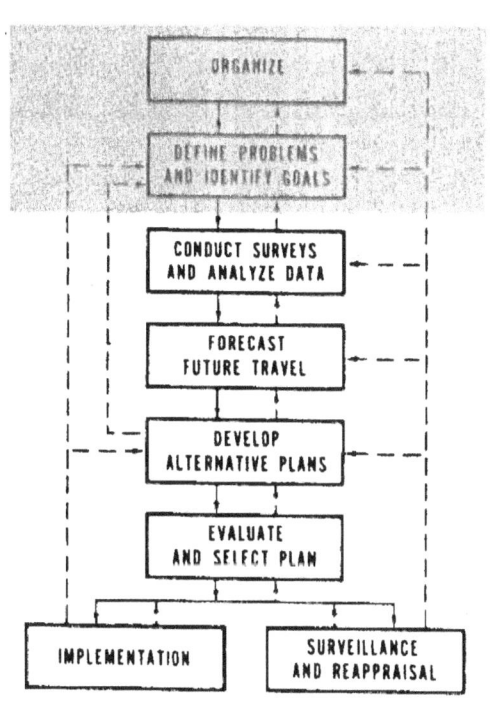

The cornerstone of the thoroughfare plan **is the existing street system.** Today's adequate street system, when projected to the design year, may become inadequate. **The thoroughfare plan should lead to a design that will efficiently handle traffic volumes of the average weekday peak-traffic hours for the design year.** These peak-hour flows usually are highly directional, with heavy inbound traffic in the morning and heavy outbound traffic in the evening. Occasionally, other time periods will determine a design for community service and retail-facility areas.

SURVEYS

SURVEYS are conducted to gather data on the present condition and traffic characteristics of an installation's roadways. These **data** are **analyzed** to estimate the traffic demands on the roadways and, as necessary, to redesign, evaluate, and program a road system to meet those demands.

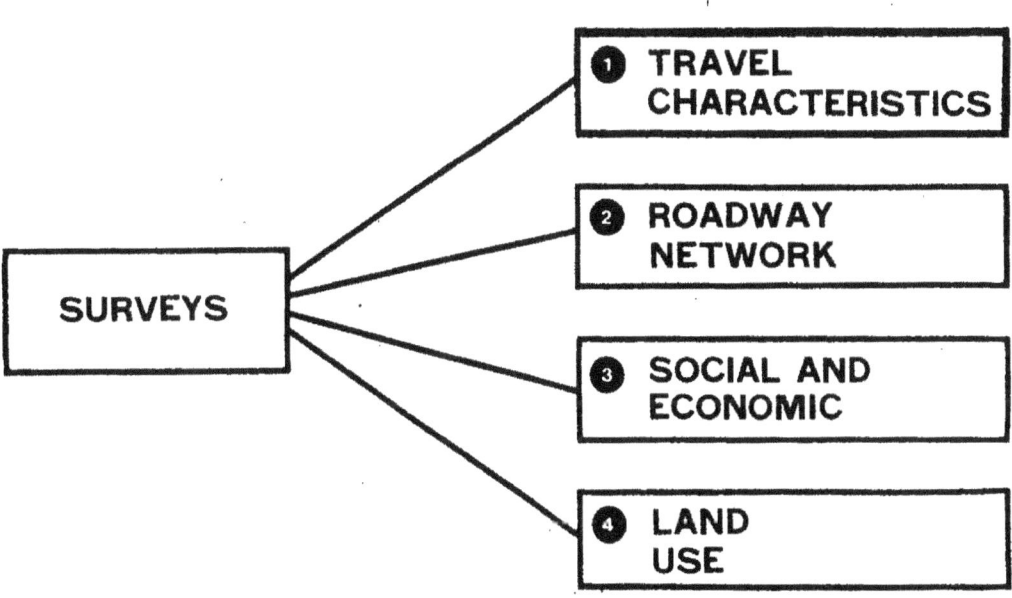

3-4

1. TRAVEL CHARACTERISTICS

These surveys determine how many people use the road system, who they are, and their travel patterns. Data are gathered primarily from studies on traffic volume, vehicle occupancy, travel time and delay, and trip origin and destination. Of major interest to the installation thoroughfare planner is the employee home-to-work trip.

ESTABLISHES ROAD USAGE

2. ROAD NETWORK

These surveys determine the condition and capacity of the roadway. Enough detail should be collected about the physical and operating characteristics of each segment of the route to calculate its capacity, as well as to determine its general level of service and accident history.

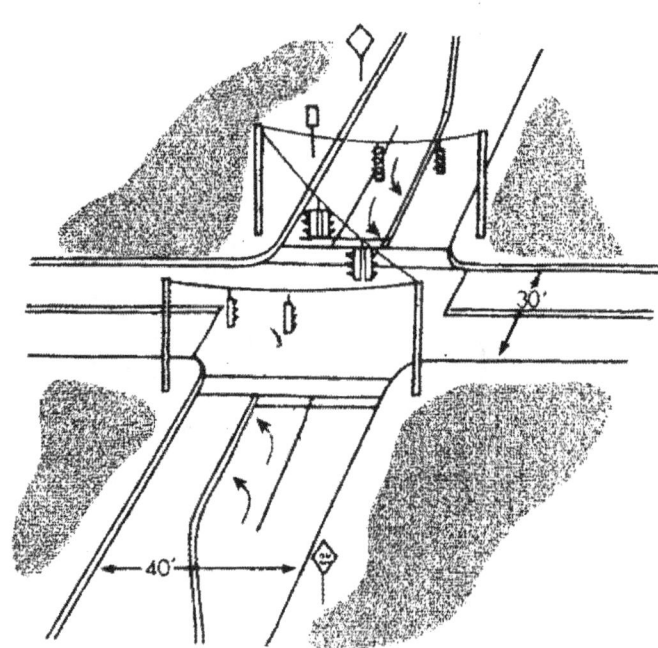

ESTABLISHES ROAD CONDITIONS

③ SOCIAL AND ECONOMIC

These surveys establish past and present facts about the installation road user. Typical data collected include population, employment, duty hours, housing, social services, security measures, and carpool programs. These data are used primarily as a basis for forecasting growth potential. The data are used also for origin and destination surveys and as variables to determine trip generations.

ESTABLISHES ROAD USER CHARACTERISTICS

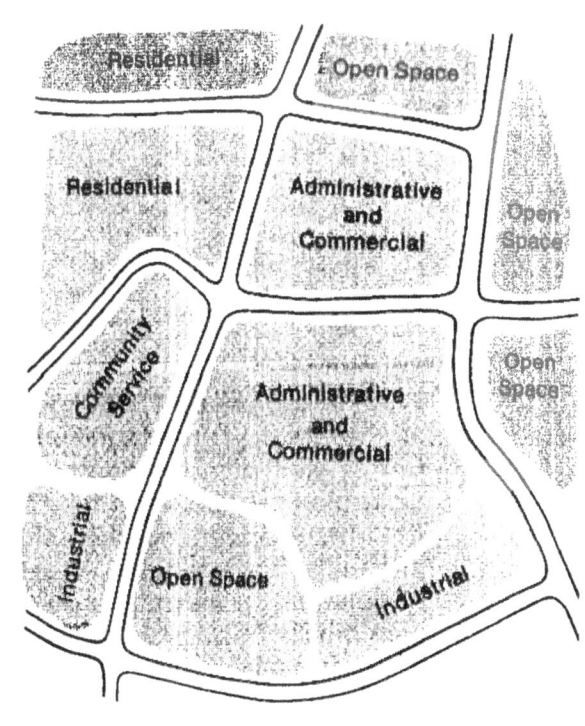

④ LAND USE

Land patterns delineate the function of the land and are basic factors in determining traffic demands of an installation.

A simplified land-use classification system should include at least five categories:

RESIDENTIAL — single-family housing, apartment housing, bachelor officer and enlisted quarters.

ADMINISTRATIVE AND COMMERCIAL — offices, training centers, and exchanges.

INDUSTRIAL AND OPERATIONAL — maintenance and production facilities, ranges, motorpools, airports, and waterfront facilities.

COMMUNITY SERVICE — dependent schools, parks, churches, and recreational facilities.

OPEN SPACE — undeveloped acreage, forest, and streams.

DELINEATES LAND FUNCTION

FORECAST

TRAVEL FORECASTS *are used to determine the transportation service NEED that will result from a change in land use.* For example, what roads will be needed to service a new housing area. Travel forecasts can include home-based, nonhome-based, work, nonwork, person, vehicle, and other type trips. Therefore, **the key to reducing the complexity of a travel forecast** *is to limit the forecast to only what is NEEDED to establish the maximum travel demand.* At a military installation, maximum travel demand is generally created by the highly directional employee home-to-work vehicle-trip that occurs during the morning or evening peak rush hour. Travel forecasts often need to establish only this type demand. A notable exception to this criterion is facilities that generate large traffic volumes not associated with the work trip, such as commercial and community facilities.

TRAVEL FORECASTS QUANTIFY FUTURE TRAFFIC DEMAND

THE FORECAST PROCESS starts with the **proposed road network and land use**, along with a **thorough understanding of existing traffic flow patterns.** Based on this information, **a prediction** is made of the number of future trips to and from an activity **(trip generation)**, where these trips begin and end **(trip distribution)**, and over which routes the trips are to be made **(trip assignment)**. This process is then used to **evaluate** various alternative road systems. After each numerical evaluation, all forecasts are examined to determine if they are reasonable. If the forecast is unreasonable, the assumptions and procedures used to predict the trips should be reexamined and appropriate changes made.

3-7

**SURVEYS
Existing Conditions**

① LAND USE
Where will activities and roads be located?

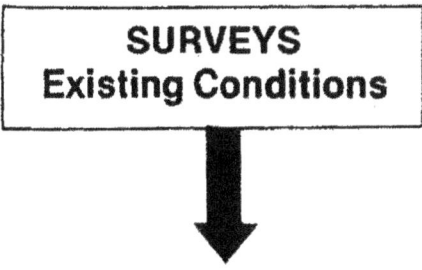

② TRIP GENERATION*
How many trips begin and end at the activity?

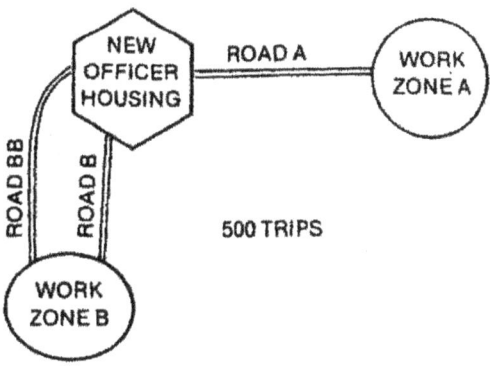

③ TRIP DISTRIBUTION*
How many trips will be made between activities?

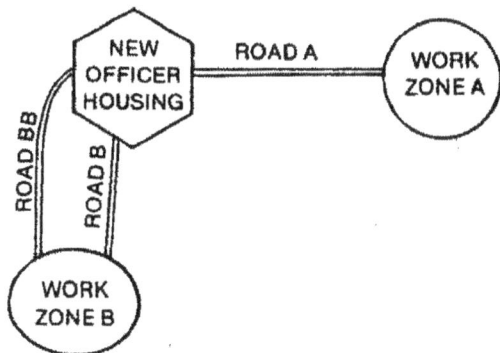

④ TRIP ASSIGNMENT*
Over which routes will trips between activities be made?

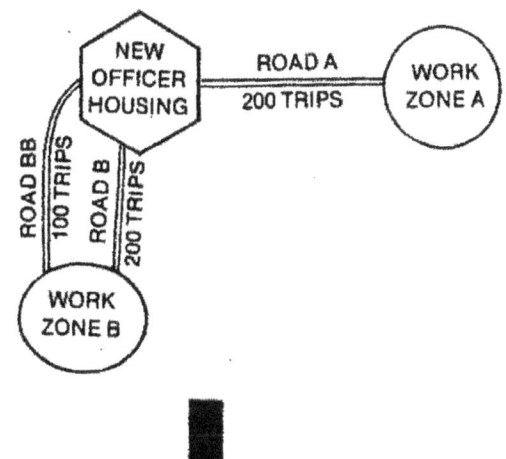

TRAVEL PROJECTIONS

*Only peak-hour trips in direction of maximum flow are shown.

① LAND USE — Where will activities be located?

LAND-USE FORECASTS *provide estimates of future land development — location and type. These estimates* include not only *land usage,* but also *socio-economic variables, such as population, dwelling units, retail sales.* On military installations, this information is obtained from the installation master development plan. However, a major consideration in selecting locations shown on the development plan is the accessibility of that location. Therefore, as the road system is developed, proposed land uses shown on the development plan should be reexamined and changed, if necessary, to achieve a desirable future travel pattern. In every case, the road plan should provide a circulation system that maximizes access for movements between activities, giving due consideration to safety, comfort, and convenience, as well as cost.

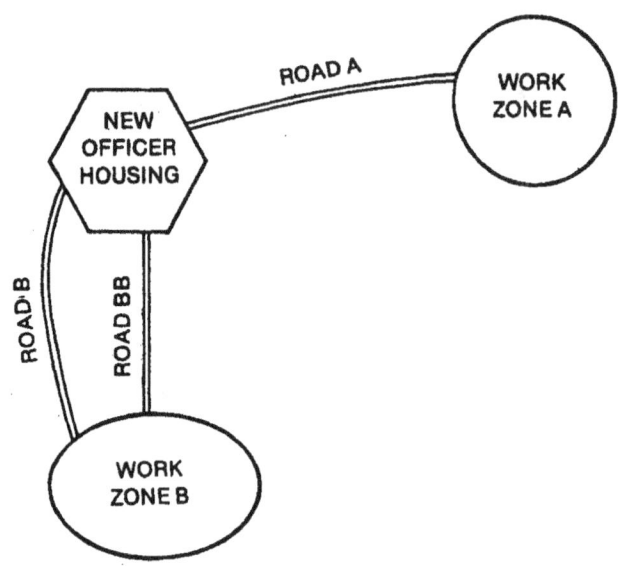

PREDICTIONS OF FUTURE TRAVEL ARE BASED ON FUTURE LAND USE

AND USE PLANNING OBJECTIVES

- Plan for people — not for automobiles and buildings.

- Arrange facilities to achieve the most attractive working and living environment.

- Improve internal traffic flow and external access.

- Consolidate various functional activities.

- Lay out commercial facilities in a way that will bring the patrons close to as many stores as possible once they have parked.

- Locate industrial sites adjacent to transportation facilities so that access is as convenient as possible.

- Provide space for future expansion of facilities and for offstreet parking.

- Locate pollution- and noise-emitting facilities away from residential and commercial areas.

- Route as much traffic as possible around dwelling areas.

- Separate pedestrian and vehicle flows.

- Provide locations that are convenient to residential areas for supplemental services — parks, schools, shops, and chapels.

3-10

② TRIP GENERATION — How many trips begin or end at an activity?

TRIP GENERATION ANALYSIS is a way to *estimate the number of future trips that will begin or end at an activity*. Trip generation analysis provides information on the peak volume of cars to be parked and the peak volume of traffic to be moved onto the road system at any one time.

Trip generation predictions are usually based on trip-making rates that are observed at existing facilities. Because of the many variables affecting traffic generation, specific generation rates have not been developed in this guide. However, for most military installations, trip-making rates can be determined from simple counts of vehicles entering and leaving driveways at existing similar facilities. When establishing generation rates, three characteristics of land use should be evaluated: intensity, character, and location of activity. "Intensity of land use" helps relate how many people will use the land and is expressed in such terms as "employees," "1,000 square feet of floor space," and "dwelling units." "Character of land use" refers to the type of land use, such as residential or industrial; whereas, "location of activity" generally refers to either a central built-up area or a remote area. When using existing facilities to estimate trip generation rates, both facilities should be similar in intensity, character, and location.

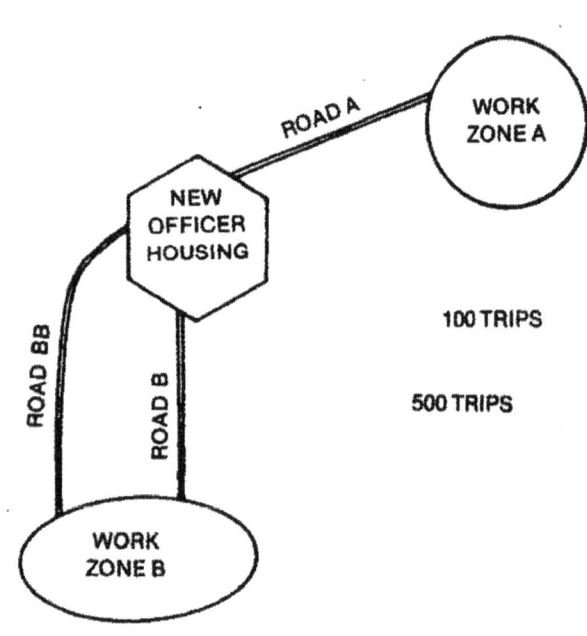

TRIP GENERATION DETERMINES PARKING AND ACCESS NEEDS

TYPICAL GENERATION UNITS

LAND USE	UNIT	LAND USE	UNIT
Bank	1,000 sq ft GFA*	Industrial	employee
Bank, drive-in	drive-in window	Institutional (schools)	student & employee
Barracks	person	Library	1,000 sq ft GFA*
Bowling alley	1,000 sq ft GFA*	Military installation	employee
Cafeteria	seat	Office building	employee
Chapel	seat	Recreation facilities	military strength
Clubs	member	Research facility	employee
Commercial	1,000 sq ft GFA*	Restaurant	seat
Dental clinic	dental chair	Service station	pump
Family housing	dwelling unit	Theater	seat
Golf club	member	Visitor center	employee
Guest house	bedroom	Warehouse	employee
Hospital	outpatient & employee	*Gross floor area	

EXAMPLE GENERATION*

A. **STATE PROBLEM AND NEED**

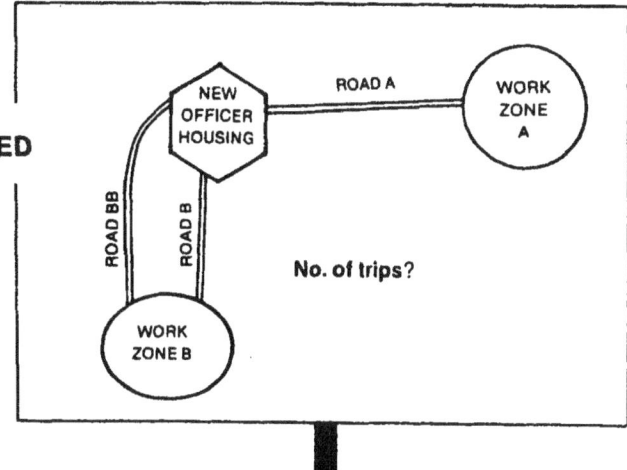

B. **IDENTIFY LAND-USE FACTORS**
- LOCATION
- CHARACTER
- INTENSITY

- BUILT-UP AREA
- RESIDENTIAL
- 500 HOUSES

C. **DEVELOP GENERATION RATE**
(Relation between trip making and land use at similar facility)

SURVEY AT SIMILAR FACILITY
- BUILT-UP AREA
- 400 HOUSES
- RESIDENTIAL
- 400 CARS EXITING IN PEAK HOUR
- TRIP RATE = 1.0 TRIPS/HOUSE

D. **APPLY RELATIONSHIP TO FORECAST**

- PEAK-HOUR ACCESS DEMAND = (500 HOUSES) (1.0 TRIPS/HOUSE)
  = 500 TRIPS

* Only peak-hour trips in direction of maximum flow are shown.

3. TRIP DISTRIBUTION — How many trips will be made between activities?

TRIP DISTRIBUTIONS *are analyzed to establish the number of trips that will be made between specific activity areas.* Two basic types of *mathematical models* are used to predict future trip distribution: *growth models and distribution models. Growth models* expand existing trips between zones based on an anticipated growth rate; whereas, *distribution models* estimate travel patterns based on the number of trips generated by the various zones, and then distribute these trips among the zones. The better known traffic models include the Fratar, Gravity, Intervening Opportunities, and Competing Opportunities. However, since these models require sophisticated data collection and analyses, they are not generally used at relatively small military installations.

TRIP DISTRIBUTION AT A MILITARY INSTALLATION generally can be *accomplished through* two methods. *An average-growth factor method* is used where significant changes in the zonal characteristics are not expected. When areas are almost completely undeveloped, a *proportional distribution method* is used. Both methods present reasonably accurate predictions of the future home-to-work trip. The average-growth method projects future trips between two zones by applying an average of the two zonal growth rates to the existing trips between the zones. On the other hand, the distribution method simply proportions the trips to be generated at a new facility in relation to existing concentrations at trip origins. Relationships for use in these models can be developed from origin and destination studies and/or peak-hour traffic counts.

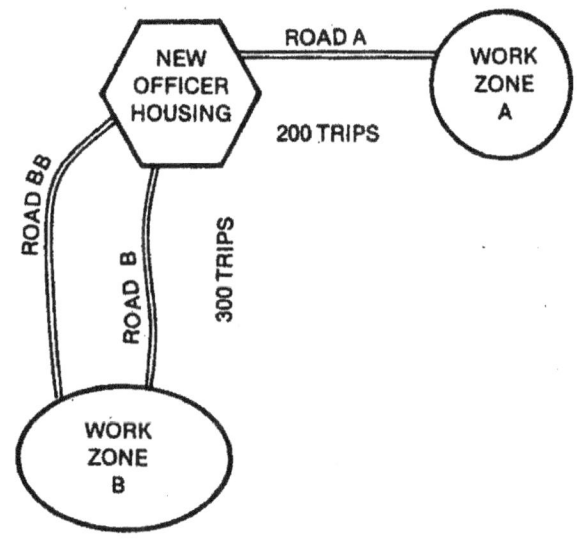

TRIP DISTRIBUTION DETERMINES TRAFFIC CORRIDOR

EXAMPLE DISTRIBUTION *

I. GROWTH MODEL

Where:

$$T_{ij} = t_{ij}\left(\frac{F_i + F_j}{2}\right)$$

T_{ij} = future trips between i & j
t_{ij} = existing trips between i & j
F_i = growth factor at i
F_j = growth factor at j

(A) DETERMINE NUMBER OF EXISTING TRIPS BETWEEN ZONES

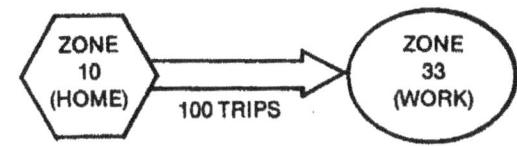

(FROM ORIGIN AND DESTINATION SURVEYS)

(B) ESTIMATE GROWTH RATES FOR BOTH ZONES

$$F_{10} = 1.6$$
$$F_{33} = 1.4$$

(INSTALLATION GROWTH ESTIMATES FROM MASTER DEVELOPMENT PLAN)

(C) COMPUTE FUTURE TRIPS

$$T_{10,33} = t_{10,33}\left(\frac{F_{10} + F_{33}}{2}\right)$$

$$= 100\left(\frac{1.6 + 1.4}{2}\right)$$

$$= 150 \text{ TRIPS}$$

*Only peak-hour trips in direction of maximum flow are shown.

II. DISTRIBUTION MODEL

Where:

$$T_{ij} = T_j\left(\frac{P_i}{\sum_{i=1}^{n} P_i}\right)$$

T_{ij} = future trips between i and j
T_j = future trips generated at j
P_i = existing trips produced at i
$\sum_{i=1}^{n} P_i$ = total trips produced

(A) DETERMINE TRIPS TO BE GENERATED AT NEW FACILITY

500 HOUSING UNITS WILL GENERATE 500 TRIPS

(B) FROM TRAVEL SURVEYS DETERMINE WHERE EXISTING TRIPS ARE DISTRIBUTED

(C) DISTRIBUTE FUTURE TRIPS PROPORTIONATELY

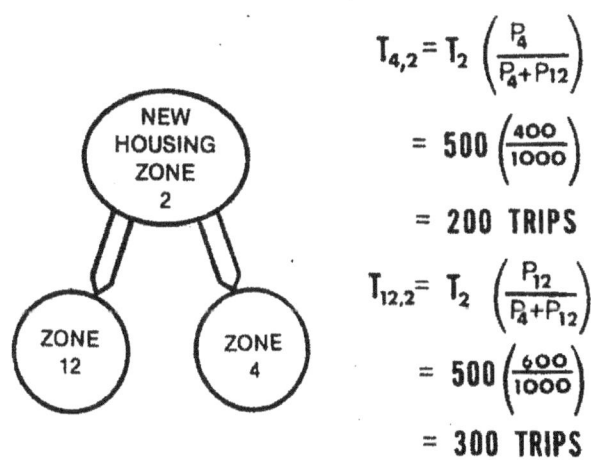

$$T_{4,2} = T_2\left(\frac{P_4}{P_4 + P_{12}}\right)$$

$$= 500\left(\frac{400}{1000}\right)$$

$$= 200 \text{ TRIPS}$$

$$T_{12,2} = T_2\left(\frac{P_{12}}{P_4 + P_{12}}\right)$$

$$= 500\left(\frac{600}{1000}\right)$$

$$= 300 \text{ TRIPS}$$

④ TRIP ASSIGNMENT — Over which routes will trips between activities be made?

The final phase of forecasting the travel demand is THE ASSIGNMENT OF VEHICLE TRIPS BETWEEN ZONES TO VARIOUS TRAFFIC ROUTES. One method of trip assignment is to simulate, from input on the travel pattern or desires of motorists, the extent to which a proposed system would be used. This technique is very complex; therefore, its use should be limited to those familiar with it.

On a military installation, the *primary technique for assigning traffic* is the *"all or nothing with capacity restraint."* In this technique, trips are allocated between zones to the one single path or route that represents the best path for a certain number of vehicles. Assignment thereafter is made to the second or next best alternate route. Frequently, the maximum traffic on a roadway is established as that capacity at which traffic can flow with only limited congestion, allowing the motorist to travel at his desired pace within legal limits. To achieve a balance in all zone-to-zone traffic, a trial-and-error assignment method generally is used; that is, minimum paths are calculated, assignments are made, roads are analyzed for travel comfort and convenience, then new assignments are made. This process continues until traffic is balanced on all routes between zones.

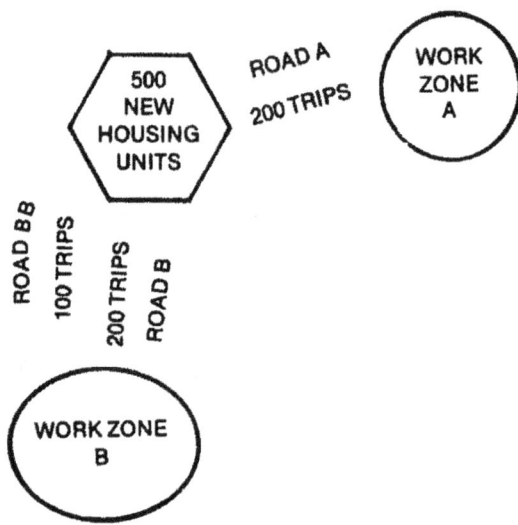

TRIP ASSIGNMENT DETERMINES ROAD WIDTH

FACTORS INFLUENCING ROUTE SELECTION

TANGIBLE	INTANGIBLE
Travel time	Human nature
Travel distance	Relative comfort and ease
Operating cost	
Frequency of stops	Esthetics
Safety	Geometrics

COMPONENTS OF ASSIGNED TRAFFIC

INDUCED TRAFFIC — new trips enticed

DIVERTED TRAFFIC — existing trips diverted from other paths

FACILITY-CREATED TRAFFIC — sightseers or traffic developed because of changes in land use

CONVERTED TRAFFIC — change in mode, such as bus to auto or auto-pool to driver

SHIFTED TRAFFIC — existing trips that show new origin and/or destination

NATURAL GROWTH TRAFFIC — result of natural growth rate

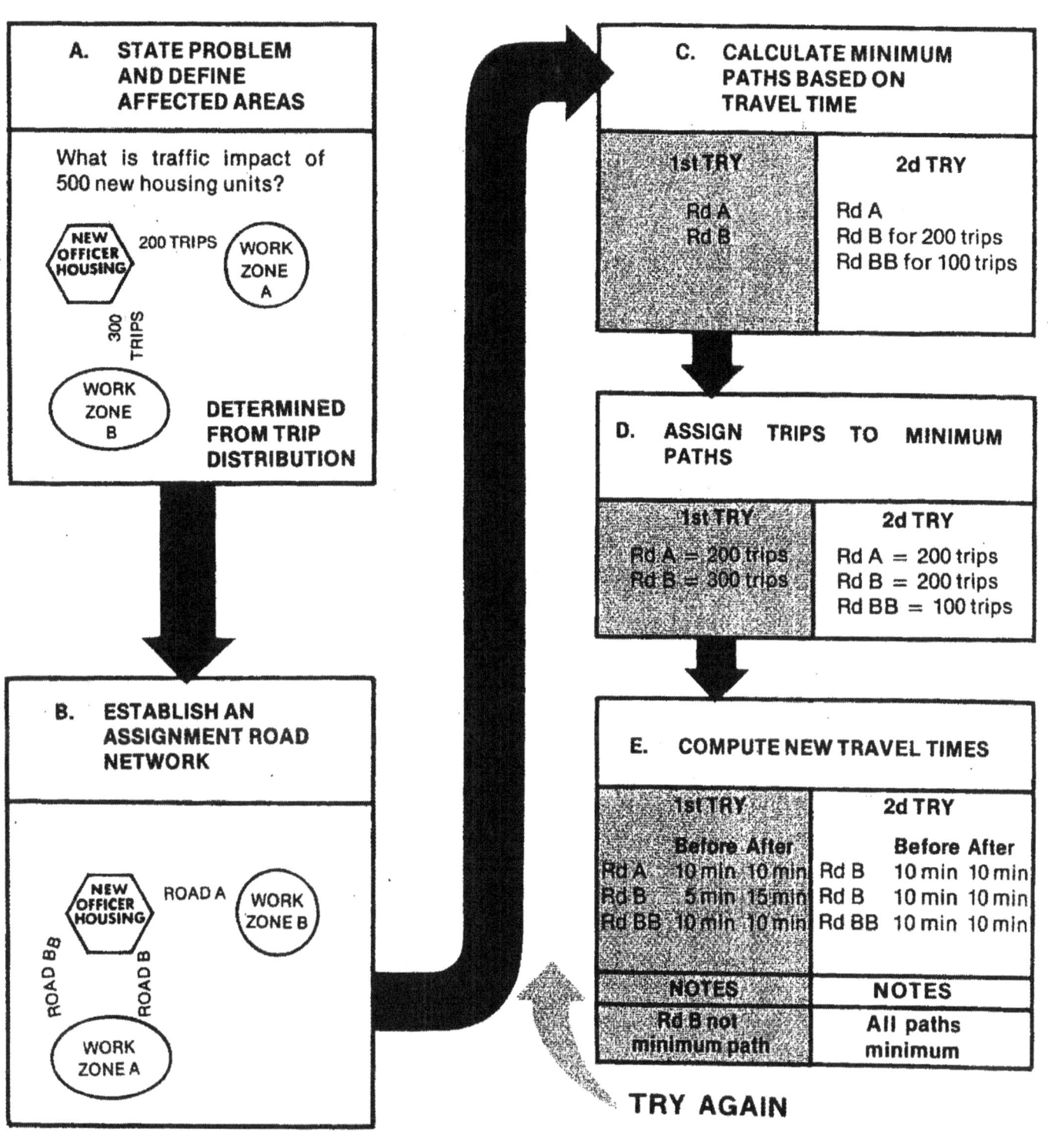

THIS PHASE OF ROAD DESIGN concerns **reducing traffic surveys and travel forecasts into various acceptable road systems.** The goal statements discussed in chapter 2 provide a basis for determining an acceptable system.

The development of alternatives, which by nature is a creative function, usually begins by estimating future travel on the existing road system. From these travel projections, problem areas and road needs can be identified. Assuming that this measure shows problems, a new trial road system is designed.

Once **one or more alternatives** are developed, the road plans are then tested to examine their performance. Congestion should be tested first. As alternatives pass the congestion test, they should be measured in more detail, such as travel time, travel distance, safety, parking, user costs, and environmental impact. The development and testing should end with a manageable number of alternatives that are acceptable in all phases of the roadway plan test. These alternatives then pass into the selection stage.

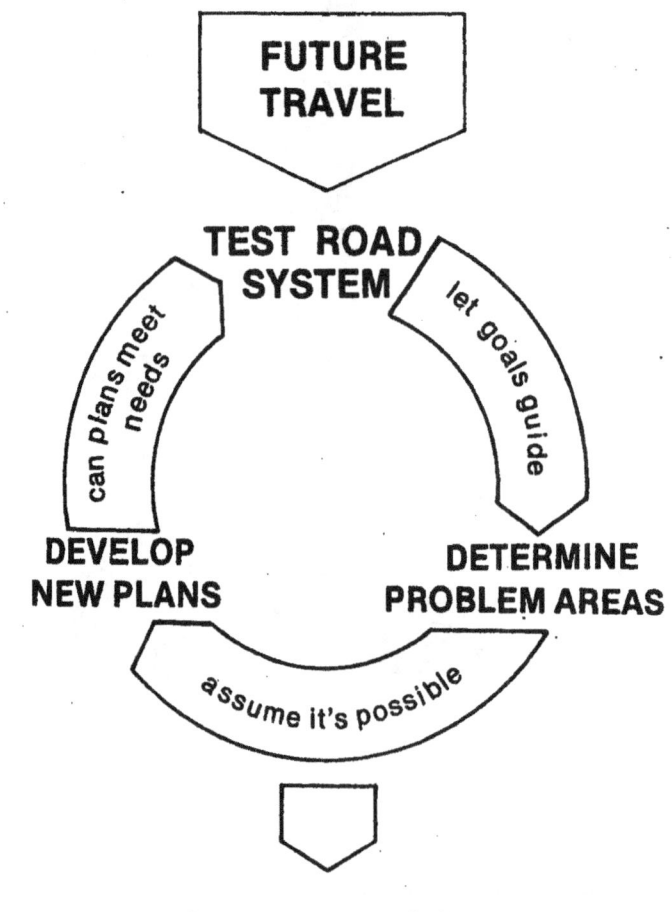

DEVELOPMENT OBJECTIVES

Although development is a creative function, the following objectives should be used to enhance the creative capacity of the road designer.

1 REDUCE CONGESTION

The test of any road system starts by measuring its capacity to handle projected traffic volumes. To eliminate capacity problems, the planner should not only insure that the congested roadways are improved, but should also consider improving remote routes in the vicinity, or even adding entire segments. For example, a bypass road can help relieve congestion on routes that are remote from it.

2 SERVE TRIP DESIRES

Analysis of vehicle trips — their origin, destination, length, and other characteristics — helps to determine installation roadway network, access-road needs, and entrance gate locations.

3 PROVIDE LAND-USE ACCESS

Alternate road systems should be developed to serve access needs identified by the installation master development plan.

4 PROVIDE SYSTEM CONTINUITY

Geometric configurations of the alternate road system should be limited to provide travel continuity, as well as practical construction and operation. When new routes are constructed, they should connect to the existing system where sufficient capacity exists to absorb the additional demand.

DEVELOPMENT OBJECTIVES

1. Reduce congestion
2. Serve trip desires
3. Provide land-use access
4. Provide system continuity

EVALUATION

IN THE EVALUATION, *all acceptable alternatives are considered and compared with one another to determine the best roadway plan.* The plan selected should provide the installation with a traffic corridor system that shows a road type or improvement for each traffic corridor. At this stage, the road plan does not show exact road location. However, each plan presented for evaluation has been found acceptable in the development phase, based on a preliminary look at the possibilities for location and design. In the evaluation phase, one plan is selected; then, in the implementation phase, the final plan is refined to show roadway location and design.

The most common method of evaluating a roadway is simply **to examine the measures of each alternative and make a judgment-based decision.** This decision usually requires trade-offs. For example, "X" minutes saved in travel are worth "Y" dwelling unit removals. As an aid in evaluating trade-offs, a weighting system applied to each evaluation criterion is suggested.

ALTERNATIVE A   ALTERNATIVE B

EVALUATION

BEST PLAN
ALTERNATIVE A

EVALUATION DETERMINES BEST PLAN

EVALUATION METHOD

① ESTABLISH CRITERIA

- Accident rates
- Travel time
- Travel distance
- Exposure to pollution

② DETERMINE WEIGHT OF EACH CRITERION

CRITERIA	WEIGHT
Accident rate	4
Travel time	3
Exposure to pollution	2
Travel distance	1

③ SPECIFY RELATIVE PERFORMANCE OF EACH ALTERNATIVE IN EACH CATEGORY

CRITERIA	PERFORMANCE RATING	
	ALT A	ALT B
Accident rate	2	1
Travel time	2	1
Exposure to pollution	1	2
Travel distance	1	2

④ MULTIPLY THE WEIGHT OF EACH CRITERION BY THE PERFORMANCE RATING, THEN SUM PRODUCTS

CRITERIA	ALT A	ALT B
	WEIGHT × PERFORMANCE RATING = PRODUCT	WEIGHT × PERFORMANCE RATING = PRODUCT
Accident rate	4 × 2 = 8	4 × 1 = 4
Travel time	3 × 2 = 6	3 × 1 = 3
Exposure to pollution	2 × 1 = 2	2 × 2 = 4
Travel distance	1 × 1 = 1	1 × 2 = 2
Total	17	13

⑤ SELECT BEST PLAN

ALT A

IMPLEMENTATION

ROADWAY IMPLEMENTATION includes location, design, right-of-way acquisition, and construction. It is not a part of the roadway planning process. Planning is only a tool for making decisions today that will meet the roadway needs of tomorrow. However, continual planning provides data and assistance for the implementation. For example, a major service is the supply of base data for locating and designing the roadway within the traffic corridor.

SURVEILLANCE AND REAPPRAISAL

ONE CHARACTERISTIC OF TRANSPORTATION PLANS is that the analysis of a few years ago may be almost obsolete today. Obsolescence of the transportation plan may be caused by changes in goals, shifts of emphasis among goals, changes in funding, changes in administration, and improvements in transportation planning. Obsolescence of the plan is also frequently caused by radical departure from some part of the plan. Each installation should monitor changes that affect the transportation plan and should estimate their effect on the validity of the plan, changing the plan as necessary.

TRAFFIC ENGINEERING

ROAD DESIGN: DESIGN CRITERIA

CONTENTS

	Page
I. TRAFFIC CHARACTERISTICS	2
1. The Road User	2
2. The Vehicle	3
3. Traffic Data	
II. ELEMENTS	8
1. Cross Section Elements	8
2. Highway Alignment	13

DESIGN CRITERIA

TRAFFIC CHARACTERISTICS

ELEMENTS

ROADWAY DESIGN, pertains to converting the planning decisions of Sections I and II into geometric form. However, **before geometric designs can be drawn, the designer must first understand the characteristics of the traffic to be served and the capability of the roadway to carry traffic.** These criteria can then be used to select appropriate design elements for the roadway, such as sight distance, horizontal alignment, and cross-section widths.

DESIGN CRITERIA
DETERMINE
ROADWAY GEOMETRICS

I. TRAFFIC CHARACTERISTICS

Before a roadway can be designed, the capabilities of the road user and the vehicle must first be understood. These characteristics, along with **road traffic demand, vehicle speed, and roadway capacity, govern roadway design.** These features are briefly reviewed in this section.

- **① ROAD USER**
- **② THE VEHICLE**
- **③ TRAFFIC DATA**

① THE ROAD USER

THE ROAD USER is one of three main ELEMENTS in automobile transportation. THE VEHICLE and THE ROAD are the other two. Since the user — driver or pedestrian — is a major part of the system, human limitations and behavior must be understood and considered in all roadway designs. Because of their complexity, user characteristics are not discussed in this guide. However, consideration for the user is found throughout the guide, since human factors affect every phase of roadway design. For example, driver perception and reaction times are considered in the determination of safe-stopping sight distances, passing sight distances, safe approach speeds at intersections, and other driving maneuvers.

HUMAN FACTORS AFFECT ROADWAY DESIGN

2 THE VEHICLE

A "DESIGN VEHICLE" *is a motor vehicle whose weight, dimensions, and operating characteristics are used to establish design controls.* For example, *the minimum turning radius and physical dimensions of the design vehicle usually are larger than those of most other vehicles expected to use the roadway.* Generally, one or more of six design vehicles should be used to control geometric design. These vehicle classifications include: passenger car (P), single unit truck (SU), single unit bus (BUS), semitrailer intermediate (WB-40), combination large (WB-50), and semitrailer/full trailer combination (WB-60). For most roadways, **designs to accommodate single unit trucks should be used.** However, on major arterials the pavement should be wide enough to accommodate semitrailer combinations or large buses even for occasional use. In all cases, a design check should be made to insure that the largest expected vehicle can negotiate the designated turns, particularly if pavements are curbed. In special cases, designs may have to accommodate vehicles larger than the WB-50.

ROAD DESIGNS ARE MADE TO ACCOMMODATE VEHICLES

3 TRAFFIC DATA

TRAFFIC DATA *form the basis for engineering analysis.* Types of traffic and future volumes largely determine the kind of roadway and the geometric design.

The following discussion presents typical traffic information used in the design of roadways.

AVERAGE DAILY TRAFFIC (ADT)

AVERAGE DAILY TRAFFIC *is the total daily traffic during a given time period divided by the number of days in that time period.* Although the ADT volume is essential in justifying expenditures, in designing structural elements, in estimating future traffic, and in ranking the relative importance of roadways, it has little direct application to geometric design. Instead, the peak-hour traffic volumes are used for roadway design.

DESIGN HOUR VOLUME TRAFFIC (DHV)

DESIGN HOUR VOLUME TRAFFIC for installation roadways *is the peak traffic flow that occurs during a 1-hour time period on an average day.* For the usual condition, this volume is found during the afternoon work-to-home peak. Occasionally, the peak traffic period of a land use does not correspond with peak employee work-to-home trips. In this case, two design volumes may be required—one to reflect traffic flow during the installation's peak traffic period, and the other to reflect travel during the peak hour for the specific land use. For example, the peak traffic period of a chapel is significantly different from the peak hour for home-to-work trips.

DIRECTIONAL DISTRIBUTION (D)

THE DIRECTIONAL DISTRIBUTION *is the percent of the design volume that travels in the direction of maximum flow.* A D factor is used to convert two-way DHV's into directional flows. This knowledge of the traffic flow is essential for determining lane requirements and intersection design. For example, consider a DHV of 4,000 vehicles per hour (VPH) in both directions. If, during the design hour, the directional distribution is even (D = 50 percent), two lanes in each direction may be adequate. However, if 80 percent of the volume is in one direction, three lanes in each direction will be required for the 3,200 VPH.

THE DIRECTIONAL DISTRIBUTION OF TRAFFIC DURING THE DESIGN HOUR should be determined by field measurements on the facility under consideration or on a similar facility. As a general rule, the D factor tends to be more equally divided near the built-up area, where a value of 55 to 60 is common. In the vicinity of entrance gates, a D factor of 80 to 95 is not unusual. Due to this wide variation, directional splits should be developed separately for each facility and each area of the installation.

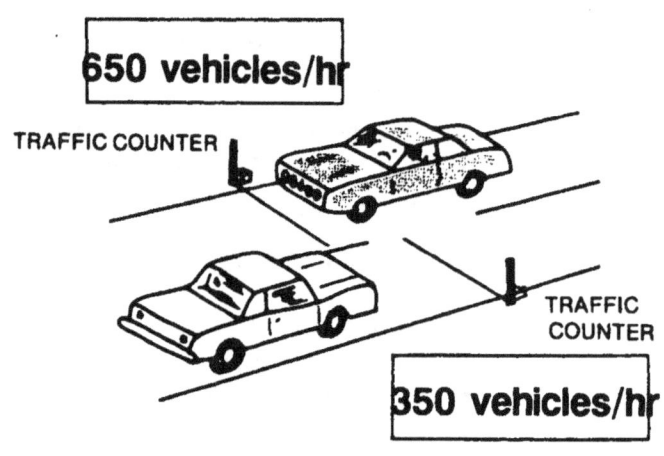

5

K=DHV/ADT

RATIO OF DHV TO ADT (K)

Traffic projections for future street networks are sometimes expressed as ADT volumes as a result of the planning process used. However, ADT volumes have little use in geometric design and must be converted to DHV traffic. This conversion may be made by applying a representative percentage to the ADT. In making this conversion, a K factor is used. This factor represents a ratio of DHV to ADT and generally ranges between 5 and 15 percent installation-wide; however, it varies widely, with highs of 25 percent observable at gate areas. Therefore, the K factor, when used, should be developed independently for each facility and each area of the installation. For example, roadways serving primarily entrance gates usually have a high K factor; whereas, roadways providing service within the built-up area have a low K factor.

PERCENTAGE OF TRUCKS (T)

T = 5%

Vehicles of different sizes and weights have different operating characteristics that must be considered in design. For geometric design and capacity studies, traffic is grouped into passenger cars and trucks — buses are considered as trucks, and light delivery trucks are considered as cars. THE COMPOSITION OF TRAFFIC, then, normally *is expressed as the percentage of trucks during the design hour, and generally is less than 5 percent*. The percentage of trucks used as a basis for design should be obtained by field studies during hours of peak-traffic flow. Where the proposed improvement follows or closely parallels an existing highway from which vehicles will be diverted, the existing route may be considered applicable. Where a new route is being designed, traffic composition on similar routes should be studied. In most cases, T values based on current traffic are applicable also to future traffic volumes.

DESIGN SPEED

DESIGN SPEED *is the maximum safe speed that can be maintained over a specified section of roadway.* It is one of the most important factors used to select geometric features in roadway design. For example, design speed is used in selecting superelevation rates, critical lengths of grade, intersection curbs, sight distance, and alignment. When selecting design speeds for installation roadways, speeds in the range of 30 to 60 miles per hour should be used. Lower speeds in this range apply to local and collector streets and to major streets in the built-up area, while the higher speeds apply to arterials in outlying areas. Generally, as high a design speed as practicable should be used, preferably a constant value for any one roadway. However, where the terrain varies or where other physical controls exist, changes in design speed for some sections of roadway may be necessary. Good alignment and flat profiles should always be sought in the design of major installation streets. Such practice improves safety and operating characteristics, particularly during off-peak periods. On the other hand, less-than-desirable design speeds are sometimes required to avoid disruption of neighborhoods, to preserve major buildings, or to reduce construction costs.

DESIGN SPEED		
ROADWAY TYPE	DESIGN SPEED (mph)	AVERAGE RUNNING SPEED* (mph)
Arterial		
Built-up Area	30–40	25–35
Outlying Area	40–60	30–50
Collector	30–40	25–35
Local	20–30	15–28

*Average running speed represents the speed that approximately 50 percent of the vehicles on the road will travel. As such, this speed varies considerably with design speed, traffic volume and roadside interference. Therefore, in the range given, the lower speeds represent typical high-volume, peak-hour conditions, and the higher volumes represent typical off-peak, low volume conditions.

DESIGN CAPACITY

DESIGN CAPACITY *is the maximum volume of traffic that a proposed roadway would be able to serve without congestion rising above a preselected level.* This information is used at the design level in assessing the adequacy of roadways to serve current and future traffic and in selecting roadway type and dimensional needs.

Technical details regarding design capacities are presented in the *Highway Capacity Manual*, 1965. However, the chart below can be used for rough estimates of design capacities.

DESIGN CAPACITIES	
TYPE ROAD	**DESIGN CAPACITY** (Passenger cars per hour per 12-foot lane)
Outlying arterial with moderate interference from cross traffic and roadsides	700-900
Outlying arterial with considerable interference from cross traffic and roadsides	500-700
Arterial in built-up area with isolated signalization	400-600
Arterial in built-up area with multiple signals	Governed by capacity of critical intersections

II. ELEMENTS

Common to all types of roadways are **elements of design,** such as **alignment, lane width, medians, and shoulders.** The design of each of these elements depends on the road usage. For example, roads with higher design volumes and speeds require more lanes, flatter grades, and more gentle curves. Nevertheless, the design standards that apply to all roadways are discussed in this section and are further developed in the chapters for each roadway type.

ELEMENTS

| CROSS SECTION | HIGHWAY ALIGNMENT |

CROSS SECTION ELEMENTS

THE ROADWAY CROSS SECTION is made up of the **lane widths, cross slope, shoulders, curbs and side slopes, medians, borders and sidewalks, and drainage.** Together, these elements determine the right-of-way required for a particular road.

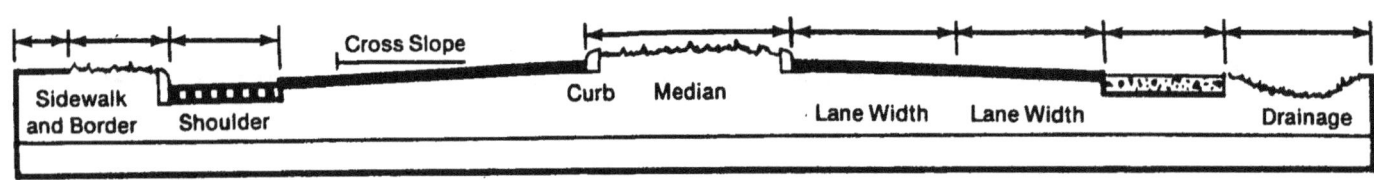

LANE WIDTH

For safe and efficient traffic operation, **lane widths should be 12 feet.** Lanes this wide provide *freedom* and ease *of operation* consistent with high-volume traffic. However, for low-volume roadways or those with restricted right-of-way, narrower lanes may be used, but in no case should a lane be less than 10 feet wide.

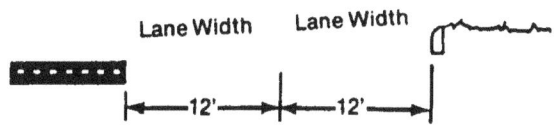

AUXILIARY LANES *consist of turning lanes at intersections, parking lanes, and climbing lanes.* At intersections, turning lanes should be as wide as the through lanes, but never less than 10 feet. As a general rule, parking on arterial streets should be discouraged. However, if parking is required, parking lanes should be at least 10, but preferably 12 feet wide. Climbing lanes for trucks on sustained grades should be 12 feet wide.

SHOULDERS

On all arterial streets in built-up areas, **shoulders or parking lanes are desirable for accommodation of stopped vehicles, for emergency use, and for lateral support of base and surface courses.** Shoulders are important links in the lateral surface runoff systems and *should be pitched sufficiently to drain surface water rapidly,* but not to the extent that vehicular operation would be hazardous.

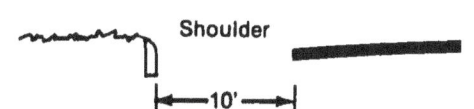

In general, a right shoulder width should be no less than 10 feet; however, in mountainous terrain, where the cost of full shoulders is prohibitive, a width of 6 feet is often used. A usable shoulder width of no less than 4 feet, and preferably 6 or 8 feet, should be considered on low-type roadways. An additional width of about 2 feet outside the usable shoulder should be provided where guardrails, guide posts, walls, or other vertical elements are used. On divided roadways, a paved shoulder strip 4 feet wide is usually adequate for the left edge.

MEDIAN

A MEDIAN *is that portion of a roadway separating traffic in opposing directions.* It may *vary in scope from a simple traffic stripe to a green area of varying width between two roadways and may be either* **depressed, raised, or flush.** A depressed median, generally used in outlying areas where adequate space is available, allows efficient snow removal and drainage. A raised median typically is used on arterial streets where left-turn movements are regulated. Also, it is used frequently where a narrow median is to be planted. A flush median, used to some extent on all arterials, is especially useful as a center left-turn lane. A center lane reserved for left turns from both directions is sometimes preferable to a barrier/raised-type median. On major streets in built-up areas, with numerous driveways on each side of the street, a barrier/raised-type median is operationally undesirable, even if sufficient width is available. Such a median without frequent openings eliminates many of the left turns. Drivers are then forced to enter and leave by right turns only, and some are required to make U-turns or travel around the block to reach their destination. This type of operation might offer more interference than direct turns at the driveways.

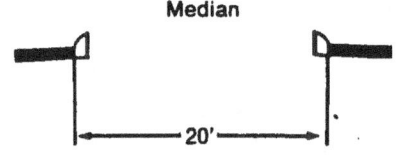

THE PRINCIPAL FUNCTIONS OF A MEDIAN are to provide: *freedom from interference of opposing traffic, a recovery or stopping area for out-of-control vehicles and other emergencies, speed change and storage for left- and U-turning vehicles, minimum headlight glare, and an open green space for aesthetics.* The median width, desirably 20 feet, is the dimension between through-lane edges, including the left shoulders. Where space is limited, widths of 16 to 18 feet permit arrangements for left-turn lanes. For medians less than 16 feet wide, few openings if any should be provided, except at intersections.

Cross Slope
1/8 in./ft.

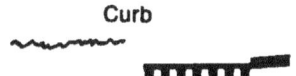

Curb

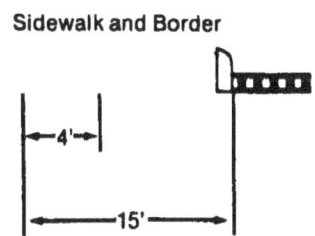

Sidewalk and Border

CROSS SLOPE

THE CROSS SLOPE AND CROWN ARRANGEMENT of the pavement *function to drain the surface.* The slope may be formed by *plane surfaces, curved surfaces, or a combination of the two.* The rate of cross slope should be as low as practicable, but generally ranging between one-eighth to one-quarter inch per foot. Cross slopes greater than one-quarter inch per foot should be avoided on high type pavements.

CURBS

CURBS are used on all highways *to control drainage, to deter vehicles from leaving the pavement at hazardous points, to protect pedestrians, to delineate the pavement edge, to present a more finished appearance, and to assist the orderly development of the roadside.* Curbs are of two classes: **barrier and mountable.** Barrier curbs are designed to inhibit or discourage vehicles from leaving the road and should not be used where speeds exceed 50 mph. Mountable curbs are designed so vehicles can cross them and are used primarily for drainage purposes. Both types of curbs may be designed with gutter sections to form the principal drainage system. Where gutters are used, a gutter of color and texture different from that of the travel lane should not be considered part of the lane width. On the other hand, a gutter of the same color and texture as the travel lane and not much steeper in cross slope may be considered part of the traffic lane.

BORDER AND SIDEWALK

BORDER AREAS *separate the roadway from the buildings and provide space for* SIDEWALKS. The width of a border may vary considerably; however, it should be kept as wide as possible.

Sidewalk widths may vary from 4 to 8 feet, and may be even wider in school areas. The width of the grass strip between the sidewalk and roadway should be 8 to 12 feet; however, narrower strips 3 to 4 feet wide may be used in restricted areas.

DRAINAGE

DRAINAGE is an integral part of roadway design, because it not only *prevents soil erosion,* but also *reduces accident potential caused by storm water.* In built-up areas and along arterials, the drainage system should be designed to intercept storm water from surrounding slopes before it reaches the roadway, as well as to remove road surface water without disrupting traffic flow or causing a safety hazard. Drainage inlets should be of the type and location to prevent undue spread of water onto travel lanes and pedestrian crossings.

Where topography requires that the terrain be cut or filled for road construction, certain values must be considered in the design, such as safety, appearance, and economy in maintenance. Therefore, the design should provide reasonably flat side slopes, broad drainage channels, and liberal rounding of the cross section. Design criteria for side slopes are best obtained by individual study. However, where terrain permits, roadside drainage channels built into the earth should have side slopes no steeper than 4:1, and a rounded bottom at least 4 feet wide. When the height of the cut or fill does not exceed 4 feet, a side slope of 6:1 is desirable. In either case, side slopes should be rounded and gradually flattened toward the end of the cut or fill section.

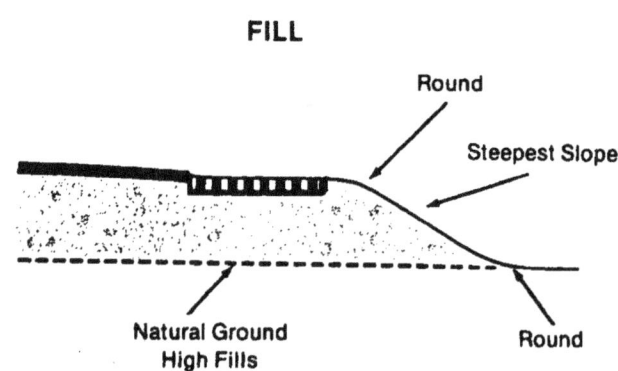

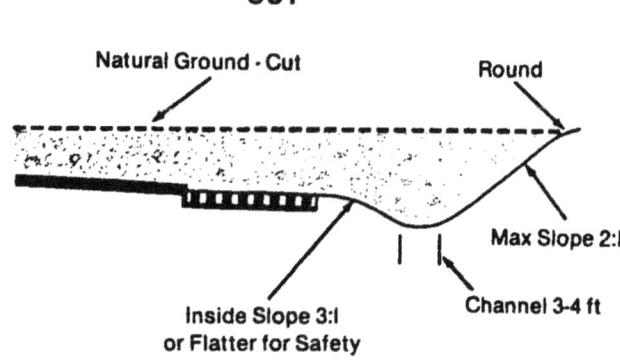

UTILITIES

In roadway design, special consideration should be given to potential joint usage of right-of-way. UTILITY LINES *should be located in a way that will minimize the need for lateral adjustment to accommodate future road improvements and to permit the servicing of such lines with minimum roadway-traffic interference.* To the extent feasible, utility line crossings should be perpendicular to the road alignment and should conform to the clear-area requirements.

HIGHWAY ALIGNMENT

HIGHWAYS MAY BE ALIGNED EITHER HORIZONTALLY OR VERTICALLY, depending on the terrain. The elements of alignment, such as degree of curve and percent, and length of grade, should conform to standards recommended by the American Association of State Highway and Transportation Officials in *A Policy on Geometric Design For Rural Highways.*

HORIZONTAL ALIGNMENT

VERTICAL ALIGNMENT

HORIZONTAL ALIGNMENT

- Alignment should be as straight as possible, consistent with topography. A flowing line that conforms generally to the natural contours is preferable to one with long tangents that slash through the terrain; exception may be made on two-lane highways where passing sight distance should be maintained over as much of the highway length as feasible. In general, the number of short curves should be minimal.

- Use flat curves whenever possible. Also, avoid the use of maximum curvature for the design speed.

- Alignment should be consistent. Sharp curves at ends of long tangents and sudden changes from straight alignment to sharp curves should be avoided.

- Curves should be long enough to avoid the appearance of a kink; they should be at least 500 feet long for a central angle of 5 degrees, and should be increased 100 feet for each 1-degree decrease in the central angle.

- Tangents or flat curvature should be used on high, long fills.

- Compound curves with large differences in radius should be avoided. If they are used, the radius of the flatter arc should be no more than 50 percent greater than the radius of the sharper arc. Where this alignment is not feasible, the necessary transition can be provided by an intermediate curve.

VERTICAL ALIGNMENT

- A smooth grade line with gradual changes, consistent with the type or class of highway and the character of terrain, is preferred to a line with numerous breaks and short grade lengths.

- The "roller-coaster" or the "hidden-dip" type of profile should be avoided by using the gradual grades made possible by heavier cuts and fills or by introducing some horizontal curvature on relatively straight sections.

- Alternating positive and negative grades, involving substantial lengths should be appraised for their momentum effect on traffic operation since they may result in undesirably high downgrade truck speeds.

- A broken-back grade line should be avoided.

- On long grades, the grade near the top of the ascent should be lowered, particularly on low design speed highways.

- Where at-grade intersections occur on highway sections with moderately steep grades, the gradient through the intersection should be reduced.

- Climbing lanes should be considered where the critical length of grade is exceeded and where the DHV exceeds the design grade capacity by 20 percent on two-lane roads or by 30 percent on multilane roads.

16

COMBINED HORIZONTAL AND VERTICAL CONTROLS

> HORIZONTAL AND VERTICAL ALIGNMENT SHOULD COMPLEMENT EACH OTHER. BOTH TRAFFIC OPERATION AND OVERALL APPEARANCE OF THE ROADWAY SHOULD BE CONSIDERED IN DESIGN.

- Sharp horizontal curvature should not be introduced at or near the top of a pronounced crest vertical curve.

- Only flat horizontal curvature should be introduced at or near the low point of a pronounced sag vertical curve.

- On two-lane highways, the need for safe passing sections at frequent intervals over an appreciable percentage of the highway length often supersedes the general desirability for coordination or horizontal and vertical alignment.

- Horizontal curvature and profile should be made as flat as feasible at highway intersections.

- On divided roadways, each side of the roadway may be treated separately; thus, median width and vertical and horizontal alignments may be varied.

SIGHT DISTANCE

SIGHT DISTANCE *is the length of roadway ahead that is visible to the driver.* The three most important *sight distance requirements are for stopping, for passing, and for visibility at intersections.* **Sight distance at every point should be as long as possible and at least equal to the stopping sight distance.**

DESIGN STOPPING SIGHT DISTANCE *is the minimum distance required for a vehicle traveling near the design speed to stop before reaching an object in its path.* It is the sum of the distance traveled during perception and brake reaction time and the distance traveled while braking to a stop on wet pavement.

DESIGN PASSING SIGHT DISTANCE *is the distance required to make a safe passing maneuver on a two-lane roadway.* This distance should be provided over as large a percentage of the roadway length as feasible. The percentage should be greater on roads with high volumes than on those with low volumes.

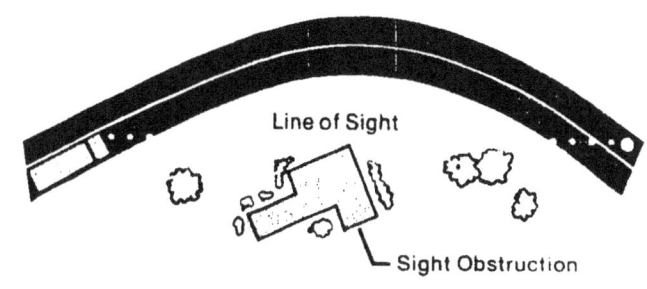

HORIZONTAL CURVE

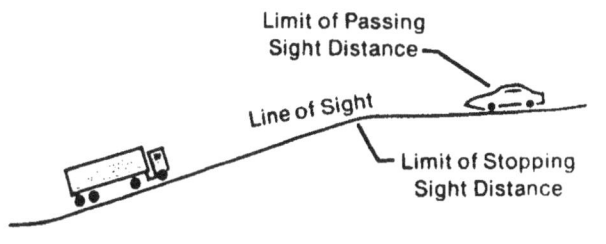

VERTICAL CURVE

SIGHT DISTANCE		
DESIGN SPEED (mph)	DESIRABLE STOPPING (ft)	MINIMUM PASSING 2-LANE ROADS (ft)
30	200	1100
40	300	1500
50	450	1800
60	650	2100

TRAFFIC ENGINEERING

TRAFFIC ROUTE LAYOUT

CONTENTS

	Page
I. SYSTEMS	1
GRIDIRON	2
RADIAL	3
II. CLASSIFICATION	1
ARTERIAL	2
COLLECTOR	2
LOCAL	3
III. LOCATION	1
DEVELOPING ALTERNATIVES-TRAFFIC SERVICE	2
DEVELOPING ALTERNATIVES-THE ENVIRONMENT	4
EVALUATION	5

TRAFFIC ROUTE LAYOUT

I. SYSTEMS

GRIDIRON

RADIAL

GOOD STREET SYSTEMS follow one of two basic patterns, or a combination of the two. One is the **GRIDIRON** pattern; the other, a **RADIAL-CIRCUMFERENTIAL** pattern.

Most military installations show a gridiron pattern, with traffic corridors extending outward from the central area. The headquarters and/or administrative units remain the major traffic generators. Any major shopping facilities are usually located adjacent to an arterial and, compared with administrative units, generate an insignificant amount of peak-hour traffic.

GRIDIRON PATTERNS COMMONLY FORM STREET SYSTEMS

GRIDIRON

The gridiron system, resembling a checkerboard, *is a series of streets located at approximate right angles to each other.* These streets produce blocks that are either *square or rectangular.*

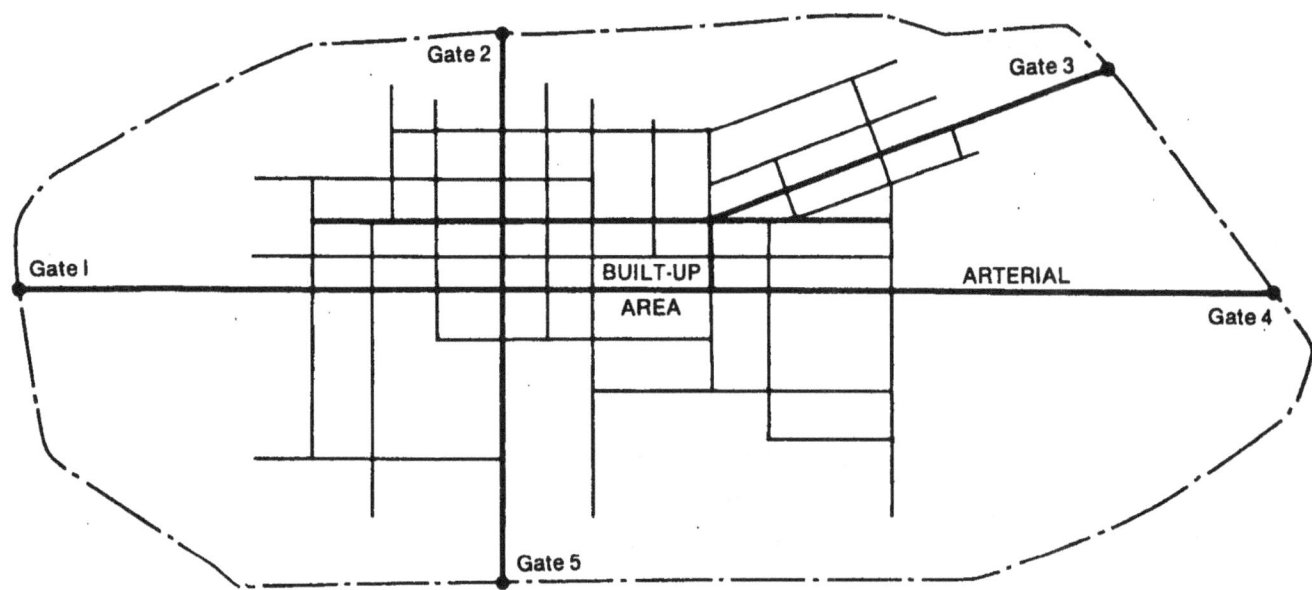

ADVANTAGES	DISADVANTAGES
Roads are easy to design and lay out. Roads can be extended indefinitely. Straight roads generally simplify the design of utilities. Rectangular blocks created by the street system are easy to subdivide. The street system is easily understood, named, and numbered.	The system does not adapt well to irregular topography. Travel between destinations located diagonally opposite each other is inconvenient and indirect. Most of the streets must be designed for high-volume traffic and have heavy-duty pavement, because every street is a through street and therefore capable of developing into a major thoroughfare. Shifting traffic and general dispersion of through traffic can spoil the entire area for best residential use, with little compensation in convenience or directness.

LOCAL

ALL ROADWAYS that are not classified as either arterial or collector are classified as LOCAL STREETS — that is, RESIDENTIAL and BUSINESS/INDUSTRIAL. *The chief function* of these streets is *to provide direct access to abutting land and to the higher road systems.* Local streets should not be developed as major traffic streets.

RESIDENTIAL STREETS

THE CHIEF PURPOSE OF RESIDENTIAL STREETS *is to provide access to housing units, as well as to serve as a channel for local utilities.* Therefore, they should be designed so that they will not become thoroughfares or major streets. They should be short and should follow the topography. Many are cul-de-sac, dead-end, or loop streets.

As its function is to serve abutting property, the residential street should be designed not to carry high-volume traffic, but to adequately meet the needs of the abutting property. The average traffic volume for a residential street varies from 250 to 500 vehicles per day, with a maximum volume of approximately 2,000 vehicles per day.

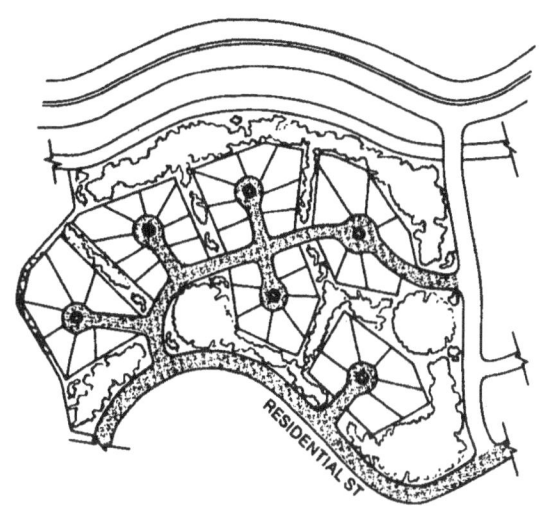

BUSINESS AND INDUSTRIAL STREETS

BUSINESS-AREA STREETS *serve business-area traffic.* These streets should be designed to permit easy movement from one location of the business area to another and to and from entrance gates.

INDUSTRIAL STREETS *serve abutting property as well as vehicular traffic.* These streets are used frequently by large commercial vehicles; therefore, the accumulation of trucks and peak-hour employee movements should be given particular consideration.

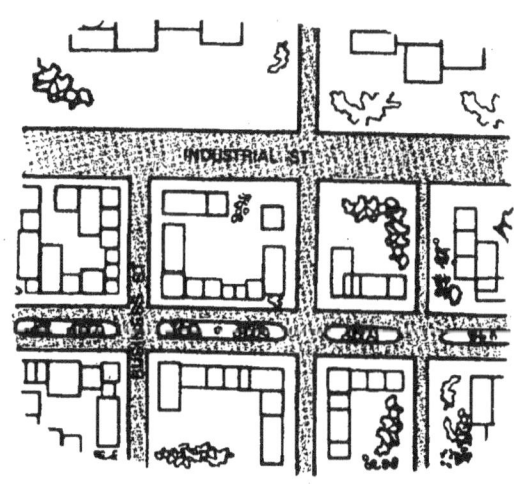

GUIDELINES FOR CLASSIFICATION

CRITERIA	ARTERIAL	COLLECTOR	LOCAL
Trip Length (mi)	1–3	1	1/2
Traffic Volume (vpd)	8,000–25,000	2,000–8,000	Less than 2,000
Service to Activities	High Volume Generators (Should not penetrate neighborhoods)	Local Areas Neighborhoods	Individual Sites
Spacing (mi)	1/4–2	1/8–1/2	NA
Access Control	Limited – Extensive	None	None
Service to Through Traffic	Moderate – High	Low	Low

II. CLASSIFICATION

ARTERIAL

COLLECTOR

LOCAL

THE CLASSIFICATION OF ROADS BY TYPE *is necessary for communication among engineers, administrators, and the general public.* Different classification methods are used for different purposes. One method commonly used for military installations divides the road system into four general categories based on their relative importance: primary, secondary, tertiary, and patrol roads. For planning, the main considerations for classifying roads are travel desires of the road user, land service needs based on existing and expected future land use, and the overall road-system continuity. Therefore, the functional classification used in this guide divides roadways into three groups by function: arterial, collector, and local. Each group carries a set of suggested minimum design standards. These standards are in keeping with the importance of the roadway system and are governed by the specific service the system is expected to provide.

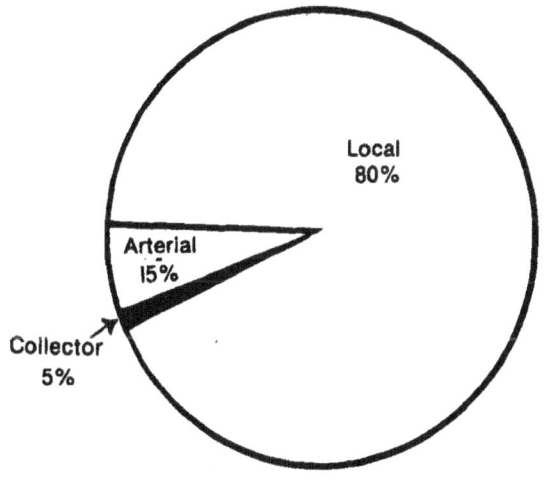

DISTRIBUTION OF STREET MILEAGE

Local 80%
Arterial 15%
Collector 5%

ARTERIAL

THE ARTERIAL SYSTEM may be of several types, depending on the size of the installation, but *the fundamental objective is the same for all: to move large volumes of traffic as safely and quickly as possible.* By design, the arterial system should carry a high volume of the total area traffic over a minimum mileage, without serving abutting property.

In their ultimate development, *arterials* may be either *freeways or expressways.* Freeways have only grade-separated intersections and prohibit access to abutting property. Expressways may have at-grade intersections, but they, too, usually prohibit land access.

At most military installations, *arterials are simply existing streets that place more emphasis on high-level traffic service than on land access.*

Arterial traffic volumes generally range from 8,000 to more than 20,000 vehicles per day. These roadways should be designed for a minimum of four and a maximum of six traffic lanes. When the traffic volume substantially exceeds 20,000 vehicles per day, some of the traffic should be diverted to another roadway. If diversion is impracticable, grade separations will be required at major intersections. Furthermore, roadways with traffic volumes approaching 25,000 vehicles per day will normally warrant a design for six traffic lanes and a median.

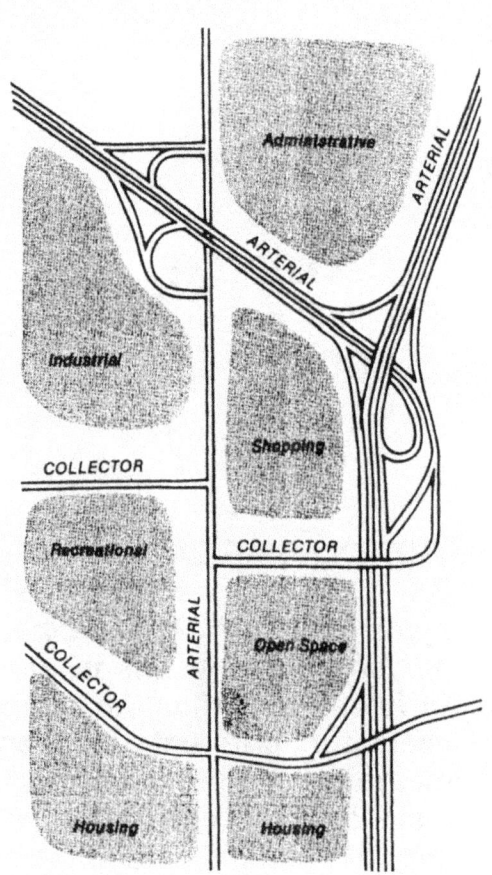

COLLECTOR

THE PRIMARY PURPOSE OF COLLECTOR STREETS *is*, as the term implies, *to collect traffic from the residential or commercial areas and move it to or from the arterial streets. These streets are of several types, but generally are of the same classification since they all serve abutting property and carry traffic of a type different from that of local streets. Collector streets carry traffic volumes ranging from 2,000 to 8,000 vehicles a day and should have from two to four traffic lanes.*

RADIAL

THE RADIAL-CIRCUMFERENTIAL SYSTEM consists of *a series of major streets radiating from the central, or built-up, area of an installation.* These radials are supplemented *by a series of circumferential streets that encircle the built-up area.* With such a street system, it is very important to have an innner loop around the built-up area — because, if all radial streets were to cross at one point in the built-up area, intolerable congestion would result. With an inner loop, traffic can flow on the radials toward the built-up area, then follow the loop around the built-up area to a point opposite its destination; it can then turn into or toward its built-up area destination. Usually, the radials terminate at the inner loop, except one or two in each major direction cross the built-up area. The built-up area usually is a gridiron pattern, which best serves built-up area traffic.

RADIAL STREETS provide direct travel between the outskirts and the built-up area of an installation. These routes adapt easily to topography and, therefore, usually are established quite naturally except where prevented by deliberate planning.

CIRCUMFERENTIAL STREETS, on the other hand, permit travel from one point to another in the outskirts of the installation without going through the built-up area. The alignment of circumferential streets, like radial streets, usually is either irregular or straight, not circular as the term implies.

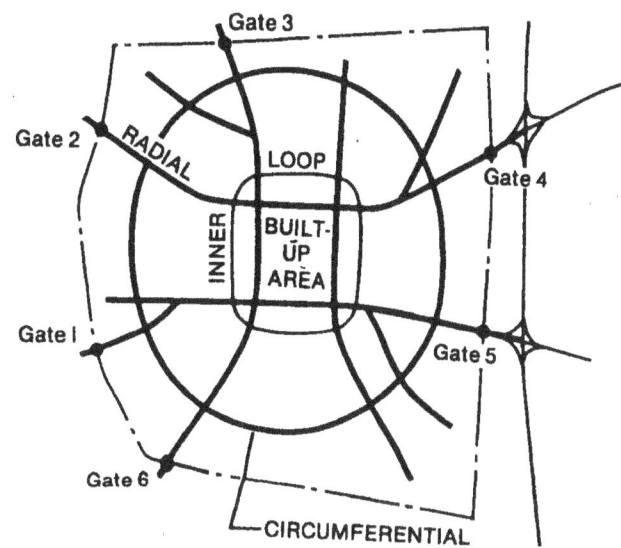

ADVANTAGES	DISADVANTAGES
Travel between any two points on an installation usually can be more direct. The system design permits good adaptation of the streets to the topography. A major street can be easily distinguished from a minor street. Each street is designed for one particular purpose, which leads to traffic stability. Cost savings in street construction and maintenance programs can result, because this system requires less actual street mileage than the gridiron requires.	Streets are more difficult to layout than in the gridiron system. Street layout leaves irregularly shaped parcels of land that may be hard to subdivide. Road layout complicates utility installations. Development of circumferential streets, which relieve congestion in the built-up area, is often neglected.

ROAD SYSTEM OBJECTIVES
Concentrate most of the traffic on a few well-designed arterial roads.
Locate arterial roads to serve the built-up area.
Supply an adequate number of nonarterial streets.
Provide direct travel from entrance gates to work areas.
Insure compatible related land use.

III. LOCATION

DEVELOPING ALTERNATIVES

TRAFFIC SERVICE

THE ENVIRONMENT

EVALUATION

THE PURPOSE OF THE ROAD LOCATION PROCESS *is to position a road within a strip of land in such a way that it will satisfy traffic demands and environmental considerations.* This process starts with *route requirements* and *selected traffic corridors identified in the planning process.* From this information, alternative road locations are prepared and evaluated. The best alternative is then selected. The process takes place after the planning phase and prior to the design phase, but blends into both.

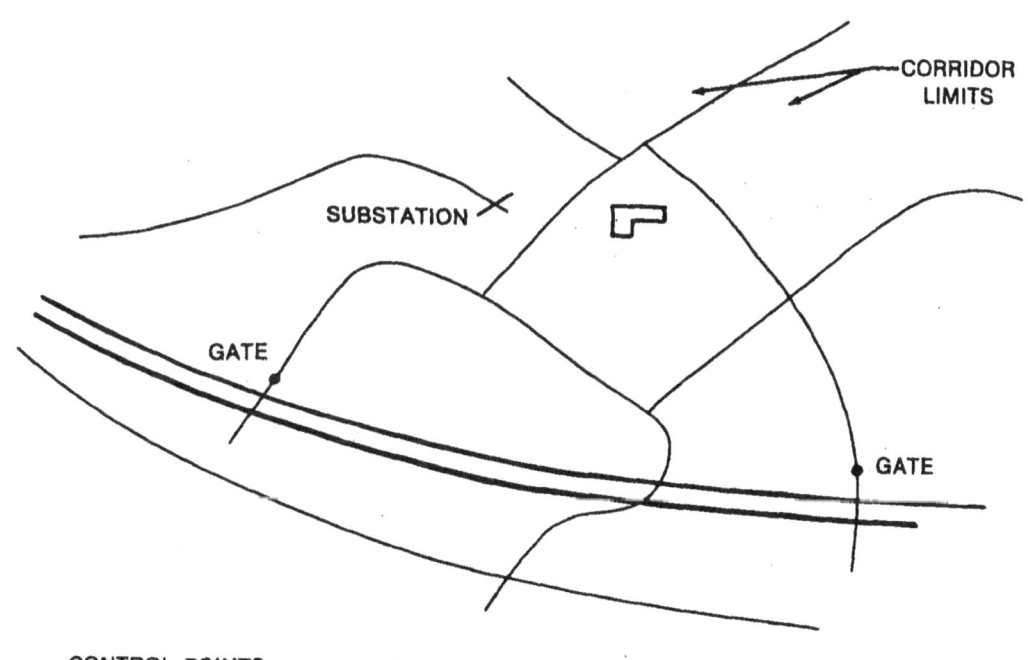

CONTROL POINTS

DEVELOPING ALTERNATIVES

THE TRAFFIC SERVICE

IDENTIFY CONTROL POINTS AND CORRIDOR LIMITS.
IDENTIFY TRAFFIC DESIRES.
PLACE TRIAL LINES ON MAP.
LAY OUT TURNING MOVEMENTS AT CROSSROADS.
ESTIMATE NUMBER OF TRAVEL LANES.
REVISE ALIGNMENT FOR OPERATIONAL IMPROVEMENTS.

IDENTIFY CONTROL POINTS AND TRAFFIC CORRIDOR LIMITS

The first step in the location process is to identify as many control points as possible within a traffic corridor. *A traffic corridor is a strip of land through which a road can be developed to satisfy traffic demands and environmental considerations.* Control points include such features as streets to be intersected, buildings to be retained, environment to be protected, parks and recreational areas to be maintained, and residential and industrial areas to be developed. Information for this step is generally developed in the planning process.

IDENTIFY TRAFFIC DESIRES

Provision of service for the estimated and assigned volumes is a **major control of location design.** Forecasted traffic largely determines the type of roadway required; whereas, the general desire lines of traffic indicate the preferred location.

DEVELOPING ALTERNATIVES IS LARGELY TRIAL AND ERROR

PLACE TRIAL LINES ON MAP

Once traffic assignments and the location of major traffic generators are known, a trial line for through movements should be superimposed over a map of the corridor. The initial trial line should connect the topographic and development control points, as well as conform to the general direction of the true traffic desires.

LAY OUT TURNING MOVEMENTS AT CROSSROADS

The selection of crossroads to be intersected or interchanged is usually done *concurrently with or following the initial layout.* Good main line operating characteristics favor widely spaced connections, uniform intersection design, and continuity of the through traffic. Spacing between connecting roads should safely accommodate weaving, turning movements, and signal progression. As a "rule of thumb," **minimum spacing of intersections on arterials should be 400 to 500 feet, and on collector streets, 300 feet.**

With general alignment and connecting crossroads chosen, the next step is to design turning movements. The design should provide a high level of service and safety not only to turning traffic, but also to through traffic. This can be done by designing for uniformity of turning movements and for continuity. **A standard intersection design should be developed and consistently applied except for the extreme cases.** Furthermore, for continuity, every attempt should be made to allow through traffic to flow naturally without being confronted with decision points.

ESTIMATE NUMBER OF TRAVEL LANES

After a trial line and turning movements have been drawn out, **the number of lanes should be estimated.** This estimation is based on design traffic volumes that will allow the driver to operate his vehicle on the road with certain minimum speeds, maximum traffic densities, and vehicle delay. For initial location, the roadway should be divided into segments of relatively uniform conditions. Two-directional traffic forecast for each segment can then be divided by the design traffic volume for that type of highway and rounded to the next higher even number of lanes. Given this estimated number of lanes and the type of roadway, the width of right-of-way necessary to construct the roadway cross section can be estimated. This width of land needed should be estimated for each alternative so that the land, improvements taken, and cost involved can be identified.

REVISE ALIGNMENT FOR OPERATIONAL IMPROVEMENTS

After completion of the location layout, **the proposed roadway should be reviewed for possible operational improvements.** The adequacy of turning, merging, weaving, capacity, and spacing should be reevaluated. Frequently, the layout of the number of lanes and turning movements may show a need to change the intersection location in order to eliminate or add an intersection to satisfy user service.

DEVELOPING ALTERNATIVES-THE ENVIRONMENT

The previous discussion concerned locating a roadway where it would provide safe, efficient, and economical transportation. However, it is also necessary to consider *the roadway as an element of the total environment. Roadways can and should be located and designed in a way that will complement their environment.*

TYPICAL ENVIRONMENTAL CONSIDERATIONS

Hold heavy cut and fill to a minimum. The roadway that flows with the topography will minimize erosion and sedimentation problems.

Evaluate soil strength and settlement information to identify potential problem areas.

Locate roadways to enhance accessibility of natural areas.

Locate roadways to minimize stream crossings and channel changes.

Mark corridor maps to portray such factors as land use, soil drainage, vegetation, wildlife preservation, surface and ground water, and potential recreation areas.

Avoid noise-sensitive areas altogether, or reduce noise effects through buffer zones, restrictions on truck traffic, avoidance of long and steep grades, or other special construction measures.

Make location decisions that will aid in the control and reduction of traffic-generated air pollution and energy consumption.

Locate new roadways, where feasible, in alignment with established geometric patterns.

Minimize disruptions of residential neighborhoods, schools, parks, shopping areas, industrial complexes, and medical centers.

Preserve areas of historical or architectural value.

Consider retaining unique areas or those that should remain the focal point.

Include a citizen participation program as part of the planning and location process.

Consider the need for vehicle access, including emergency vehicles, to health services, residential areas, industrial areas, parks, commercial areas, and employment centers.

5 EVALUATION

THE BASIS FOR SELECTING ONE ROADWAY LOCATION OVER ANOTHER WITHIN THE SAME CORRIDOR *is a judgment as to the location that will best achieve the traffic goals of the installation.* **These goals include: reduced travel time and cost, increased safety, improved travel comfort and convenience, and desirable social and environmental development.** At small installations, many times an intuitive judgment is a sufficient basis for decisions. However, at large installations, this intuitive approach or the "try and see" approach is generally not practical because of the enormity and permanence of road works. A comprehensive evaluation is essential in these instances.

In the location evaluation process, it is necessary *to place values on the benefits, costs, and consequences associated with the alternatives considered.* Placing these values is obviously a difficult task. However, identifying and ranking the relevant evaluation criteria *help to increase the probability of achieving the optimal choice.*

A first step in ranking the various alternates *is through an economic evaluation.* Of course, the most economical route may not necessarily be selected as the "best" because of adverse social and environmental consequences. However, this evaluation will permit the decisionmaker to narrow the alternatives to the one that is "best" in monetary terms. Furthermore, *the economic evaluation can often be used to decide whether or not to proceed, defer, or terminate a project.* For example, if the economic evaluation indicates a high prospective rate of return or benefit to cost and if the social and environmental consequences are of minor importance, a decision can easily be made to authorize construction. For marginal projects, the decision to authorize construction will require that an environmental evaluation be made. This evaluation considers those factors that cannot be given a monetary value. Although this evaluation is usually quite arbitrary, the decisionmakers can rank all the elements involved, and thus, review and evaluate the factors in a systematic and equitable manner. *The guiding consideration throughout the process should be that the decisionmaker is making a decision on behalf of the public.* Therefore, **the best solution must consider what is right to the expert, then the consequences of implementation should be best for the average installation citizen.**

TRAFFIC ENGINEERING

ROAD DESIGN: INTERSECTIONS

CONTENTS

	Page
I. ELEMENTS	2
TURNING ROADWAYS	3
CORNER RADII	3
AUXILIARY LANES	4
CHANNELIZATION	6
SIGHT DISTANCE	8
MEDIA OPENINGS	9
II. DESIGN	10
CLASSIFICATION	10
CONTROL	12
INTERSECTION TYPES	14
INTERSECTION DESIGN IMPROVEMENTS	16

ROAD DESIGN: INTERSECTIONS

ELEMENTS

DESIGN

THE NUMBER, TYPE, AND SPACING OF INTERSECTIONS determine to a large degree the capacity, speed, and safety of most installation roadways. This chapter discusses the elements of design as well as various geometric designs that can be used to insure efficient traffic flow. *The selection of the primary geometric and traffic control designs of the intersection are dependent on the traffic pattern during one or more peak traffic periods.*

**INTERSECTIONS
CONTROL CAPACITY
AND SAFETY**

I. ELEMENTS

THE MAJOR ELEMENTS OF INTERSECTIONAL DESIGN are those *elements that have the greatest impact on vehicle operations, such as medians, channelization islands, deceleration and acceleration lanes, and corner radii.* The dimensions given in this section for those elements are based on widely accepted standards, or are as recommended by the American Association of State Highway and Transportation Officials.

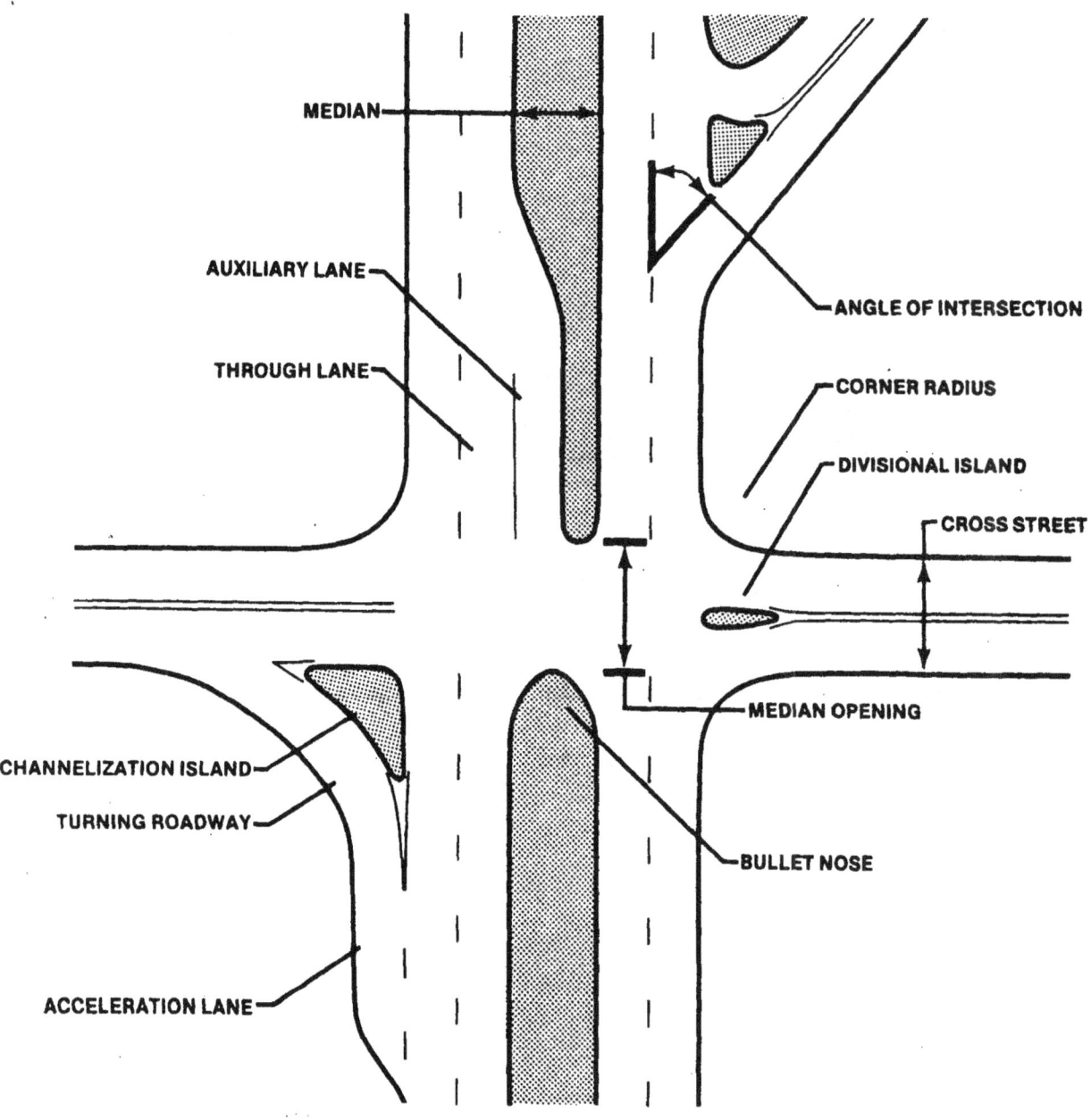

TURNING ROADWAYS

THE "TURNING ROADWAY" TECHNIQUE *connects two intersection legs. Thus, it shortens the travel path for turning vehicles, facilitates traffic control by separating turning movements, and reduces the amount of intersectional pavement by substituting islands for surfaced area.* This technique can also *reduce the frequency and severity of collision between right-turn vehicles and through traffic.* It is warranted, however, only where the main road traffic volume exceeds 10,000 vehicles per day, the road speed exceeds 25 miles per hour, and right-turn maneuvers exceed 30 per hour.

The critical elements of the turning-roadway design are the island area and location, the turning radius, and the roadway width. The island must be large enough to command attention and should be located at least 2 to 4 feet from the through lanes. A desirable 90-degree turning lane for buses and single-unit trucks would have a 70-foot radius and an 18-foot width. Angle-of-turn designs for other vehicles may be found in the American Association of State Highway and Transportation Officials publication, *A Policy on Geometric Design of Rural Highways.*

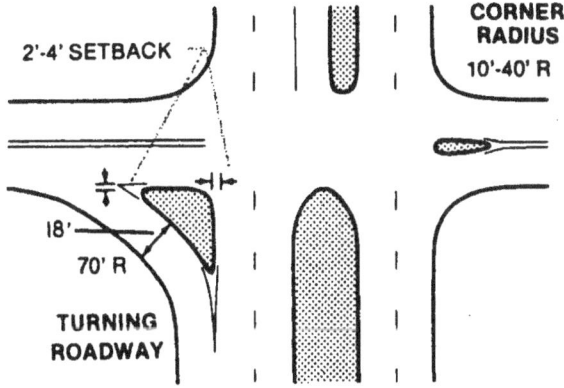

CORNER RADII

Generally, to the extent practicable, THE CORNER RADII OF INTERSECTIONS ON INSTALLATION ROADWAYS *should satisfy the requirements of the vehicles using the roadways.* However, many **factors** must be considered in **determining the corner radii** of individual intersections, such as: *availability of right-of-way, angle of the intersection, pedestrian use of the intersection, width and number of lanes on intersecting streets, and speed on the roadways.*

Radii of 10 to 20 feet may be used in built-up areas and other areas where vehicle needs must be balanced against pedestrian needs and against the need for corner setbacks.

Radii of 15 to 25 feet, adequate for passenger vehicles, may be used at minor cross streets with little truck-turning requirement. These small radii may be used also at major intersections with 10-foot-wide parking lanes at the curb and 12-foot-wide travel lanes. At these locations, even semitrailers are able to turn about a 15-foot curb radius with little or no encroachment on adjacent lanes. When using this design, parking must be restricted for at least 30 feet on the approach and 45 feet on the exit. Caution in use of these small radii is advised because traffic volumes may increase to the point where parking will be prohibited and the space used as a travel lane. Where feasible, radii of 30 feet or more should be provided at major cross streets to permit occasional truck turns without too much encroachment.

Where buses and large truck combinations turn frequently, radii of 40 feet or more should be provided. These larger radii are desirable also where speed reductions might cause problems.

AUXILIARY LANES

AUXILIARY LANES *are those lanes that adjoin the through travel lanes, but are used to supplement through traffic movement.* These lanes are used primarily as *storage for vehicles turning onto cross streets.* However, they may be used for acceleration of vehicles turning onto the major street, deceleration of vehicles leaving the major street, parking, or as climbing lanes for trucks.

The preferred design width of these lanes is 12 feet, but they may be 10 feet. The length of an auxiliary lane for turning vehicles consists of three components: deceleration length, storage length, and taper length. *The deceleration length is the distance required for a comfortable stop, and generally includes the taper. The storage length is based on the maximum number of vehicles likely to accumulate at any one time.* At unsignalized intersections, design should be based on the number of turning vehicles that arrive in an average 2-minute period within the peak hour. At signalized intersections, storage length should be based on 1.5 to 2 times the average number of vehicles that would store per cycle. In either case, the design length should be on the liberal side to avoid the possibility of through traffic being delayed by a turning vehicle.

In addition to the deceleration and storage lengths, *the taper length is an important component of the auxiliary lane.* The taper is used in transition from the normal road width to that of the auxiliary lane. For speeds of less than 30 miles per hour, a taper rate of 8:1 is standard and tapers less than 70 feet long generally are unsatisfactory.

Design for acceleration lanes is similar to that for deceleration lanes, in that widths and tapers are similar, and the total length of the lane depends on the speed difference between the through traffic and the merging traffic. A minimum length of 150 feet is recommended for these lanes.

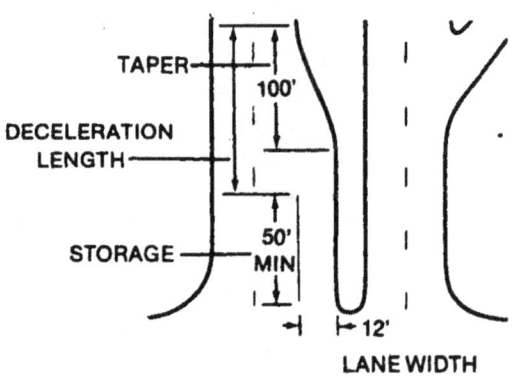

LEFT-TURN DECELERATION LANE

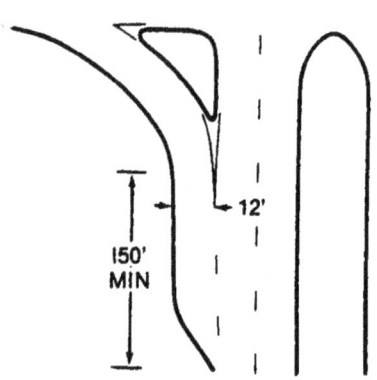

ACCELERATION LANE

DECELERATION LENGTHS (INCLUDING TAPER)

MAJOR STREET TRAVEL SPEED (mph)	LENGTH (ft)
20	160
30	250
40	370
50	500

STORAGE LENGTHS (UNSIGNALIZED)*

LEFT-TURNING VEHICLES (vph)	STORAGE (ft)
30	50
60	50
100	75
200	175
300	250

*SIGNALIZED — Storage length equals 1.5 to 2 times the average number of vehicles that would store per cycle.

ACCELERATION LENGTHS (INCLUDING TAPER)

MAJOR STREET TRAVEL SPEED (mph)	LENGTH (ft)
30	150
40	310
50	680

CHANNELIZATION

CHANNELIZATION *is the design of traffic lanes and islands in a way that will provide definite paths for vehicles to follow within the intersection. Effective channelization reduces the points of conflict in an intersection, or at least reduces the severity of any possible conflict.* In some cases, channelization can prevent wrong decisions and/or reduce the number of decisions the motorist must make. However, if improperly designed, traffic channels and islands can be not only confusing, but also exceedingly dangerous. It must be remembered that, although every intersectional detail may appear vividly in the design plan, the driver sees the intersection at a flat angle. Therefore, if it is too complicated, he may become confused in trying to interpret the intent of the channelization.

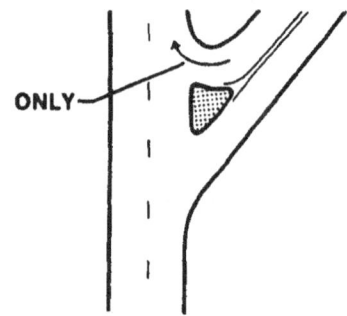

CHANNELIZATION

CHANNELIZATION SEPARATES COMPLEX INTERSECTION MOVEMENTS, AND CLEARLY DEFINES POINTS OF CONFLICT.

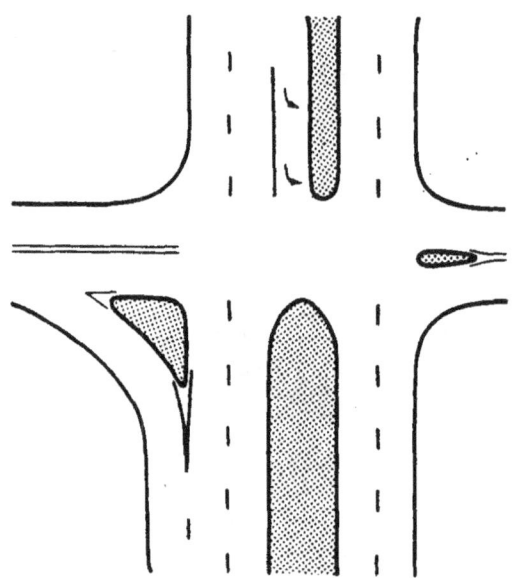

CHANNELIZATION

CHANNELIZATION REDUCES THE AMOUNT OF PAVED AREA, WHICH DECREASES VEHICLE WANDERING

CHANNELIZATION PREVENTS INCORRECT DECISIONS AND CONTROLS THE ANGLE OF CONFLICT

CHANNELIZATION FORCES RIGHT ANGLE CONFLICT GIVING MAXIMUM SIGHT DISTANCE

CHANNELIZATION

DESIGN

Traffic streams that cross should intersect at or near right angles, unless a merging or weaving maneuver is involved. In those cases, a flat angle of intersection is preferred.

Points of crossing or conflict should be well separated.

Refuge areas for turning vehicles should be provided clear of through traffic.

Prohibited turns should be blocked wherever possible.

Location of essential control devices should be established as a part of the design of a channelized intersection. Channelization may be desirable to separate the various traffic movements where multiple-phase signals are used.

Channelization islands should be designed so that the vehicle naturally moves through the islands.

Although the area of vehicle conflict should be reduced as much as possible by channelization, the number of islands should be kept to a minimum. Excessive islands can make it impossible for the driver to determine his or her course of action.

Traffic islands should be at least 4 to 6 feet wide and at least 12 to 20 feet long. Smaller islands confuse the driver.

Channelization islands should be set back 2 to 4 feet from the traffic lane so that they do not form an obstruction that tends to cause the vehicle to swerve away from the island.

CONTROL ANGLE OF CONFLICT

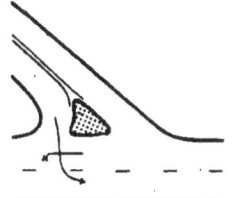

ISLAND SIZE AND LOCATION

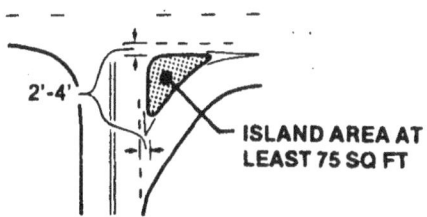

PROTECTION AND STORAGE

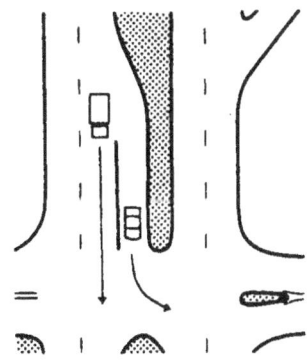

FLARED OPENINGS FOR EASY ENTRANCE

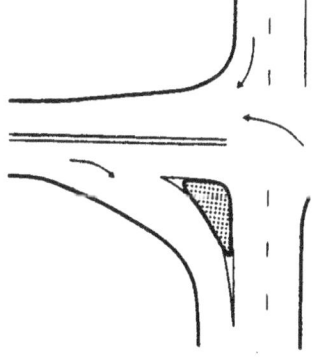

SIGHT DISTANCE

Along the roads of an intersection, as well as across all road corners, SIGHT SHOULD BE UNOBSTRUCTED FOR A DISTANCE THAT WILL ENABLE DRIVERS APPROACHING THE INTERSECTION TO SEE EACH OTHER IN TIME TO PREVENT COLLISION. The sight distance needed at a given intersection *depends on the type of traffic control at that intersection, width of the road, speed of approach, and type of vehicle.* Where no control exists, sight distance along each intersectional leg must be great enough that a driver can see any obstacle at the intersection in time to avoid it. Where cross-street traffic is controlled by STOP signs, the driver of the stopped vehicle should see enough of the major road to be able to clear the intersection before a vehicle that comes into view after he has started reaches the intersection. This distance is the basic criterion for most roadways. Where sight distance is inadequate, speed zones or signal control may be required for safety.

STOP CONTROL ON CROSS STREET		
DESIGN SPEED (MPH)	REQUIRED SIGHT DISTANCE	
	2 LANES (FT)	4 LANES (FT)
30	405	465
40	540	620
50	675	775
60	810	930

For divided roadways, medians equal to or wider than the vehicle length enable the crossing to be made in two steps. Narrower medians should be included in the width to be crossed in one step.

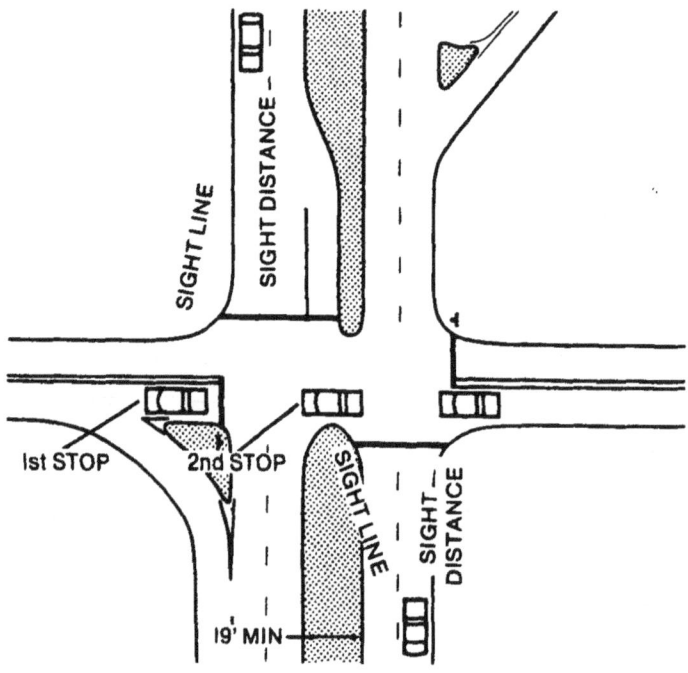

MEDIAN OPENINGS

The design of medians for intersections **depends on the character and volume of through and turning traffic.** Where nearly all vehicles travel through the intersection, and the volume is well below capacity, the simplest and least costly median opening may be adequate. Conversely, where crossing and turning movements are numerous and speeds and traffic volumes are high, the median should be of a shape and width that will permit efficient turning movements.

1 MINIMUM DESIGN

For medians requiring only a simple design, the length of the median opening and shape of the median end are determined by the vehicle turning radius. The arc of the radius is tangent to the median edge and the centerline of the crossroad. For single-unit trucks and an occasional semitrailer, a 50-foot radius with a semicircular median end is acceptable. The minimum length of the median opening should be at least 40 feet; and the maximum length no more than 100 feet.

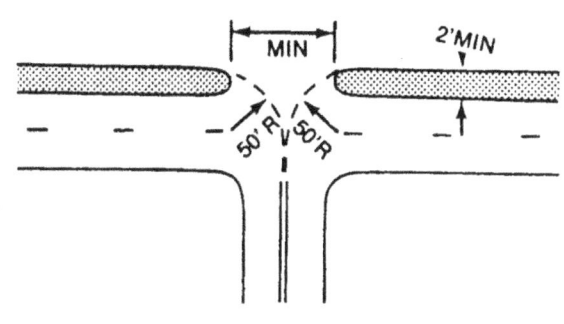

2 ABOVE-MINIMUM DESIGN

Where above-minimum designs are required, the general pattern for the simple design is used, but with larger dimensions. For example, in lieu of using a 50-foot control radius for single-unit vehicles, a 75-foot radius could be used. Also, for medians wider than 8 feet, a bullet-nose median end can be used in lieu of the semicircular end. This end treatment improves vehicle travel paths, lessens intersectional pavement, and shortens the length of the median opening.

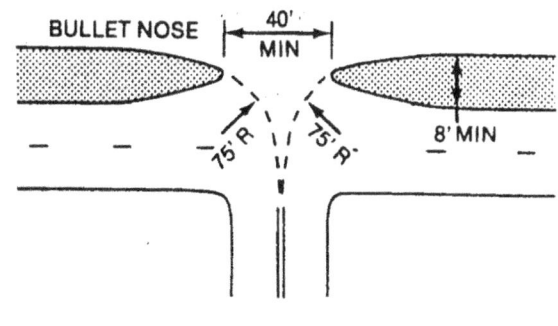

3 DESIGN FOR CROSS TRAFFIC

Where signalization is unjustified and crossing movements are unsafe, the median should be wide enough to store at least one vehicle. The controlling median width is the length of the design vehicle to be accommodated.

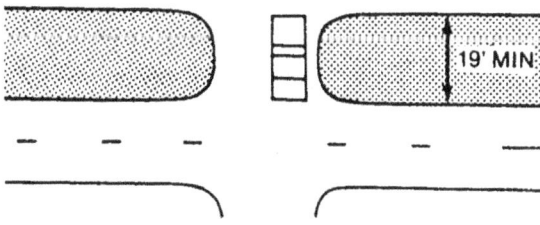

II. DESIGN

The regulated sharing of common space where two or more roadways intersect requires intersection designs and traffic controls that are drastically different from those of the open road. "INTERSECTION DESIGN" *is the process of determining the best way one traffic stream can cross another or make certain movements without conflict.* For example, where two major roadways cross, some type of bridge structure may be required to eliminate conflict. Where two minor roadways cross, however, traffic conflict may be controlled simply with a stop sign. In general, then, **traffic volume, speed, and accident rate** — *as well as the ever-present economics* — **determine the method to be applied at a given crossing.** This section illustrates various designs that can preclude conflict at roadway crossings.

CLASSIFICATION

Design requirements for intersections vary with the importance of the intersecting roadways. Therefore, the functional classification used here places *crossing roadways into three groups* in accordance with their importance: *minor/minor, major/minor, and major/major.* Each group carries a set of suggested minimum design standards, which correspond with the importance of the roadway system and the specific service each is expected to provide.

❶ MINOR/MINOR INTERSECTION

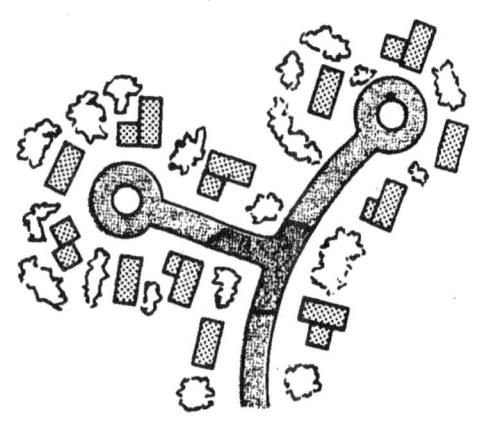

THE INTERSECTION OF TWO LOW-VOLUME ROADS should be kept *simple in geometry and traffic control.* Drivers need only to be able to see other approaching vehicles so as to judge their speed and distance. Design of this intersection should insure that: *paths on approach to and through the intersection are natural; horizontal and vertical alignment is compatible with the operation; and sight distance is sufficient.*

❷ MAJOR/MINOR INTERSECTION

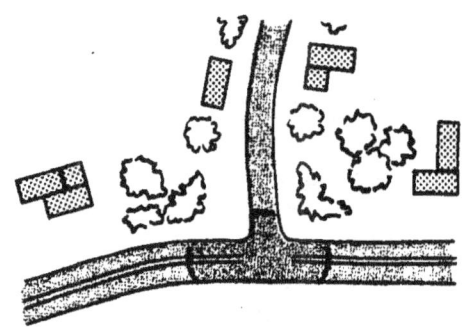

Where a low *volume road* and *a high volume road* intersect, it is basic that drivers on both roads know immediately which road is major. Also, good sight distance for both roads is essential but particularly for vehicles crossing the major road. Traffic control of these intersections generally is provided with stop signs on the minor road.

③ MAJOR/MAJOR INTERSECTION

Heavy traffic volumes where two or more roadways cross each other may require drastic changes from open road operating conditions, and capacity considerations because of the regulated sharing of common space. The configuration of the intersection is the principal determinant of operational safety and efficiency. The type of control and geometry can vary extensively. For example, *control may vary from yield signs to traffic signals, and geometry may vary from a two-lane, two-way roadway to a six-lane divided roadway with auxiliary lanes and turning roadways*. Because of extensive variations that may be required to handle heavy traffic volumes, requirements for both present and future demand should be established prior to design.

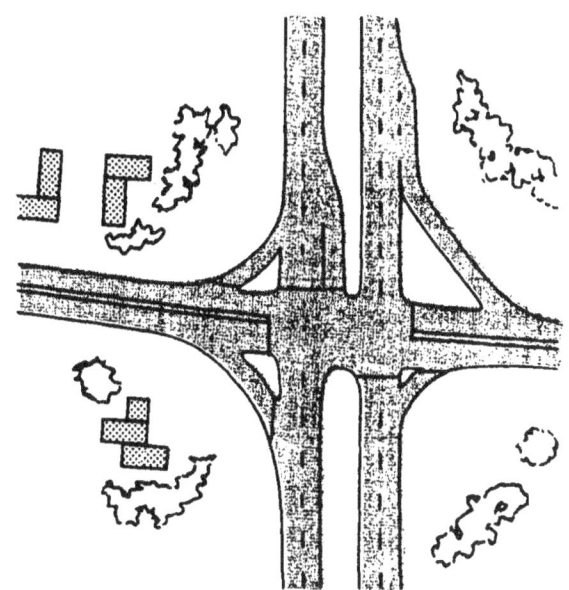

Horizontal and vertical alignment should be compatible with operational requirements.

Paths on approach and through intersection should be natural.

Traffic should be separated according to maneuvers.

Turning maneuvers should be physically accommodated.

Turning roadways should be designed for reasonable speeds.

Good transitions to turning roadways and auxiliary lanes should be provided.

Sight distances should be sufficient for conditions.

Design must be compatible with environmental conditions.

> **DRIVERS SHOULD BE ABLE TO:**
>
> - DETECT THE IMPORTANCE OF THE INTERSECTING ROADWAY.
>
> - DETERMINE THE REQUIRED LANE OR POSITION IN ORDER TO ACCOMPLISH THE INTENDED MANEUVER.
>
> - IDENTIFY AND RESPOND TO THE CONTROL DEVICE.
>
> - IDENTIFY THE REQUIREMENTS OF THE INTERSECTING TRAFFIC STREAM AND JUDGE THE CHARACTERISTICS OF THAT STREAM AS THEY RELATE TO THE MANEUVER.

CONTROL

Many methods may be used to enable one traffic stream to cross another or to make certain turning movements efficiently and safely. However, **basic crossing conflicts can be eliminated by** use of these devices: **yield signs, stop signs, and traffic signals.**

❶ YIELD SIGNS

YIELD SIGNS generally are *used where minor roads intersect, where traffic speeds are low, and/or where adequate sight distance is available.* The yield sign indicates to the driver that he must decide whether to continue through the intersection at 15 or 20 miles per hour or come to a complete stop. Thus, *sight distance must be sufficient for the driver to look in both directions, determine his course of action, and then either traverse the intersection or come to a complete stop.* This sign should never be used to protect entrances on major streets.

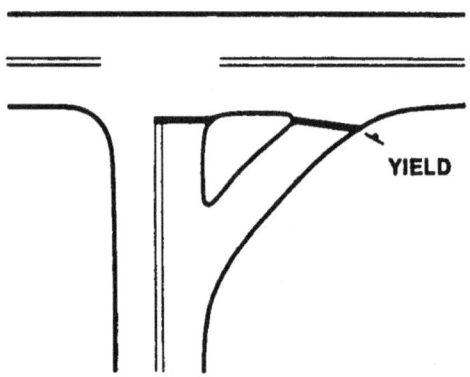

② STOP

At an *intersection of a minor roadway with an intermediate or major one,* the *crossing conflict* generally can be *controlled* by the use of a stop sign. The driver on the minor street must have sufficient sight distance to judge when it is safe to cross and must have an adequate gap in the traffic flow. It is possible to make use of a stop-and-enter crossing only when the traffic volumes on the major facility are not over approximately two-thirds of the capacity of the facility. When the major facility is flowing continuously, it will be difficult, if not impossible, to make a safe crossing. When this condition exists, more restrictive control is required.

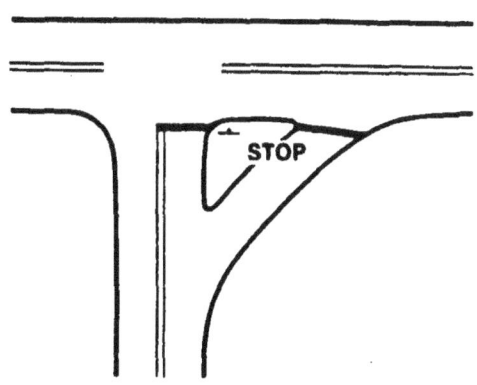

③ TRAFFIC SIGNAL

The most restrictive intersectional control — *signalization* — *should be used only at major intersections and, desirably, only where the road speed does not exceed 45 miles per hour.* The signalized intersection should be designed so as not to reduce the capacity of the street system. For example, if two major roadways are to cross at an intersection and each will operate near capacity, the traffic signal may reduce the capacity of both roads to one-half. In this case, additional traffic lanes within 1,000 feet of the intersection may be desirable.

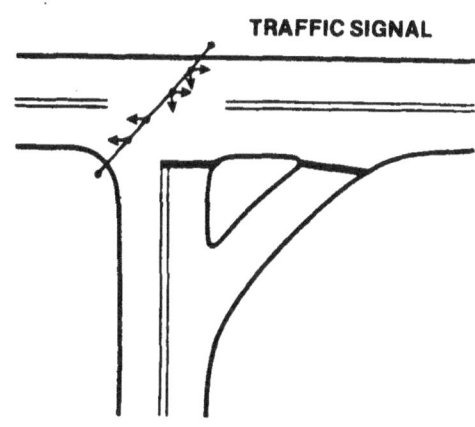

INTERSECTION TYPES

THE BASIC TYPES OF INTERSECTIONS *are determined by the number of intersecting legs;* that is, **three-leg, four-leg, multileg.** However, any one of the basic types **can vary greatly in scope, shape, and channelization.** Once the type is established, a final geometric design can be selected simply by applying the design controls and elements previously discussed. In this section, each type of intersection, with likely variations, is discussed. Traffic control for every type of intersection is not discussed; however, all types of intersections shown lend themselves to control, ranging from yield signs to traffic signals.

❶ THREE-LEGGED

Generally, this design is *used to terminate one roadway.* Where turning movements are hazardous, the intersection may be flared or designed with turning roadways. A Y-type design, an undesirable version of the T-intersection, generally results in operational problems.

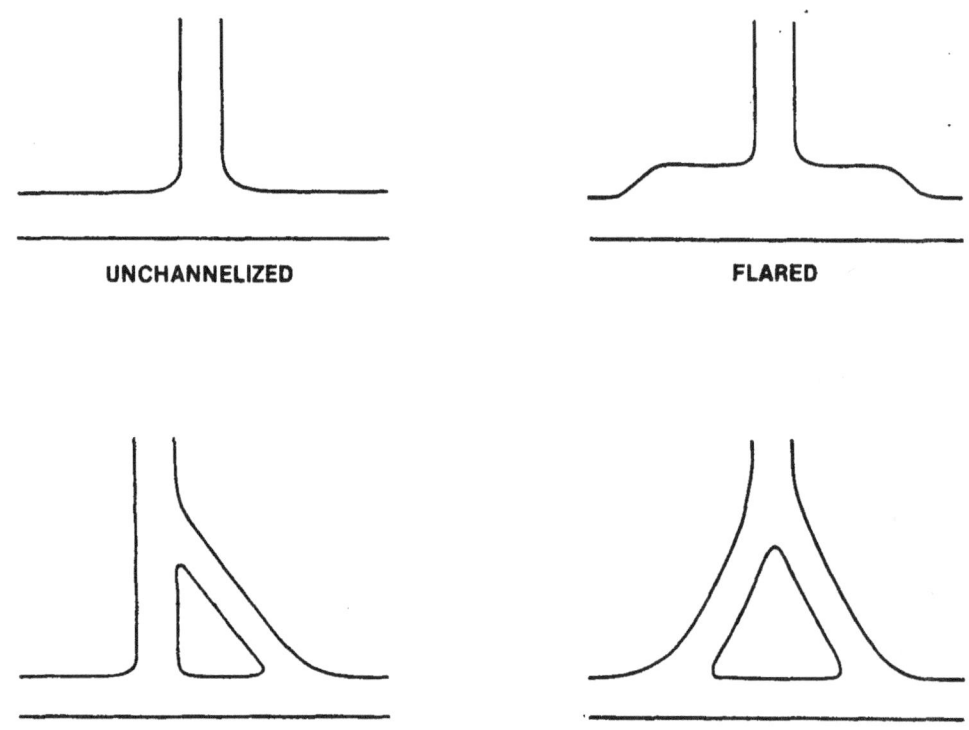

UNCHANNELIZED   FLARED

TURNING ROADWAYS

2 FOUR-LEGGED

Except that it provides for the direct crossing movement, a cross-intersection is *similar to the T-intersection.* The cross-intersection has many variations, depending on operating conditions. The *right-angle* is the common crossroad type; however, the crossroad may be skewed, even though this is undesirable.

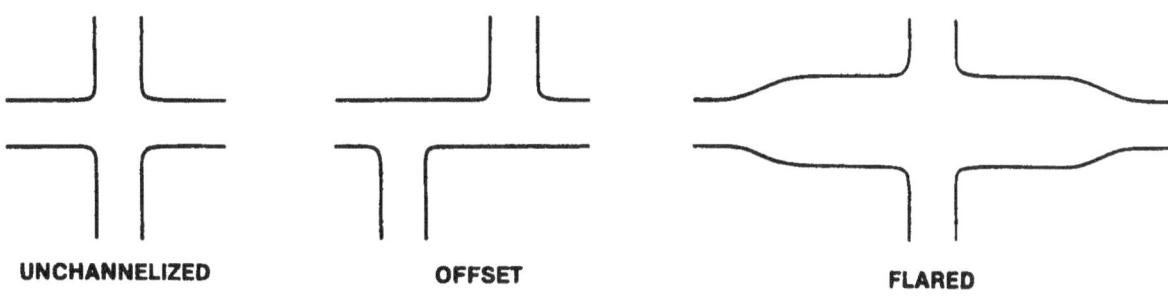

UNCHANNELIZED **OFFSET** **FLARED**

3 MULTILEGGED

This type of intersection generally *represents a total compromise of operational requirements.* Generally, either some form of channelization and signalization should be used, or one leg of the intersection should be eliminated. However, the rotary type intersection has been used for multisided intersections with heavy turning movements and low speeds. The rotary design operation depends upon weaving, and the success of such an operation depends upon the length of the weaving section in relation to traffic volume and operating speeds. In some cases, a rotary design can be improved by routing the through traffic directly through the middle of the rotary and forcing all turns onto the rotary. Minor street and turning movements may be either stop-and-enter or signalized, depending upon the volumes of traffic to be handled.

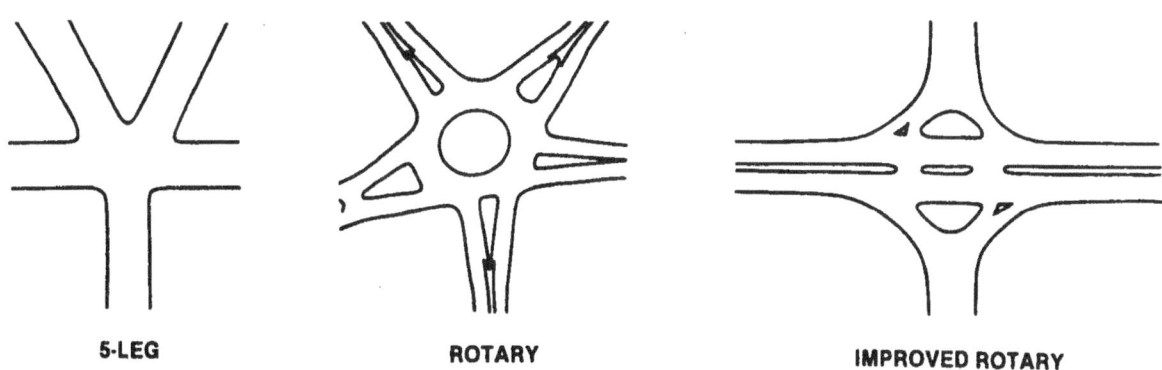

5-LEG **ROTARY** **IMPROVED ROTARY**

INTERSECTION DESIGN IMPROVEMENTS

THE TYPES OF INTERSECTION IMPROVEMENTS include a wide range of minor and major changes to intersections. For purposes of this guide, these IMPROVEMENTS have been grouped into four categories: **realignment, widening, and left- and right-turn provisions.** Not all types of improvements are included here — only the most common ones.

DESIGN PRINCIPLES

The layout should be visible to the driver, and the moves he must or can make should be apparent. A "bird's eye" or "drawing board" view is not available for a driver to study.

Intersection layouts should be simple. All drivers must be able to sense what to expect so that they are not required to hesitate or to decrease relative speeds while passing through an intersection.

Intersectional design should incorporate the informational signing necessary to guide vehicles through. Problems resulting from inadequate sign position and sign message can often be avoided by good initial design of all essential components.

The intersection should have adequate capacity for present and future traffic demands.

The intersection should be easy to cross. Excessively skewed intersections should be avoided because of the difficulties involved in crossing them.

Intersections should be planned to permit installation of additional control devices as traffic flow increases.

DESIGN IMPROVEMENTS

1. REALIGNMENT
2. WIDENING
3. LEFT TURN
4. RIGHT TURN

① REALIGNMENT

Offset intersections — that is, intersections whose opposite halves are not in direct alignment — constitute a major traffic engineering problem. For the two halves to operate as two intersections, the offset needs to be at least 150 feet in built-up areas and at least 500 feet in outlying areas. Redesign of the intersection to match the two halves usually will reap large benefits in safety and efficiency of operation.

Intersections with high skew angles also are troublesome. The classical solutions to this problem are either: to realign or reduce the skew angle; or to separate the two halves of the intersection into two individual intersections by realigning the halves into T-intersections. Either of these realignments will reduce the potential for near head-on collisions that are inherent in the "before" condition. With either design, however, the tradeoff is a probable increase in the frequency of minor accidents.

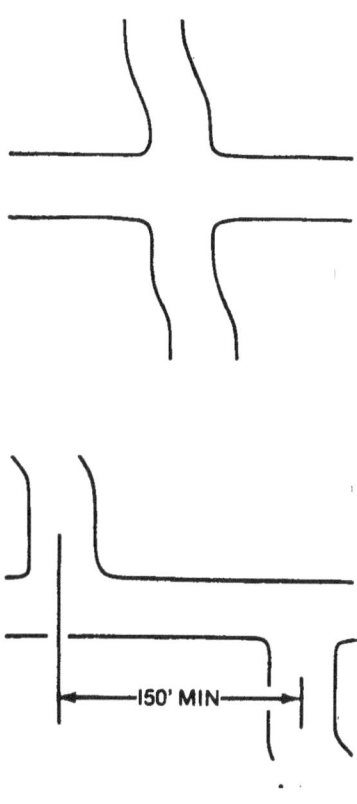

② WIDENING

The intersection is commonly the lowest capacity element of an arterial street system. Thus, intersectional modifications that increase the number lanes in the intersectional area can more effectively balance the capacity of the facility. Flaring is an effective intersection treatment that increases the capacity, while improving operations, of the intersection. Flaring involves increasing the width of the pavement approaching the intersection. This is accomplished usually by adding a left-turn lane or, a right-turn lane, or both, as discussed under left- and right-turn provisions. Flaring can be used also to increase the number of through lanes. However, great care must be exercised to guard against operational problems downstream. To truly be effective, the merging operation downstream requires 300 to 500 feet of taper, which usually indicates midblock lane additions as well as the intersectional improvements. For this reason, flaring usually provides space for turn lanes.

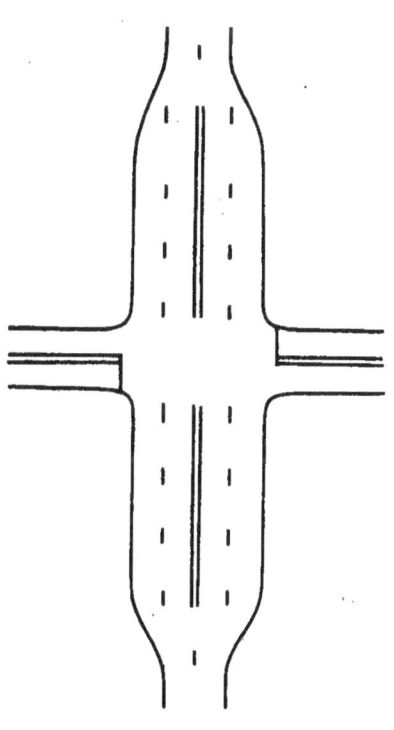

③ LEFT-TURN PROVISIONS

In general, A VEHICLE THAT LEAVES A MAJOR ROAD VIA A LEFT TURN *must come to a complete stop.* The **addition of left-turn lanes**, whether **by flaring or by taking space from an existing median,** can substantially increase the capacity and safety of the intersection by reducing the conflict between left-turning vehicles and through lanes.

SINGLE TURN

For normal **two-lane facilities, the roadway at the intersection must be widened to provide the "deceleration" lane. For a four-lane divided road, portions of the division strip may be removed to provide a median lane.** Median widths of 20 to 25 feet are desirable for median lanes; however, widths of 16 to 18 feet are adequate. A 10-foot lane with a 2-foot separator, either curbed or painted, may be used where speeds are low and the intersection is signal-controlled.

Typical traffic volumes warranting use of this technique should exceed 8,000 vehicles per day on the major road, with 100 left-turn vehicles during the peak hour.

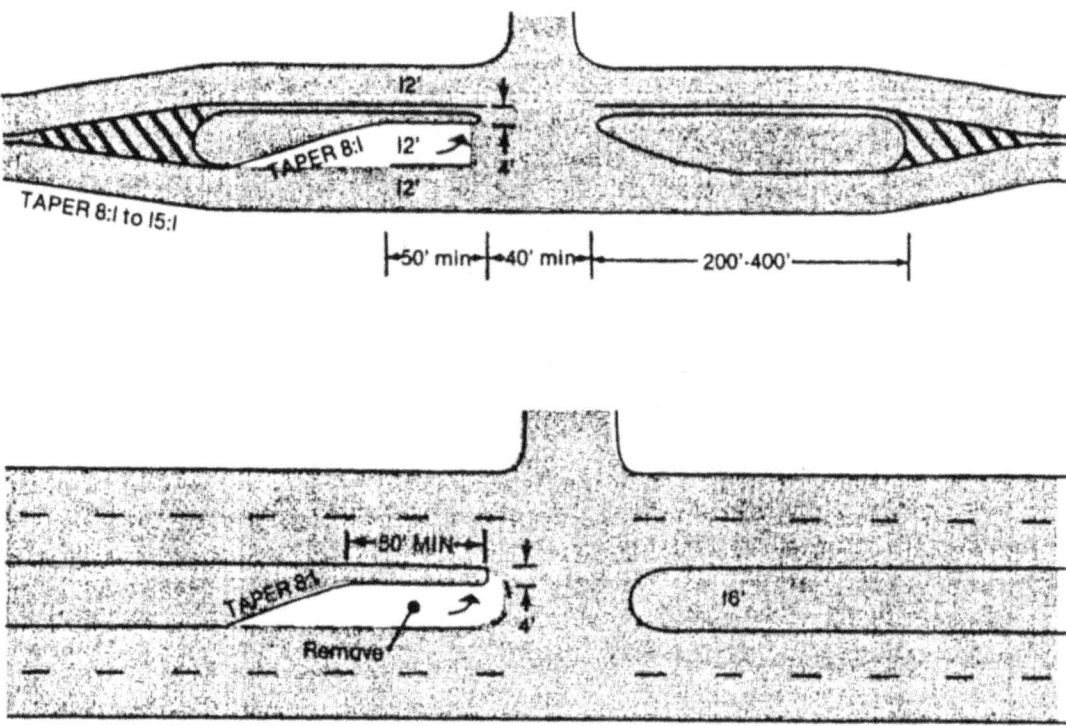

DUAL TURN

Where the capacity of a single left-turn lane is insufficient to accommodate the demand volume, a dual left-turning lane should be considered. Generally, the capacity of the approach controls the capacity of the intersection; thus, to maximize the flow through an intersection and to determine the quality of service afforded, a capacity analysis is necessary. However, a 75- to 80-percent left-turn capacity increase may be predicted by adding a second left-turn lane.

To provide a *left-turn bay* for a dual left-turn situation, it is necessary to *provide a wide continuous median or to "neck down" the lanes farther downstream*. Two through lanes in both directions and two left-turn lanes (all 12-foot lanes) would require a minimum pavement width of 76 feet, including a 4-foot median at the nose of the left-turn bay. This would then result in a 28-foot median downstream if the right-of-way were not narrowed. This width is desirable but often unavailable, especially in the more centralized areas where frequent dual left-turn lanes are needed. It is important, though, to provide a wide enough *"throat"* at intersection-entrance lanes to allow motorists to reach their lane safely and comfortably after a turning maneuver, without encroaching on another lane, the median, or curb. The operation of dual left-turn movements must be signalized, and is generally more favorable if the left turns have their own signalized phase, or if they are controlled on a leading or lagging green indication of the through phase.

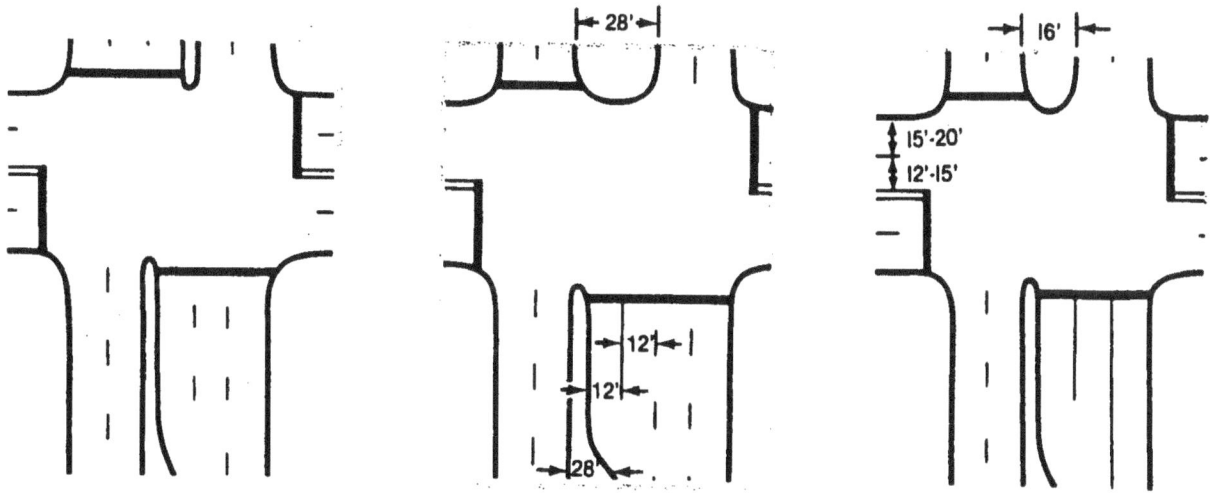

4 RIGHT-TURN PROVISIONS

RIGHT-TURNING MOVEMENTS may be enhanced by the **use of large corner radii, turning roadways, merging lanes, and deceleration lanes.** Generally, the technique that should be used is *related directly to the amount of traffic making the movement, the volume on the major street, and the vehicle speeds.*

LARGE CORNER RADII

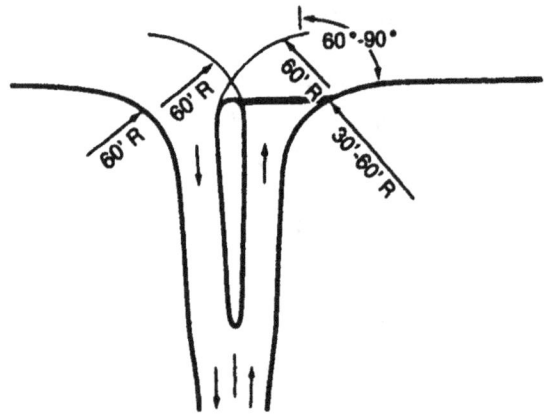

TURNING ROADWAY

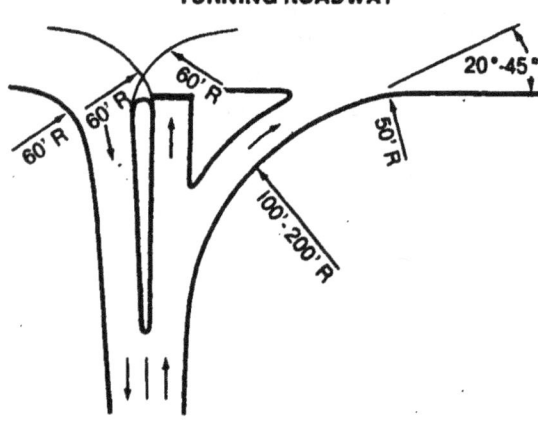

TURNING ROADWAY WITH ACCELERATION LANE

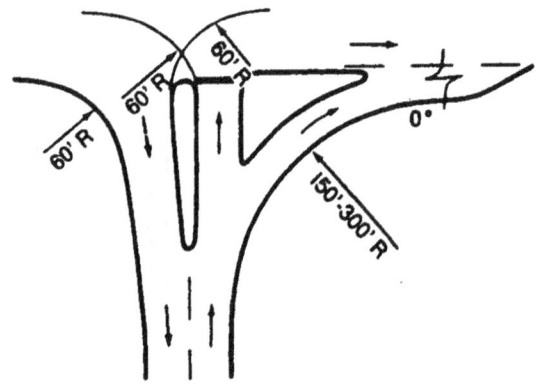

FROM MINOR TO MAJOR ROAD

Large corner radii should be used where minor volumes are making a right turn and it is desirable to minimize conflict between turning vehicles and through traffic. Where there are at least 60 turning vehicles during the peak hour and 8,000 vehicles per day on the major road, **a turning roadway** may be appropriate. With this design, the angle of entry into the road should be from 20 to 45 degrees in order for the turning vehicles to enter the through lane at a moderate speed. Finally, when major street volumes exceed 8,000 vehicles per day with at least 90 right turns from the minor road during the peak hour, it may be desirable to provide for their continuous movement into the intersection. In these cases, the angle of entry onto the through lane should be zero degrees, and vehicles must be provided with an **additional lane** that extends a sufficient distance for the vehicles to weave into the main stream of traffic. In some cases, this additional lane may be added for over a thousand feet. Where turning roadways are inappropriate, intersections may be improved by adding a **special right-turn lane.** As a general guideline, consideration should be given to installing this lane when the average number of right-turning vehicles exceeds 2 per signal cycle or 120 per hour during the peak period.

FROM MAJOR ROAD TO MINOR ROAD

Vehicles leaving a major facility via a right turn **should be permitted to make their exit at a reasonable speed so that they will not be forced to slow down to a point that will hold up traffic or create unsafe conditions.** On moderate speed routes, where traffic volumes are not in excess of 8,000 vehicles per day, the right turn can be made from a "taper" and a circular curve. *The length of the taper and the radius of the curve will depend upon whether the right-turning vehicle must come to a complete stop before merging into the minor street traffic.* Where traffic volumes are at least 8,000 vehicles per day and speeds exceed 30 miles per hour, a separate deceleration lane should be formed for the turning traffic. In general, this deceleration lane and the turning radius must be related so that the vehicle can come to a complete stop, if necessary, at the entrance to the minor road.

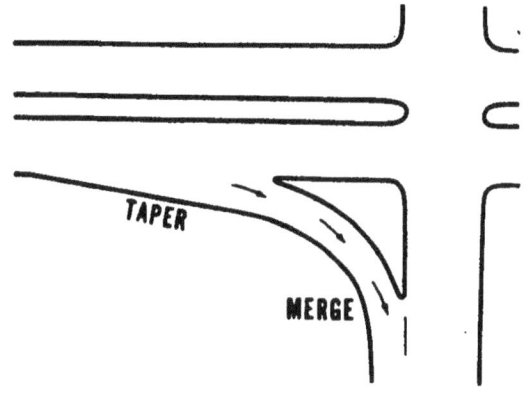

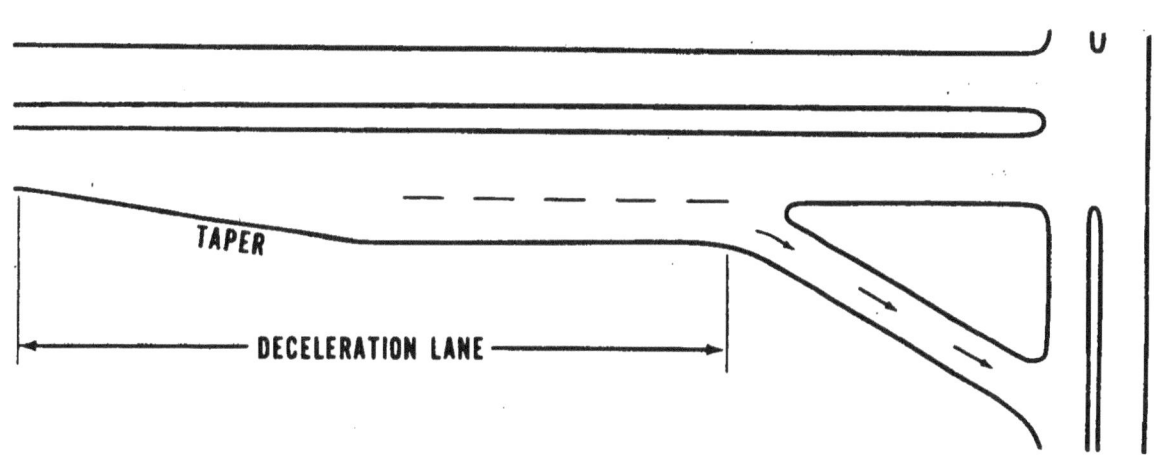

TRAFFIC ENGINEERING

ROAD DESIGN: CATEGORIES OF STREETS

CONTENTS

	Page
I. ARTERIALS	1
ACCESS CONTROL	2
ELEMENTS	6
STAGE DEVELOPMENT	8
II. COLLECTOR AND LOCAL STREETS	9
COLLECTOR	10
LOCAL	11
III. RESIDENTIAL STREETS	12
CLASSIFICATION	13
LAYOUT	14
ELEMENTS	17

ROAD DESIGN: CATEGORIES OF STREETS

I. ARTERIALS

ACCESS CONTROL

ELEMENTS

STAGE DEVELOPMENT

ARTERIALS are those streets that provide high-volume traffic service. In the development of an installation road network, the routes selected for arterials usually include portions of existing street systems originally designed to provide land access. This access function conflicts directly with that of providing high-volume traffic service; that is, **for arterial streets, unlimited access equates to poor traffic service in terms of travel time and safety.** This chapter discusses techniques for controlling access to existing arterial streets and provides guidelines for designing new arterials.

ARTERIALS PROVIDE HIGH LEVEL TRAFFIC SERVICE

ACCESS CONTROL

"**ACCESS CONTROL**" refers to *techniques for reducing traffic interference from intersections and driveways;* it can **vary from full control to none at all.** *Full control is provided with frontage roads and grade separations; partial control, with curb-cut restrictions. No control permits unlimited access from intersections and driveways.* Since most installation arterials must provide some form of land access, this section prescribes ways to provide quality access as related primarily to safety. Quality access can be achieved by improving whole roadway sections or individual intersections and driveway connections.

This chapter describes the techniques for controlling access along roadway sections that have closely spaced driveway connections.

ACCESS CONTROL
REDUCES TRAFFIC
INTERFERENCE

INSTALL TWO-WAY, LEFT-TURN LANE

This technique *removes left-turning vehicles from the through traffic lanes.* Its major design requirement is a center lane that is at least 14 feet wide. The technique is warranted on multilane roads that meet all of the following criteria: the roadway connects with closely spaced driveways that have per-mile left-turn maneuvers totaling 20 percent of through volume during peak travel periods; the road volume exceeds 10,000 vehicles per day and the road speed exceeds 30 miles per hour. Locations with high accident rates resulting from left-turn maneuvers, will warrant this technique even if they do not meet the criteria required above. A 35-percent reduction in the accident rate can be expected where this technique is used.

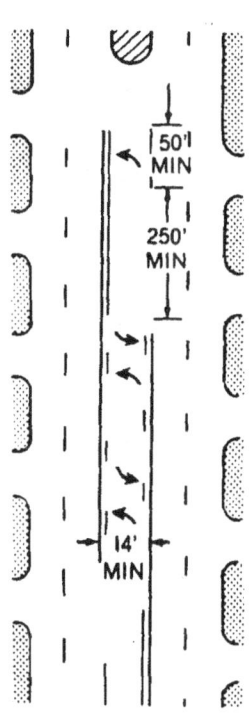

INSTALL RAISED MEDIAN DIVIDER WITH LEFT-TURN DECELERATION LANES

This median treatment *controls access by permitting left turns at major driveways only.* This tight control should yield a 50-percent reduction in total accidents. The price for such safety, however, is the increased travel time and the inconvenience resulting from circuitous travel paths, plus the expense of widening the existing roadway to accommodate median construction. The minimum roadway width for this technique, to accommodate four 11-foot through lanes and a 12-foot median, is 56 feet. A more desirable design requires a road width of 70 feet, with four 12-foot through lanes and a 22-foot median. This technique generally is warranted at locations where the ADT exceeds 10,000 vehicles per day, the travel speed ranges from 30 to 45 miles per hour, and left-turn movements exceed 150 vehicles per hour per mile during the peak period; or where warranted by a high accident rate.

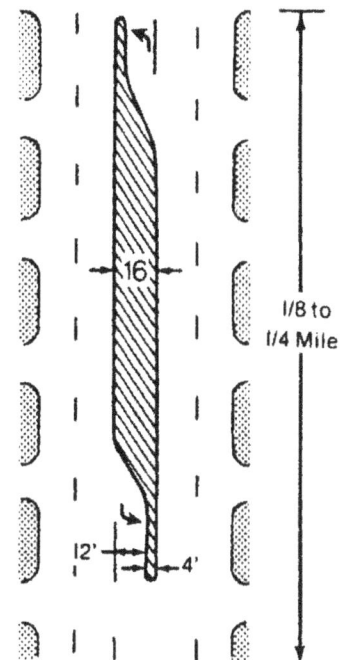

INSTALL ALTERNATING LEFT-TURN LANE

This technique *provides a separate left-turn lane for one direction of traffic at a time into closely spaced driveways.* It has the advantage of requiring a center lane only 12 feet wide, versus the usual 14 feet. This lane design normally can be provided on arterial sections where the traffic volume and travel speeds exceed 10,000 vehicles per day and 30 miles per hour, respectively, and where left turns per mile exceed 15 percent of through traffic during peak traffic demand, or where warranted by accident rates resulting from left-turn maneuvers. In either case, this technique will be used only when other left-turn techniques are infeasible. This technique should produce a 25-percent reduction in the accident rate.

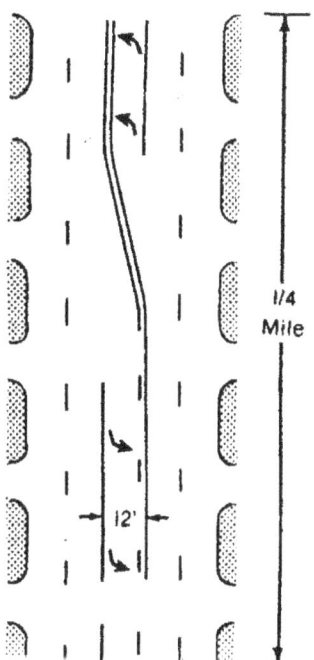

CHANNELIZE THE MEDIAN

This technique controls driveway access by providing a physical barrier to prevent left turns. Median channelization is warranted on arterial sections with 30 driveways per mile, with a travel speed between 30 and 45 miles per hour, and with an ADT of at least 5,000 vehicles per day, but with no more than 100 prohibited left turns per day. In particular, it is warranted where safety is hampered by a few left-turn maneuvers. As this technique causes circuitous routings, the total circulation pattern should be analyzed before the technique is implemented. When it has been determined that median channelization is appropriate for an arterial roadway, the technique can be implemented by three methods.

The first method extends the median to physically prevent left turns from a driveway onto the arterial. This method, common on divided roads with left-turn deceleration lanes at major driveways, should reduce accident rates by 20 percent. For this design, the median must be at least 14 feet wide.

The second method channelizes the median to prevent left turns from the arterial into driveways; but permits left turns from driveways onto the arterial. This method, generally associated with an existing opening in a narrow median, is estimated to reduce accident rates by 30 percent.

The third method closes the median, thus preventing all left turns. This method, common for narrow medians, can be expected to reduce the accident rate by 50 percent.

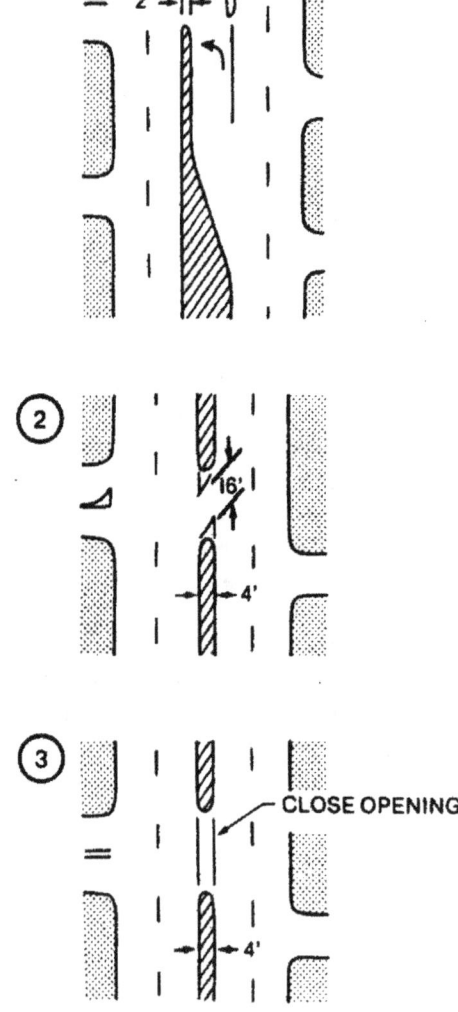

INSTALL CONTINUOUS RIGHT-TURN LANE

A continuous right-turn lane removes turning vehicles from the through traffic stream, thereby reducing the frequency and severity of rear-end collisions. The design is essentially a right-turn lane extended to accommodate several nearby driveways. However, to operate as intended, the continuous lane should be no longer than one-quarter mile; it should be limited to arterial sections with more than 60 driveways per mile, with an ADT exceeding 15,000 vehicles per day, with a travel speed exceeding 30 miles per hour, and with right turns per mile exceeding 20 percent of the ADT.

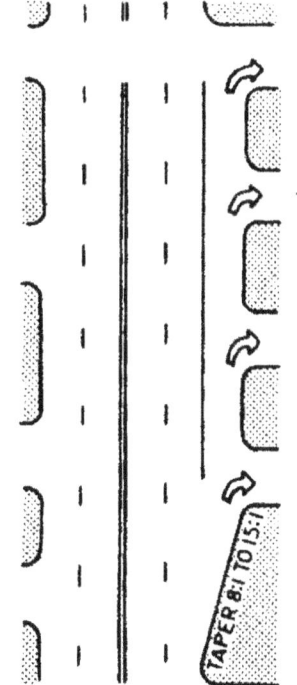

INSTALL ONE-WAY TRAFFIC FLOW

The implementation of one-way operation on arterial sections is an alternate to the previously described medial design techniques and should be considered where insufficient right-of-way exists for widening the arterial. This technique, which eliminates opposing left-turn conflicts, can *increase capacity* by as much as *50 percent* and improve safety significantly. A *25-percent reduction in total accidents* may be expected after converting to one-way operations.

One-way operations can be initiated usually by converting all traffic lanes to one direction of travel. Of course, use of this technique depends on the availability of a suitable arterial to carry reverse-direction traffic. A pair of closely spaced, one-way streets is suggested.

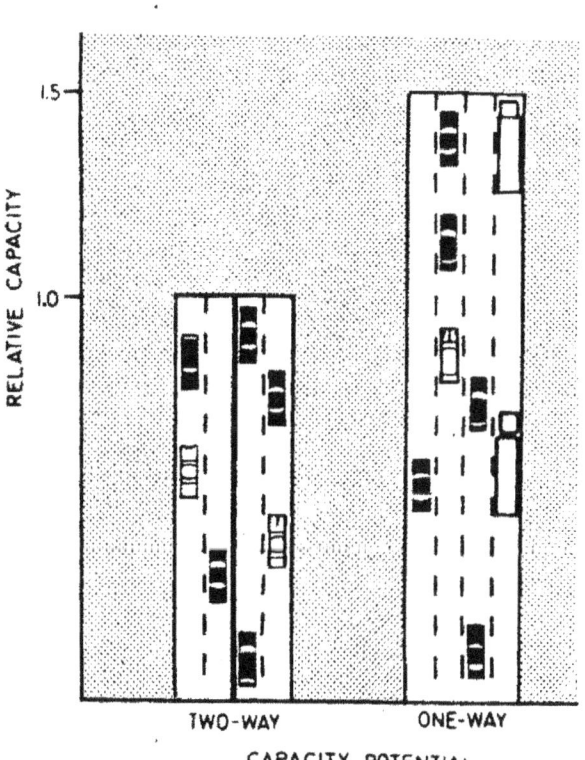

ELEMENTS

ARTERIALS usually **carry a large percentage of the total traffic**, with traffic volumes ranging from 8,000 to more than 20,000 vehicles per day; therefore, their **geometric design** should afford high capacity and relatively high speeds. The travel speed along arterials should average between 25 and 35 miles per hour during peak traffic. Therefore, design speeds should range from 40 to 60 miles per hour, with an average design speed of 50 miles per hour. A lower design speed may be used in built-up areas or, particularly, for restrictive conditions.

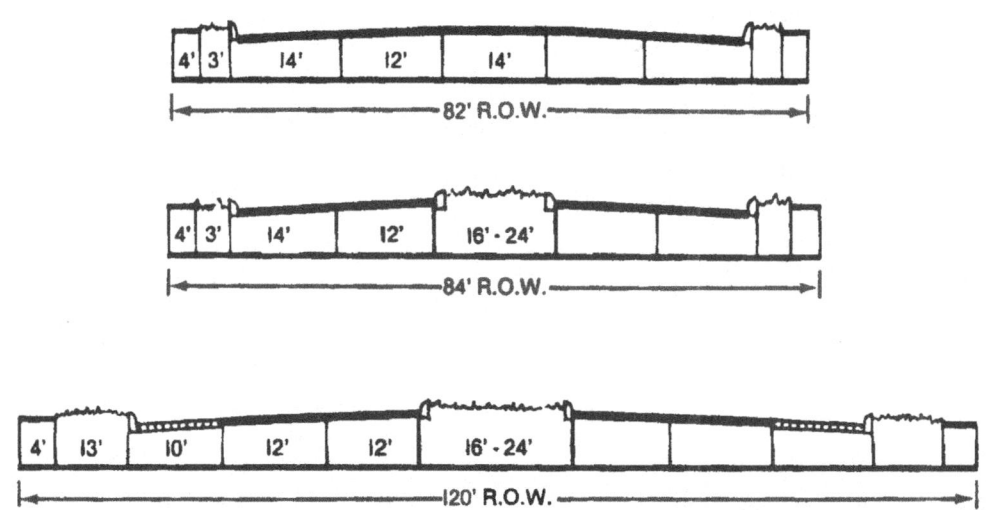

TRAFFIC LANE

Traffic lanes desirably should be 12 feet wide, although 11 feet is acceptable under restricted conditions. The number of traffic lanes will vary depending on traffic demand and availability of right-of-way; however, a capacity analysis should be used to determine the proper number. Use of the road for on-street parking should be avoided, as it decreases capacity, impedes traffic flow, and increases accident potential. Where parking must be permitted, 12-foot-wide lanes should be used. A lane this wide can then be converted to an additional traffic lane during peak hours or if future traffic volumes warrant. Also, improved sight distance at driveway entrances can be obtained without removal of parking, by inserting a no-parking zone, 8 to 10 feet long, between two parking stalls. This added space also facilitates entering and leaving the parking space.

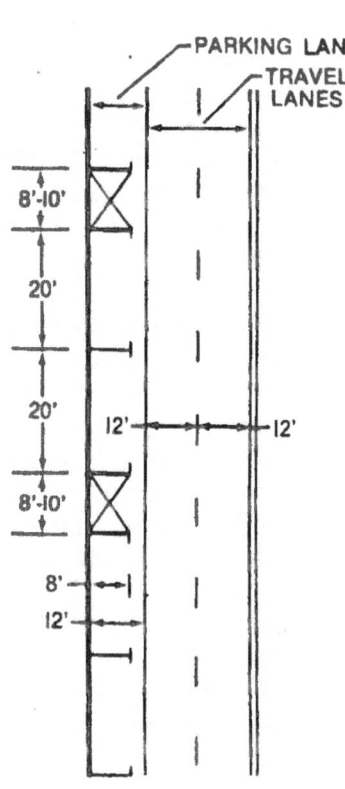

SHOULDERS, CURBS, AND BORDERS

SHOULDERS are an asset to any arterial street. They **enhance safety, serve as speed change lanes for turning vehicles, and provide storage for plowed snow.** On existing arterials, shoulder use may be limited because of restricted right-of-way or the necessity to use available right-of-way for traffic lanes. However, for new roadways with available right-of-way, 10-foot-wide shoulders should be included in the ultimate cross section. Also, every effort should be made to provide borders at least 8, but preferably 12 or more, feet wide. On the other hand, curbs should be omitted unless necessary to control drainage.

SHOULDERS SHOULD BE WIDE ENOUGH TO ACCOMMODATE STOPPED VEHICLE

MEDIANS

MEDIANS, like shoulders, greatly improve the safety of arterials and should be provided as space and funds permit. Limited space and funds add importance in the allocation of space to borders, traffic lanes, and medians. For example, where land access from the roadway is vital, a two-way, left-turn lane may be superior to a raised median. Conversely, where intersections are widely spaced or where lack of space precludes a center lane, the median is preferable, even if it is only a few feet wide. *The most important element of the median is width,* desirably 22 feet to allow U-turns. However, a 16-foot-wide median will provide a 12-foot-wide storage lane and a 4-foot-wide medial separation.

MEDIAN FUNCTION	MINIMUM WIDTH (FT)	DESIRED WIDTH (FT)
Separate opposing traffic	4	10
Pedestrian refuge and sign locations	6	14
Left-turn storage	16	20
U-Turns	22	24
Protection for crossing vehicles	25	30

STAGE DEVELOPMENT

Because of their enormous construction cost, arterial roadways sometimes **are developed over a period of years.** Also, when new roadways are constructed, traffic volumes may not warrant major-street design. In such cases, stage construction is appropriate. The initial construction can consist of only a 24-foot-wide pavement, offset 8 feet from the center line of a 120-foot-wide right-of-way. At a future date, two lanes can be added to the other side of the center line; also a separate left-turn lane in each direction can be provided from the median at major intersections. The final stage of construction would be the addition of two travel lanes to provide a total of three travel lanes in each direction. Relatively speaking, the ultimate cross-section capacity would be almost five times the initial capacity.

FOUR-STAGE ARTERIAL DEVELOPMENT

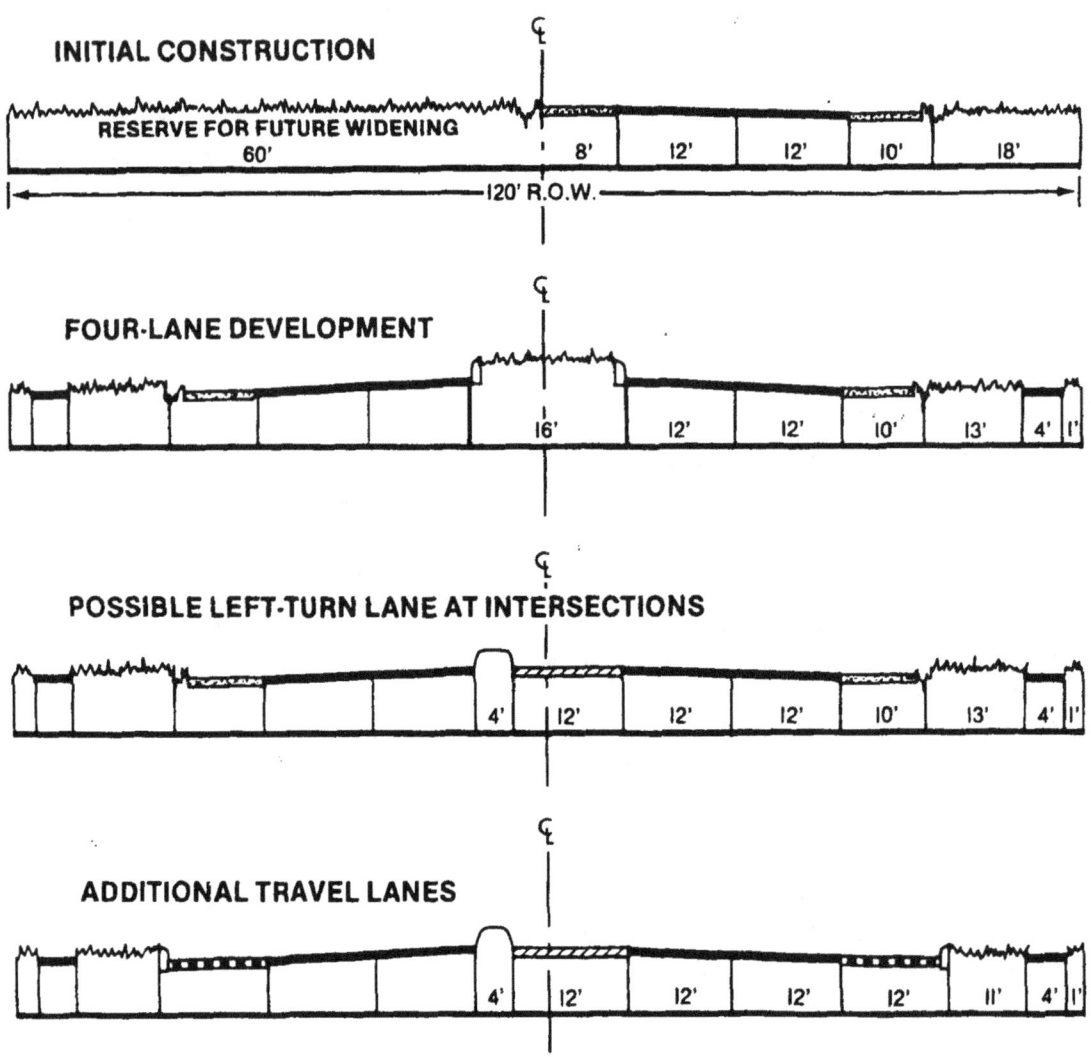

II. COLLECTOR AND LOCAL STREETS

COLLECTOR

LOCAL

Within the classification system for installation roadways, there are **three categories of streets: arterial, collector, and local.** Design of arterial streets, which serve as through streets with limited access, was discussed in chapter I. This chapter discusses design criteria for collector and local streets. **Collector streets** should be designed to serve, about equally, the functions of access to abutting property and through movement; whereas, **local streets** should be designed primarily as access streets for abutting property, and their function as a through street should be minimal.

COLLECTOR AND LOCAL STREETS PROVIDE ACCESS TO ABUTTING PROPERTY

COLLECTOR

Local streets carry limited traffic volume at low speeds; whereas, arterial streets are designed to carry high volumes over greater distances at higher speeds. Design standards for collector streets fall between these two extremes. **Four types of collector streets** are discussed in this guide: **residential, commercial, industrial, and neighborhood.**

RESIDENTIAL

RESIDENTIAL COLLECTORS *are designed to handle traffic volumes of up to 2,000 vehicles per day, while providing access to abutting property and on-street parking.* Such streets are necessary adjacent to multi-family residential developments, schools, and local retail and public facilities. They are required also when more than 50 dwelling units or residential lots must utilize the street for access to the collector/arterial street system. *Major entry streets to a residential community normally will be set up as residential collector streets.* The right-of-way should be 60 feet wide, and the pavement, 44 feet wide.

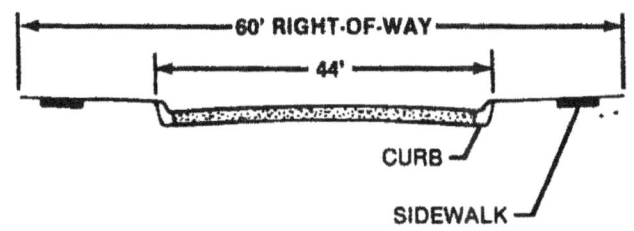

INDUSTRIAL/COMMERCIAL

A COMMERCIAL OR INDUSTRIAL COLLECTOR is one serving as principal access to a commercial development or an industrial site. The length of such a street should not exceed two miles. Direct residential frontage should be discouraged to prevent a conflict between residential and commercial traffic. Multi-family development, BOQ's or BEQ's, can front onto a commercial collector if ample off-street parking is provided and access is limited. For industrial streets, the right-of-way and pavement widths are 80' and 64 feet, respectively; and for commercial streets, 60 and 44 feet, respectively.

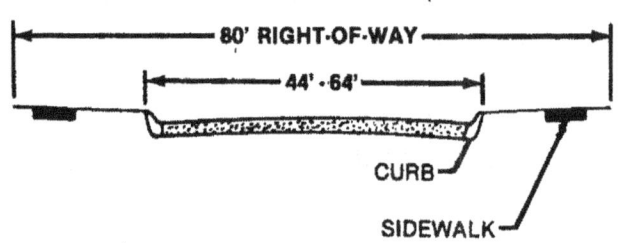

NEIGHBORHOOD

A NEIGHBORHOOD COLLECTOR STREET is designed to traverse distances from one-half to two miles, to serve a variety of land uses, and to handle traffic volumes of up to 8,000 vehicles per day. On-street parking usually is prohibited or restricted on neighborhood collectors; access to abutting property is limited, and uses may include multifamily dwelling units; schools; and retail, office, and community service facilities. Streets in a residential area serving more than 200 dwelling units should be designated as neighborhood collector streets. The right-of-way should be 70 feet wide and the pavement 44 feet wide. At major intersections, left-turn lanes may be required in addition to four through lanes. Where left-turn lanes are required, pavement must be 64 feet wide with an 80-foot-wide right-of-way.

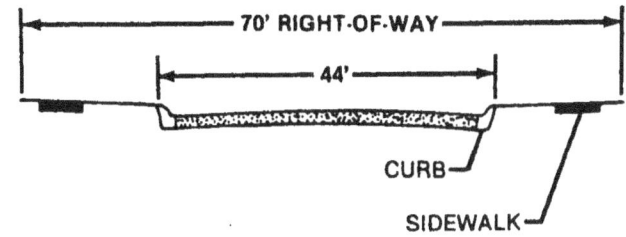

LOCAL STREETS *provide access to abutting property, and parking on these streets is usually permitted.* The main function of these streets is to **link the collector/arterial system and the low-density residential development**, as shown in chapter 10. Also, a few business and industrial streets can be considered in this class. However, due to the potential for increased development along these streets, most commercial streets should be designed as collectors.

Traffic volumes on local streets should be less than 2,000 vehicles per day, and their length less than 3,000 feet. The right-of-way requires a width of 54 feet, and the pavement should have a width of 34 feet.

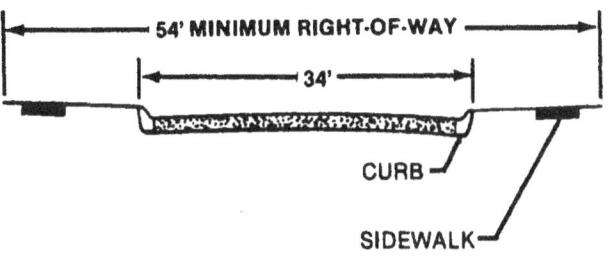

III. RESIDENTIAL STREETS

CLASSIFICATION

LAYOUT

ELEMENTS

RESIDENTIAL LIVING can be enhanced significantly through proper design of the "neighborhood unit," as this *area encompasses most of the major facilities required by its resident population.* Besides the family dwellings themselves, these facilities include elementary schools, churches, shopping centers, recreational facilities, utilities and, not least, streets. This section provides guidance for designing local streets for use in a residential environment.

DESIGN RESIDENTIAL
AREAS FOR
TODAY'S NEEDS

CLASSIFICATION

Residential streets usually have four classifications: **place, lane, subcollector,** or **collector.** Each is discussed below.

PLACE

A PLACE is a *short street, cul-de-sac, or court,* whose primary function is to conduct traffic to and from dwelling units to other streets within the neighborhood. Usually, a place is dead-end, with an ADT of less than 100 and with limited on-street parking.

LANE

A LANE is *similar to a place in design and function,* the primary difference being that a lane occasionally branches to connect two or three other lanes or places. Like a place, a lane does not serve through traffic, but its ADT range (75 to 350) is higher than that of a place.

SUBCOLLECTOR

A SUBCOLLECTOR, with an ADT ranging between 200 and 1,000, *provides access to places and lanes and conducts traffic to an activity center or to a street of higher classification.* The subcollector may be a loop connecting one collector or arterial street at two points, or it may be a fairly straight street conducting traffic between collector and/or arterial streets.

COLLECTOR

A COLLECTOR *conducts traffic between arterial streets and/or activity centers.* It is a principal traffic artery within residential areas and carries a relatively high ADT, ranging between 800 and 2,000 vehicles.

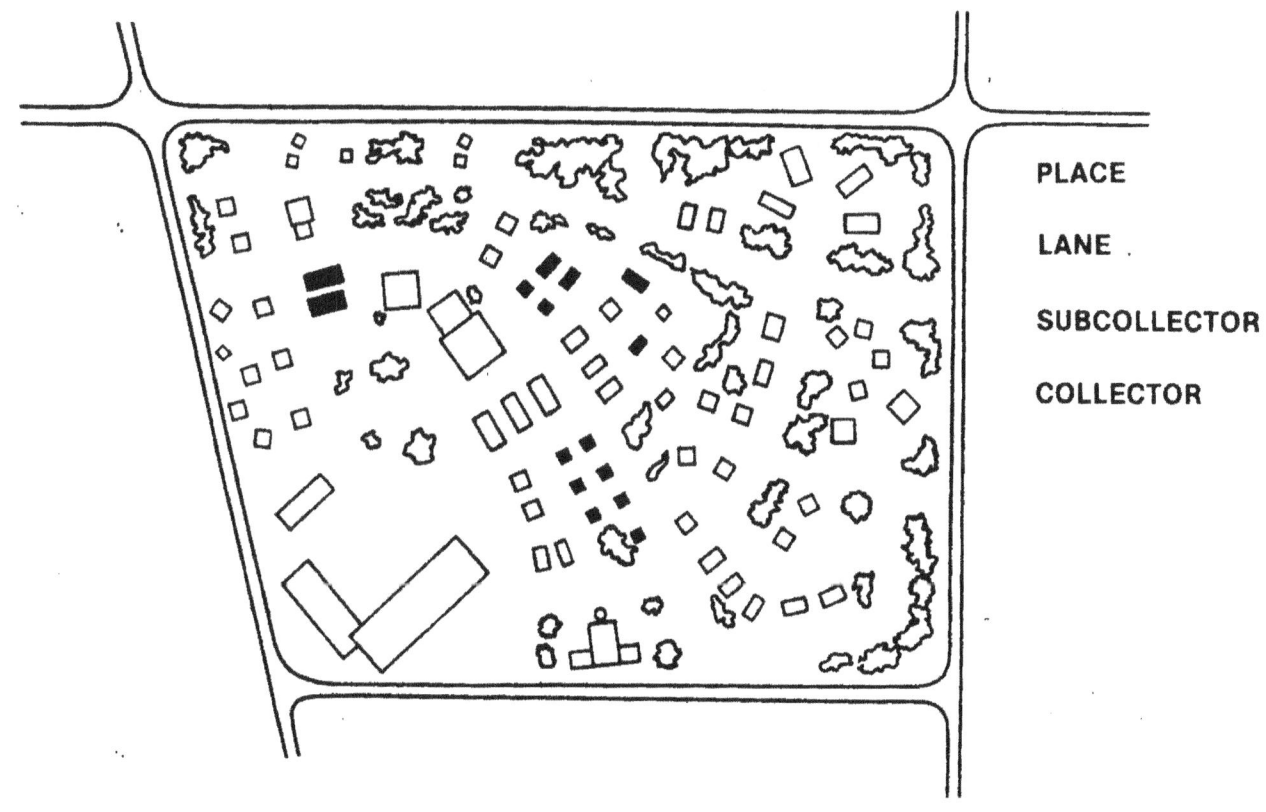

PLACE

LANE

SUBCOLLECTOR

COLLECTOR

LAYOUT

THE BASIC CONCEPT OF A NEIGHBORHOOD is to group land uses away from, but conveniently accessible to, through-traffic arterials.

DESIGN CRITERIA

- The use of through streets, as well as the rectangular grid pattern, should be avoided in the residential network design. Through traffic can be discouraged by creating discontinuities in the street pattern, such as loops and cul-de-sacs.

- Street patterns should be reasonably repetitive or should conform to the topography. Streets that wander or turn back toward themselves should be avoided.

- The specific function of residential streets should be clearly indicated in their design and construction.

- Whenever possible, four-way intersections should be avoided in the residential street layout. Well-spaced T-intersections, at least 150 feet apart, are preferable.

- All dwellings should be accessible to emergency and service vehicles.

- The residential street must be accessible to the traffic it is intended to serve. Driveway grades should not be more than 10 percent; that is, the street should not be more than 5 feet above or 10 feet below the housing unit.

ACCESS CONTROL

TRAFFIC CIRCULATION SYSTEMS AND LAND DEVELOPMENT PATTERNS within the residential area *should not detract from the efficiency of bordering arterial roadways.* Driveway entrances should be avoided on arterial streets and, wherever possible, on collector streets. Intersections along arterials should be placed as shown below for efficient control.

ACCESS DESIGNS

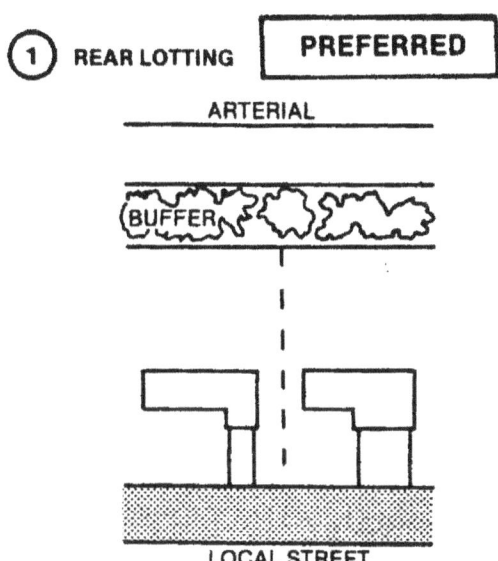

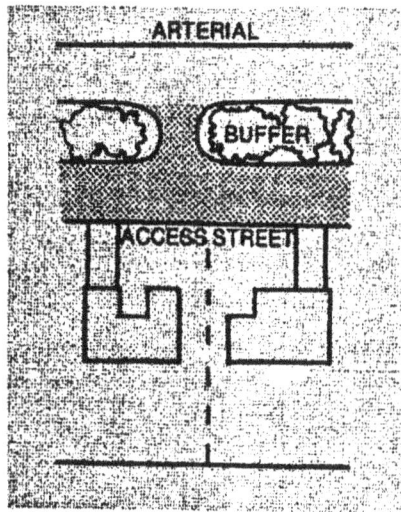

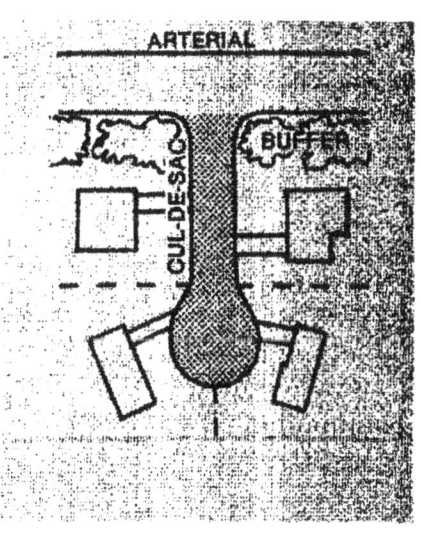

ARRANGEMENT

The arrangement of **LOCAL STREETS** should permit practical patterns, shapes, and lot sizes.

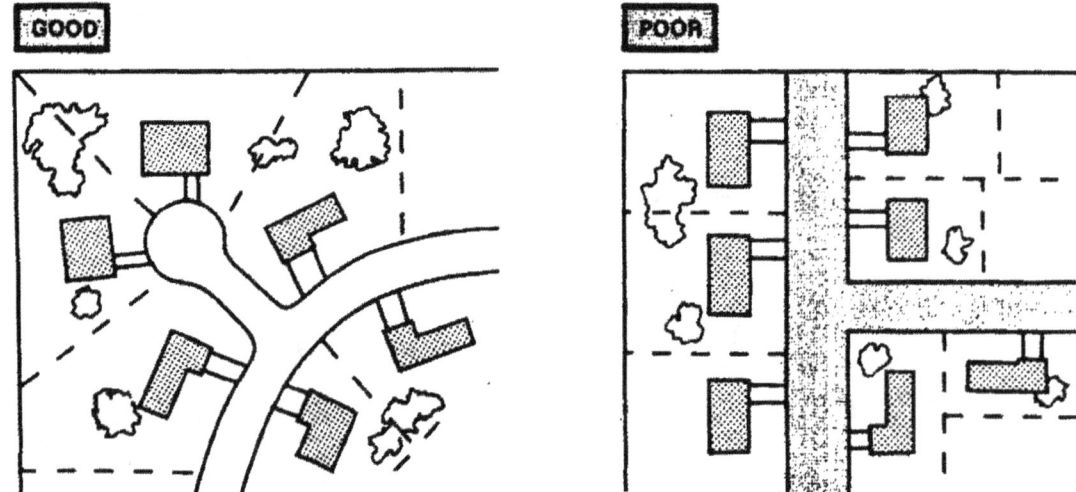

If streets are not to be extended at the corner of the residential area, use curved or cul-de-sac streets.

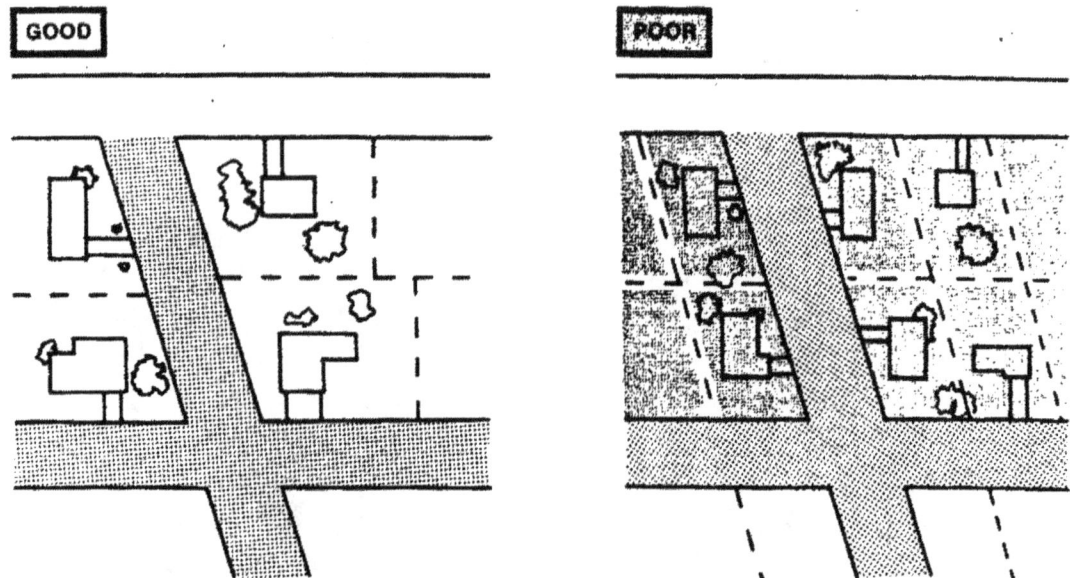

When flat-angled streets must be used, keep lots perpendicular to the major streets.

ELEMENTS

RIGHT-OF-WAY *must be sufficient to contain the elements of pavement and curbing, sidewalks where required, and street utilities.* In extreme northern climates, additional width may be required for snow plowed from the roadway. Allowance for future street widening should be unnecessary in most well-planned neighborhoods. Where future widening is anticipated, right-of-way allowance should be based on the installation master plan.

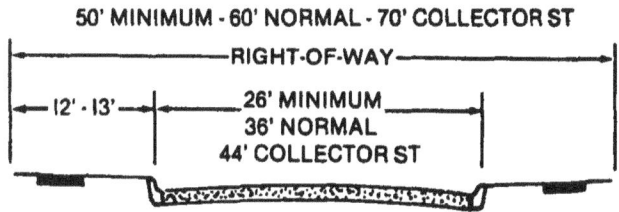

PAVEMENT WIDTH

THE PAVEMENT WIDTH FOR RESIDENTIAL STREETS *varies from 26 to 44 feet.* A 36-foot width, which provides two travel lanes and two on-street parking lanes, is the most common. In restricted areas and low-density housing areas, a 26-foot width is acceptable, as it assures one free-moving traffic lane even when vehicles park on both sides of the street. However, the narrower width should be used only on streets whose travel distance to the nearest collector street is less than 1,500 feet. A pavement width less than 26 feet is not recommended for residential areas. While the pavement is too narrow to permit parking on both sides and still provide one free-moving travel lane, it is wide enough to tempt drivers to park on both sides.

For collector streets, a 44-foot width is recommended, as it will provide two 10-foot-wide parking lanes and two 12-foot-wide travel lanes.

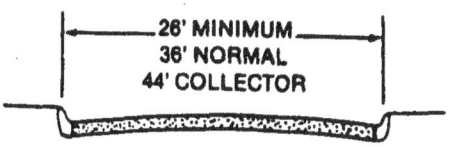

CURBS

CURBS *provide excellent control of drainage, furnish protection for pavement edge, and discourage drivers from encroaching beyond paved surfaces.* For these reasons, curbs are recommended for most residential streets. However, when the sole purpose of the curb is to furnish pavement-edge protection, alternatives to curbs should be considered.

SIDEWALKS

SIDEWALKS along most residential collector streets **are both desirable and necessary.** However, for minor residential streets, sidewalks may not be justified on both sides, or even one side, of the street. In either case, before sidewalks are installed, the expected use of the sidewalk should be evaluated. For example, when residents will include children, and paved private driveways are not planned, sidewalks on at least one side of the street should be installed.

The sidewalk should be at least 4-feet wide, but wider in school areas. Also, the walks should be placed 3 to 10 feet from the curb — the greater distance being preferred along collector streets. In any case, the maximum separation of pedestrians and vehicles is desirable.

PARKING

PARKING for residential areas should be designed so that all residents park off street and only visitor parking overflows onto the street. For low- to medium-density housing areas, at least two off-street spaces should be provided per dwelling unit, and only parallel parking should be permitted on street. For high-density areas, independent studies should be made to determine parking demand and projected needs. Parking bays constructed for these areas should be physically separated from the roadway, using a 90-degree double-bay parking layout.

Another item of increasing importance in residential parking is the recreational vehicle. These vehicles, as well as trailers and other special-purpose vehicles, should not be parked on residential streets, in front yards, or between residences. Ideally, they should be stored and maintained in separate, secured areas provided by the installation.

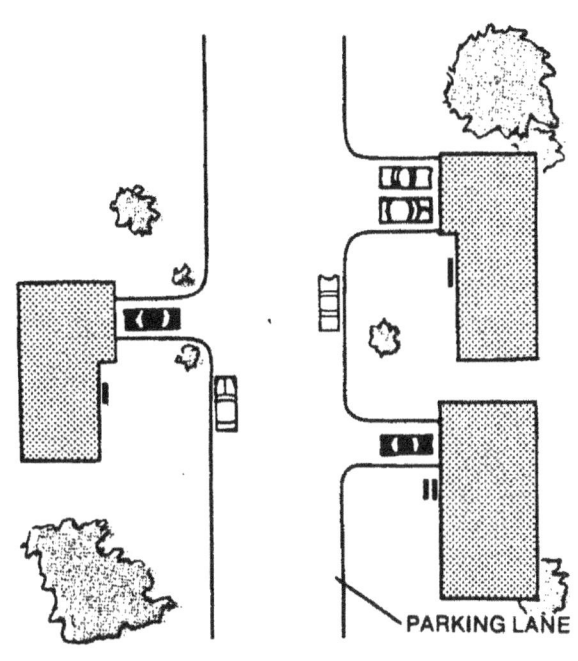

TURNAROUNDS

Modern residential design has led to increased use of CUL-DE-SACS and other DEAD-END roadways. Except on short driveways serving individual dwelling units, every dead-end roadway that might be used by large vehicles should be provided with a turning facility. To accommodate a small truck and a single piece of fire equipment, a 40-foot curb radius is considered minimum. However, where parking is to be provided within the cul-de-sac, a 50-foot radius is recommended.

The usual length of street leading to a turnaround ranges from 400 to 600 feet. When using lengths longer than 500 feet, the maximum number of dwelling units that are provided access should not exceed 20.

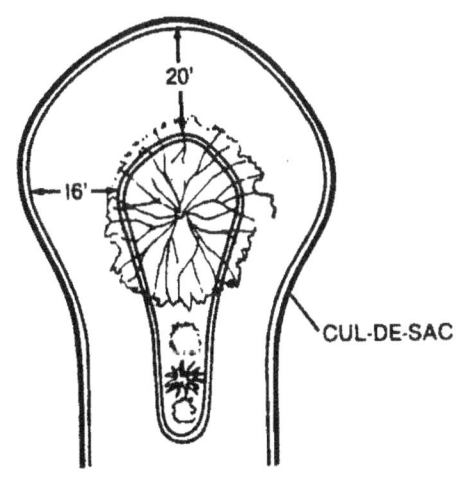

STREET LIGHTING

For safety, security, and convenience, MODERN STREET LIGHTING should be provided at every intersection. Energy savings cannot be justified when the tradeoff involves pedestrian security. To add aesthetic value, underground wiring is recommended.

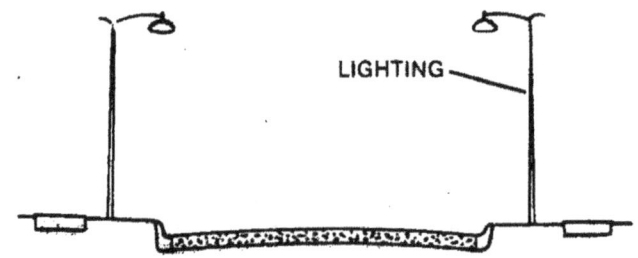

DESIGN SPEED

LOW DESIGN SPEED on residential streets is DESIRABLE. A design speed of 20 to 25 miles per hour is recommended for places and lanes, and 25 to 35 miles per hour for collector streets. The lower speeds of each class should be used for hilly terrain, and the higher speeds for flat and rolling terrain.

SIGHT DISTANCE

A residential roadway network should be designed to operate without any traffic control device, except along collector streets. The need for control devices can best be minimized by maintaining clear sight distance. CLEAR SIGHT DISTANCE, in turn, *can best be provided by properly locating buildings, fences, shrubbery, or trees, and by restricting the height of any embankment.* Sight distance can be controlled also by *intersection location.* When streets are laid out, the placing of intersections on a hilltop or slightly below a hilltop should be avoided. However, where one of these intersections must be used, the hillcrest is preferable because it offers two-directional visibility.

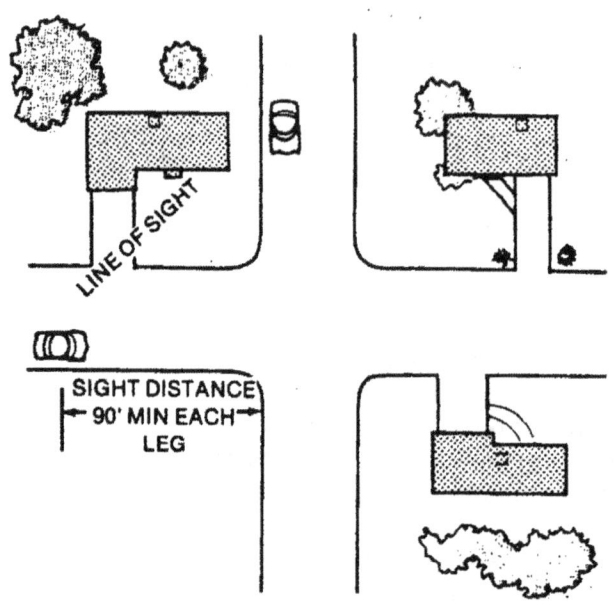

DRAINAGE

Whenever possible, *street layouts should be planned to avoid* EXCESSIVE CONCENTRATION OF STORM RUNOFF. When the residential area is constructed, the structures and the paved roads will increase the stormwater runoff. This runoff should not cross several properties, wash away front yards, or flow from the street to a building site. Therefore, careful curbed-street layout and gradient planning will help route storm runoff to avoid undue concentration on street surfaces or residential property.

STREETS PERPENDICULAR TO CONTOURS

A road that is perpendicular to the contours causes steep yards; as a result, storm runoff accumulates on properties at the bottom of the grade. Retaining walls may be necessary. Special drainage systems are needed to drain water from the lot to the street to prevent house flooding in heavy rains. Roads perpendicular to contours, with grades over 4 or 5 percent, should be avoided.

STREET PARALLEL TO CONTOURS

Roads on steep slopes running parallel to the contours will make one house too high to permit driveway connections, while the opposite house will be below street level and will have a poor lot. What's more, it may be impossible to connect the lower house to the sanitary sewer system and achieve gravity flow.

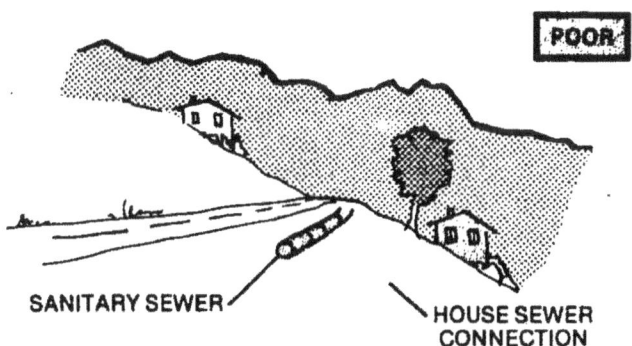

STREET DIAGONAL TO CONTOURS

As explained above, roads over reasonably steep slopes should cut diagonally across contours.

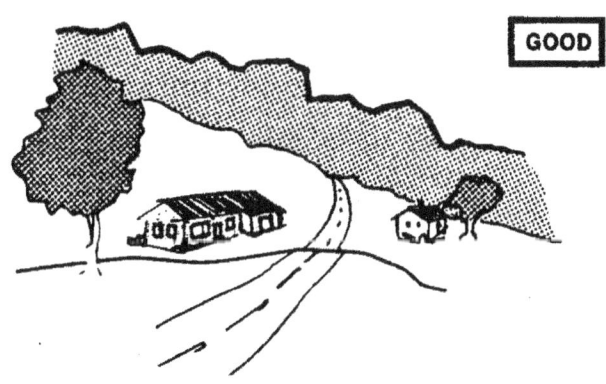